AN INTRODUCTION TO CAUSAL ANALYSIS IN SOCIOLOGY

Ian Birnbaum

Part I, Introductions to Part II and Appendices © Ian Birnbaum 1981

All rights reserved. No part of this publication may be reproduced or transmitted, in any form or by any means, without permission

First published 1981 by
THE MACMILLAN PRESS LTD
London and Basingstoke
Companies and representatives
throughout the world

Typeset in 10/12 Press Roman by
Styleset Limited, Salisbury, Wiltshire

British Library Cataloguing in Publication Data

Birnbaum, Ian
　An introduction to causal analysis in sociology
　1. Social sciences — Statistical methods
　I. Title
　300'.1'51953　　H61

ISBN 978-0-333-26112-5　　ISBN 978-1-349-16466-0 (eBook)
DOI 10.1007/978-1-349-16466-0

To my late father, Louis Birnbaum

Contents

Preface		ix
Acknowledgments		xi
Part I	*The Theoretical Basis of Causal Analysis*	1
The Theory of Causal Analysis		3
Introduction		3
A	Basic Ideas: Units of Analysis and Levels of Measurement	4
B	Some Fundamental Statistical Notions	9
C	General Regression for Two Variables	10
D	Linear Regression for Two Variables	14
E	General Regression for Three or More Variables	18
F	Linear Regression for Three or More Variables	19
G	Regression and Non-cardinal Variables	24
H	Estimating Regression Coefficients: The Method of Least Squares	27
I	Causal Analysis	30
J	Linear Causal Models: The Regression Coefficient Interpretation	32
K	Linear Causal Models: The Variance Interpretation	37
L	Standardised Linear Models	40
M	Using Discrete Variables in Causal Analysis	43
N	Estimating Path Regression Coefficients	44
O	Testing Hypotheses in Causal Analysis	51
P	An Example with Hypothetical Data	57
Q	Time and Causal Analysis	63
Part II	*Causal Analysis in Action*	67
Introduction		69
Chapter 1	Causal Models for the Study of Prevalence	70
Chapter 2	Religious Identification and its Ethnic Correlates	86
Chapter 3	Regression Analysis for the Comparison of School and Home Effects	113

viii Contents

Appendices

Appendix 1	Some Further Reading	137
Appendix 2(I)	Review of Some of the Basic Statistical Results Used in Part I	138
Appendix 2(II)	Proofs of Asterisked Results in Part I	141
Appendix 3	Matrices	150

References 160

Index 164

Preface

This book is mainly intended for students or practising social scientists who wish to use the methods of quantitative causal analysis and who require a thorough, but essentially elementary grounding in the theory and practice of this methodology.

It is assumed that the reader has had some acquaintance with descriptive statistics — for instance, the mean and standard deviation — and that he also has some idea of the concepts associated with probability and with simple statistical inference. Beyond this, all that is required is a facility with the algebra commonly found in 'O'-level mathematics courses. Any further knowledge is developed in the text or included in an appendix.

The book is divided into two parts. In the first, I give a thorough theoretical introduction to the assumptions and methods of quantitative causal analysis. Considerable attention is paid to the basic theory of regression, and in particular linear regression (by which I mean linear in the data as well as the parameters) and the development here makes a careful distinction between what I call constrained and unconstrained regression. Causal analysis is then developed from regression theory, the additional assumptions being carefully explained. The path analysis interpretation of coefficients in terms of 'proportion of variance explained' is examined and it is concluded that path coefficients are more meaningfully interpreted as standardised regression coefficients using the earlier development. The issue of standardisation is then considered. Throughout, the importance of the measurement level of variables is stressed.

Problems of statistical inference are considered, and methods developed, in particular the use of the likelihood ratio test for testing the causal model as a whole. This method is not widely used in practical applications of causal analysis in the literature, although it is well known to econometricians, but I do not consider it too advanced to include in an introductory account. Indeed, I regard it as a mistake to gloss over problems of estimation and testing, an error common in many introductions to the subject.

An introduction, however, must exclude something. I have restricted my attention to recursive models and I do not deal with issues like measurement error, unobserved variables or specification error. I have included few references in the text, but rather included an appendix where further reading is indicated. In Appendix 1, I mention the important topics not

x *Preface*

included in the text and make suggestions on where the interested reader might look for further ideas. A short appendix on matrix algebra is also included, although matrix methods are not used in this book, since the more advanced literature uses them. The book therefore also serves as a springboard for more advanced study.

Part II of the book contains three articles from the social scientific literature showing causal analysis in action. The main purpose of this part is to illustrate some of the diverse and imaginative ways in which causal analysis can be used. The articles are reprinted in full, since the background to the use of causal analysis discussed in each article is at least as important as the causal analysis itself. The articles should give the student unacquainted with the research literature an insight into the nature and structure of the research task.

I would like to thank Mrs Sheila Rose for her secretarial assistance.

February 1979   IAN BIRNBAUM

Acknowledgments

I wish to thank James Coleman and Academic Press Inc. for permission to reproduce 'Regression Analysis for the Comparison of School and Home Effects'; William Eaton and University of North Carolina Press for permission to reproduce 'Causal Models for the Study of Prevalence' and part of the Addendum to this article; Bernard Lazerwitz and University of North Carolina Press for permission to reproduce 'Religious Identification and its Ethnic Correlates: A Multivariate Model'.

Part I The Theoretical Basis of Causal Analysis

The Theory of Causal Analysis

Introduction and Synopsis

Causal analysis is concerned with establishing quantitative measures of causal connection between variables. It does not prove that one variable causes another but, on the contrary, can only be applied if assumptions concerning the possible directions of causality between variables are made. Moreover, as we will see below, these are not the only assumptions necessary for its correct application.

To understand causal analysis, certain statistical and methodological ideas must be established first. In this book I begin by discussing the nature of the data itself — namely the entities on which measurements are taken and the various modes of measurement available. In the causal analysis examined in this book only certain levels of measurement are applicable.

Next, certain fundamental statistical ideas are developed, by far the most important in our context being that of probability and expectation. Many of the ideas are reviewed in the first part of Appendix 2, and, depending on the level of statistical background of the reader, as much or as little as necessary can be read. Part (II) of this appendix contains proofs of results given in the text. Readers not interested in such proofs can omit this, but for those who are interested, an asterisk in the text indicates that a proof is available in that appendix.

A detailed discussion of regression follows this, since regression is the statistical foundation for causal analysis. Regression is technically called linear if it is linear in the parameters (e.g.

$$x_3 = aX_1 + bX_1^2 + cX_1 X_2 + dX_2^3 + e + u$$

is linear in this sense, since all parameters, $a, b, c, d, e,$ are not squared, cubed etc.). However, the word linear is also used to refer to regression linear in the variables defined (so that the equation in the example above is not linear in this sense), and it is in this sense that I use it in this book. Causal analysis generally uses regression which is linear in both senses, but can sometimes without serious difficulty be applied to equations non-linear in the second sense by using suitable transformations (e.g. letting $Y_1 = X_1^2$, $Y_2 = X_1 X_2$, $Y_3 = X_2^3$ in the example above). In this book, however, I devote most attention to equations linear in both senses.

After this, the road is clear for a discussion of causal analysis, and Part I ends with an example of the method with hypothetical data.

In Appendix 1, I present in broad outline some developments not discussed in the main text and give some suggestions for further reading on these and related ideas.

This book does not use matrix methods, since their use in an introductory text would present an unnecessary barrier to many readers. Nevertheless, more advanced discussions, including all the references in Appendix 1, do use matrices, and so in Appendix 3 I include a short introduction to matrix algebra and its use in the mathematical analysis of causal analysis. Any reader wishing to use this book as a starting point for further study ought to find this appendix useful.

A   Basic Ideas: Units of Analysis and Levels of Measurement

Our starting point is a set of entities on which we take various measurements. Our immediate problems are firstly to specify the entities, and secondly to determine the mode and level of measurements. Let us take these in turn.

In the social sciences, a common set of entities is a set of individual persons, but this is not necessarily the only sort. We can conceive of classes of schools, factories, households, towns or countries, for instance, as our set of entities. These latter sorts of entity might be called collectives. To call them this does not imply that all their features can be reduced to those of individuals. There is no need to take a stand here on this issue of reducibility or what is sometimes referred to as methodological individualism (though this term can cover a multitude of positions). The only relevant point here is that the set of entities need not be individual people.

The set of entities upon which we decide to take measurements in a given research setting will be called the *units of analysis* for that setting.

Now the measurements we take will be characterised by variables. As far as we are concerned, a variable takes a number of possible values pertaining to the quality or property measured. The actual values of a variable for a given unit of analysis represents the state of that property to which the variable pertains for that individual. The values need not be quantitative, though in this book most of the variables are quantitative. In practice, there will be more than one property in which we are interested for the units of analysis, and so there will be more than one variable. One of our main concerns, and the primary concern of this book, is to investigate ways of establishing relationships between the various variables for the set of units of analysis with which we are concerned.

The problems involved in actually carrying out the measurements are complex, and we will not discuss them in this chapter. The chapters in Part II, however, will contain many examples of the way in which such measurement problems are solved (indeed, real examples are a fine way of learning how to solve measurement problems in practice). One area which we must examine, however, is the classification of variables in terms of their level of measurement.

The most basic level of measurement, for our purposes, is the *nominal level*. In this case, the values of the variables are purely labels for the states of the property, but otherwise have no relational significance whatsoever. This is clear if the values of the variables are expressed in words — for example, Catholic, Anglican, Non-conformist, Jewish, Other: this is a nominal variable for the concept or property 'religion'. Note that the values of the variable are *mutually exclusive* (no individual can take more than one value) and also *exhaustive* (every individual must take a value of the variable — in this case because of the residual category 'Other'). Every variable that we shall consider will have these two properties. (Formally, a variable is a mapping from units of analysis to values, which is many to one or one to one.)

Now, in the case where nominal variables are expressed numerically, great care must be taken. As an example, consider religion again with values 0, 1, 2, 3, 4 (corresponding to the five verbal values above). Now 1 is more than 0 but this in no way implies that Anglican is somehow 'more' than Catholic. The property of *order* incorporated in the numbers must be suspended in this case. The numbers are in fact purely numerals — labels for given states. Again the distance between 0 and 1 is the same as between 1 and 2, but this property is again suspended. Similarly, the fact that 4 is twice as much as 2 is irrelevant. *Any* numerals may be chosen for values, as long as they are different. (Formally, we can say that what characterises nominal variables is that they are invariant under one-to-one mappings of any kind.)

It should also be clear that we cannot in some sense 'add' an Anglican to a Non-conformist and get a Jew! However, the case of dichotomous variables is slightly different here. Dichotomous variables are characterised by having two values only. Some 'natural' dichotomies exist, like sex — male/female — but most are formed by the values 'possessing quality A'/'not possessing quality A'. Now, again, any two numerical variables may be chosen for these, but there is a strong reason why 1 and 0 respectively should be chosen. The reason is simple. The sum of the values of the dichotomous variables over the units of analysis will give us a count of the number of A's in the set. Hence, in this case, addition has a meaning, but the meaning lies outside the concept itself. It is not that $1 + 0 = 1$ means that a person with A combined in some way with a person without A is just the same as a single person with A — this would rarely be meaningful (and in most social situations would be the opposite of the truth — consider one Jew and a thousand non-Jews, hardly the same as just one Jew). Rather, it is that the addition of the values has a meaning valid socially. Addition of the values corresponds to counting; 1 corresponds to inclusion; 0 to exclusion. This property of dichotomous variables enables them, in some instances, to be combined with 'proper' quantitative variables, as we shall see later.

The next level of measurement is the one most commonly used by individuals in society themselves — the *ordinal level*. An example is the concept of 'power', with values say 'very powerful', 'reasonably powerful', 'mildly powerful', 'lacking power'. This case differs from the nominal in that we seem to have a notion of order built in — we can talk of the strength or intensity of power, of 'moreness' and 'lessness'. Hence, we can allow the order property of numbers to be retained. For example we might choose 3, 2, 1, 0 for the values above, respectively. Now, the fact that 3 is more than 2 has meaning for the concept measured. However, the fact that the distance between 3 and 2 and between 2 and 1 is the same is not relevant, for we do not assume this of the verbal categories to which the numbers relate. Indeed, we could have chosen 94, 16, 2, 1 as values if we wished — the only property that is relevant is the order of the numbers. (Formally, a variable is ordinal if it is invariant under any order — preserving mapping.)

The next level of measurement for our purposes is the *cardinal level*. What is important in this case is that the distances between values become relevant. Before elaborating on this, however, we need to consider the difference between discrete and continuous variables. The mathematically precise formulation of this is that the possible values of a discrete variable can be counted *in principle*. There may be a hundred, a thousand or a countable infinity of such possible values, but in all cases the variable is discrete. In general, a discrete variable is a variable whose values can be put into one-to-one correspondence with the natural numbers (1, 2, 3, 4, ...). A continuous variable is then not discrete. A mathematically incorrect, but in practice far easier characterisation of a continuous variable is one where, between any two of its values, a third can be found. That is, a continuous variable allows infinite discrimination in that no matter how close we feel two values are, a third value can be found which lies between them. In this formulation, a discrete variable is one that is not continuous.

Now, in practice we can only measure discretely. No matter how fine our measuring instruments are, we have limits of precision which impose only a discrete set of measurements. Nevertheless, we can conceive of our variable as continuous, and treat the measurement as an approximation (more or less acceptable) to the 'true' value of the variable. We may, for instance, decide that 'power' is a continuous variable. Our limits of measurement will, however, impose a discrete set of measurements on us. This set is likely to be much bigger than the four values given above for 'power' but it will be discrete. In this way we can differentiate between a variable which is truly discrete and one which has underlying continuity; in both cases, however, the practical measurement set will be discrete.

We can now return to our definition of *cardinal level*. Let X_1 be a cardinal variable and x_{1i} and x_{1j} two of its values, with $x_{1j} > x_{1i}$. (Here, and in the rest of the book, I use the notation of a capital letter for a variable and a small letter for one of its values. If only one value is considered it is usual to write x_1 instead of x_{1i}. If two or more are considered, the double suffix is used, as in x_{1i} and x_{1j}.) Let $x_{1j} - x_{1i} = d_1$. Also, let x_{1k}, x_{1l} be two more values ($x_{1l} > x_{1k}$), where $x_{1l} - x_{1k} = d_2$. Then d_1 and d_2 can be interpreted meaningfully as distances between values, and if $d_2 > d_1$, then the one distance is greater than the other to the extent (d_2/d_1), which itself is meaningful. Moreover, if $d_1 = d_2$ then the distances between the values considered are equal in a substantive sense.

A distinction is sometimes made amongst cardinal level variables, between interval level and ratio level variables. The latter are characterised by having a fixed zero point whilst the former have no such fixed zero. An example of a ratio level variable is a person's age (the idea of zero here is fixed by birth and it is not meaningful to choose another starting point when talking of a person's age); an example of an interval level variable is temperature (compare the zeros for Centigrade and for Fahrenheit). What this difference amounts to is that with ratio level variables the ratio of the values themselves is meaningful, but this is not so with interval level variables. This is easily shown. If x_{1i}, x_{1j} are two values of an interval level variable X_1, then $(a + x_{1i})$ and $(a + x_{1j})$ are those values when the origin is changed to $-a$ on the scale of X_1 (i.e. the value a of X_1 becomes the origin of a new variable $X_1{}'$). It is clear that (x_{1j}/x_{1i}) does not give the same value as $[(a + x_{1j})/(a + x_{1i})]$ unless $x_{1i} = x_{1j}$. The distance between x_{1i} and x_{1j} is unchanged, however, by a change of origin.

Both interval and ratio level variables are invariant to changes of scale. This time consider bx_{1i} and bx_{1j} (a scale change is equivalent to multiplication by a constant term). If X_1 is ratio we see that $(x_{1j}/x_{1i}) = (bx_{1j}/bx_{1i})$. If X_1 is interval, then, using the notation above, d_1 and d_2 become bd_1 and bd_2 and we see that $(d_2/d_1) = (bd_2/bd_1)$.

The distinction between interval and ratio variables is somewhat academic, however, for we can always decide by convention to fix the zero point if we wish to compare values directly through ratios. Thus, temperature is interval level because we want to compare changes in temperature or temperature rises. If we want to compare quantities of heat we use a ratio level variable. In this book, we shall talk generally of cardinal level variables.

With cardinal level variables it makes sense to talk of the value of a variable being decomposed into a function of other quantitative variables, and this is of considerable value in our search for relationships between variables, as we shall see. It is possible to produce techniques for non-cardinal variables but these are necessarily less powerful. Nevertheless, it is often very hard to measure variables to a sufficient degree of accuracy so that our measurements correspond to the true cardinal variables. In these cases it may be better to treat the variables as non-cardinal and use the less powerful techniques. However, in general, a search should be made for ways of measuring cardinality, assuming the true values are indeed cardinal. *In this book, the techniques considered assume cardinality* (except in special cases where dichotomous variables can be used).

Almost all cardinal variables are assumed to have underlying continuity. This is not a characteristic of their definition, but it turns out that it is more difficult to conceive of a series of discontinuous values for the variable than to conceive of a continuum of values. The usual exception to this is a variable involving counting (like number of children in a family). As we have already said, the measurements will, of necessity, exhibit discontinuity: the assumption is generally made that the measuring instrument gives a good enough approximation. (Techniques exist for dealing with measurement error, but they are outside the scope of this book — see Appendix 1.)

Cardinal variables are so close to the properties of numbers, that it is tempting to perform the usual arithmetic upon them. To what extent the mathematical operations correspond to operations valid in the social world is difficult to judge. Each case must be taken on its merits: it is no part of a concept of a cardinal variable that arithmetic corresponds to social operations in all cases, or indeed, in any case. However, lack of correspondence (or a failure to specify correspondence) need not imply that arithmetic may not be used. If the purpose of adding, for instance, is to produce some summary measure valid in statistical terms (like the arithmetic mean), then the mathematical operation is quite meaningful at this statistical level. It is when the operations involved in producing the measure are taken to reflect social operations — so that the measure is conceived to be an outcome in social reality produced by operations corresponding to the mathematical ones — that problems can arise. In this book, no such correspondence between the mathematically meaningful and the socially meaningful will be assumed or needed.

B Some Fundamental Statistical Notions

The target set of units of analysis in which we are interested will be called the *population*. In general, we shall have access only to a *sample* from this population. Methods of sampling are outside the scope of this book, but we need say here only that we try to choose a method which produces as representative a sample as possible. The limits to this are dictated by our knowledge of which factors constitute bias in a sample; clearly we cannot ensure representativeness, for we would then have perfect knowledge of the population, but we can attempt to make the chance of bias as small as possible. Outside of the factors which we know about and can control, our sample will be effectively random. The randomness is often achieved by using methods analogous to picking various numbers of balls from various urns, guarding against systematic bias; but these methods are by no means necessary to producing a sample which may be regarded as random. The methods are in general use mainly because they provide a publicly acceptable way of choosing a sample in such a way as to minimise subjective bias.

On the basis of the data extracted from the sample, we wish to make an estimate of the various parameters of interest in the population; we may also want to test whether parameters have some hypothesised value in the population on the basis of the evidence of the sample. This is the purpose of statistical inference. (It can be argued that statistical inference is necessary in causal analysis even when we have full access to the whole population. The argument is complex and somewhat controversial: the interested reader should refer to Birnbaum (1979).) In order to use statistical inference, it must be the case that every unit of analysis in the population has some chance (no matter how small) of being included in the sample. Hence, attempting to use statistical inference to predict the future (treating the present data as a sample from data now and in the future), or attempting to generalise from, say, a town to all towns when members of only one town could be chosen (treating the data as a sample from the available geographical territory and also from unavailable territory), are simply invalid. Such temporal and spatial extrapolation is extrastatistical; theoretical reasons must be adduced to validate such generalisations. Of course, such theoretical reasons should indeed be forthcoming, or else the whole research project is very likely to be a sterile exercise in statistical technique. Nevertheless, it is essential to realise the limits of statistical inference, lest it be believed that statistics can do our scientific thinking for us.

We shall suppose that the variables of interest in our population have a probability rather than a frequency distribution. In fact, probability is a theoretical concept and is never observable in practice. That is, we can only estimate a probability — we can never measure it accurately. Probability is often said to reside in infinite populations, but since these cannot be observed, they are themselves of a theoretical nature. It is possible to give an account of probability in terms of what are called generating conditions, but this too is complex and controversial and the interested reader may again refer to Birnbaum (1979). In our case, it will suffice to suppose that the population is large enough for the relative frequencies to be sufficient approximations for probabilities.

Appendix 2 of Part I gives a brief account of probability and includes all the statistical results used in the book. The reader can read it now and/or refer to it as the need arises. *An asterisk in the text indicates a reference to Appendix 2, Part II*, where mathematical proofs are provided.

C General Regression for Two Variables

If for each unit of analysis we record observations on just two variables, X_1 and X_2, then we may wish to seek some relationship between the variables for each unit of analysis. The relationship may be construed as causal, but it is possible to make investigations without making any causal assumptions. One of our aims may simply be to measure the strength of the relationship between X_1 and X_2.

Many expressions exist to measure the association between variables, but in the case of cardinal variables the most usual expression is that called the product moment correlation coefficient (pmcc). Its most general form is as follows. Let s and t be two variables (they may each be functions of other variables). The pmcc between s and t is defined by

$$\rho(s, t) = \frac{\text{Cov}(s, t)}{\sqrt{\text{Var}(s)\,\text{Var}(t)}} \qquad \text{C.1}$$

Clearly the value of the expression will depend on s and t, but later we shall be led to choose specific functions of X_1 and X_2 to replace s and t here.

For the moment we notice that $-1 \leq \rho \leq 1^*$. If ρ is positive, the closer it is to 1 the more s and t tend to vary in the same direction from their means for each unit of analysis. Similarly, if ρ is negative, the closer it is to -1, the more s and t tend to vary in opposite directions from their means. We shall have more to say about ρ a little later.

The next step from measuring association is that of attempting to find some functional relationship between X_1 and X_2. It is unlikely that any such exact relationship holds for all units of analysis, and so we are led to search for a relationship which in some sense is as close as possible to the actual relationship in the population.

So far, we have presented the analysis in terms which treat X_1 and X_2 symmetrically. However, we usually wish to seek a relationship which will allow us to predict the value on one variable from a value on the other. To fix ideas, take X_1 to be the score on a mathematics attainment test taken at Christmas and X_2 as the score on the public examination in mathematics taken the following summer. As our units of analysis, we consider all the candidates for the exam over a five year period, where the format of the exam has remained relatively unchanged. For the purposes of this exposition we shall suppose (unrealistically) that we have access to all the data in the target population, and that all candidates had taken the mathematics attainment test. Hence we need not worry about sampling problems.

Our aim is to choose a function of X_1 which will act as a predictor for X_2. Clearly, the notion of prediction is not in fact relevant to our target population since they have already taken the public exam. Rather, we wish to use the function of X_1 that we derive from this population to make predictions about future candidates, where we have access only to attainment test results. We note immediately an extra-statistical assumption here, analogous to the one already discussed in relation to sampling. The function of X_1 will only be of use in the future if we can validly make the assumption that relevant features of the future candidates and future exams are much the same as the target population. What constitute relevant features is a difficult question in the case of the future candidates, but they should be easy to state for the examination. Of course, we can always test the predictive use of the function of X_1, but only after the public exam results are known and by then it may be too late. We may want to use the attainment test results to give employers an idea of the probable results of prospective employees in a public examination which occurs too late in the year for them to make use of it. We thus require our prediction to be as accurate as possible.

A word must be said here about causality. It is quite clear here that X_1

cannot be treated as a cause of X_2. Indeed, the causal relationship seems to be that they have common causes, and we hope, for predictive purposes, that most relevant causes of X_2 are causes of X_1. However, there is no need for us to speculate upon the causal relationship between X_1 and X_2. Our aim is a predictive one: we require only that the prediction be as accurate as possible, and for this there is no necessity to make causal assumptions. This is in marked contrast to causal analysis, examined in later sections, where our primary aim is to establish the strength of causal influence regardless of predictive value in any specific case.

How, then, should we choose our function of X_1? It is clear that if we looked at candidates with a specific score on X_1, say x_1, then there would be many different scores for those candidates on X_2. That is, given any particular score x_1 on X_1, there would be a scatter of scores on X_2, and this is likely to be so for all scores on X_1. Our problem is to choose for each score on X_1 one and only one score on X_2 which acts in some sense as the best predictor of the scatter of scores on X_2.

Let $f(X_1)$ be any function of X_1. $f(x_1)$ will be the prediction of X_2 for a score of x_1 on X_1. We can write for each individual unit of analysis

$$x_2 = f(x_1) + \tau_2 \qquad \text{C.2}$$

τ_2 is a value of the random variable T_2 which is effectively a 'residual' variable: it measures the amount by which the actual score on X_2 differs from the predicted score for each unit of analysis.

Now a very reasonable criterion for choosing $f(X_1)$ is to choose that function which minimises the residuals for each and every value of X_1. Since the residuals may be positive or negative, however, we cannot simply add them; for a small sum may conceal large negative and positive residuals. Instead, we shall square the residuals so that their signs do not affect their sum.

It is clear, then, that we wish to minimise $E(T_2^2 \mid x_1)$ for each value of x_1. Now,

$$E(T_2^2 \mid x_1) = E[\{X_2 - f(x_1)\}^2 \mid x_1] \qquad \text{C.3}$$

This is minimised if

$$f(x_1) = E(X_2 \mid x_1)*$$

that is if $f(x_1)$ is equal to the conditional mean of X_2 given $X_1 = x_1$. The conditional mean is indeed a function of X_1, and we see that this mean gives us the best function in terms of our criterion, namely that, for each value of x_1, $[X_2 - E(X_2 \mid x_1)]^2$ is, in a summation sense, as small as possible.

Now a different, but equally reasonable criterion is to choose $f(X_1)$ so that the pmcc between X_2 and $f(X_1)$ is maximised, for then we shall have found a function of X_1 which gives the maximum possible association, using the pmcc criterion, between X_2 and a function of X_1. It happens, however, that according to this criterion also, the best function is $E(x_2 \mid x_1)$.* That is, $\rho^2(f(X_1), X_2)$ is maximum when $f(x_1) = E(X_2 \mid x_1)$. Thus, again, the conditional mean is the best function.

This function is so important that it is called the *regression function*, the process of forming the predictor being termed *regression*.

Now the value of $\rho^2(f, X_2)$ is the maximum possible when $f = E(X_2 \mid x_1)$, and this value is called the square of the *correlation ratio*, designated by η_{21}^2. We have that*

$$\eta_{21}^2 = \frac{\mathrm{Var}\,[E(X_2 \mid x_1)]}{\mathrm{Var}\,X_2} \leqslant 1 \ (\text{since } \rho^2 \leqslant 1) \qquad \text{C.4}$$

It is clear that if $\eta_{21}^2 = 0$, then $\mathrm{Var}\,[E(X_2 \mid x_1)] = 0$ and so $E(X_2 \mid x_1) = E(X_2)$ for all values of x_1. This does *not* imply, however, that X_1 and X_2 are *statistically* independent since, for instance, $E(X_2^2 \mid x_1)$ may depend on x_1. We have statistical independence only if $E(h(X_2) \mid x_1) = E(h(X_2))$ for *any* function h of X_2.

Now, letting $M(x_1) = E(X_2 \mid x_1)$, we have*

$$E[(X_2 - E(X_2))^2] = E[(X_2 - M(X_1))^2] + E[(M(X_1) - E[M(X_1)])^2] \qquad \text{C.5}$$

From C.4 and C.5 we see that

$$1 = \frac{E[(X_2 - M(X_1))^2]}{\mathrm{Var}\,X_2} + \eta_{21}^2$$

and so

$$\eta_{21}^2 = 1 - \frac{\mathrm{Var}\,T_2}{\mathrm{Var}\,X_2} \qquad \text{C.6}$$

Equation C.5 shows that variation in X_2 can be split into two components: that due to variation in M and that due to variation in the residual variable T_2. Hence, from C.6, the closer η_{21}^2 is to 1, the less relative variation in T_2 there is compared to X_2 itself. η_{21}^2 is, therefore, a measure of the extent to which the predictor M accounts for X_2 in terms of its variation; and whatever this value of η_{21}^2 is, we know we can do no better by looking for another function $f(X_1)$ other than $M(X_1)$. Instead, we can include more variables, and we shall examine this later.

Notice that, from C.2,

$$E(X_2 \mid x_1) = E(f \mid x_1) + E(T_2 \mid x_1)$$

But f is constant given $X_1 = x_1$, so $E(f \mid x_1) = f$. Hence,

$$E(X_2 \mid x_1) = f + E(T_2 \mid x_1) \qquad \text{C.7}$$

But if $f = E(X_2 \mid x_1)$,

$$E(T_2 \mid x_1) = 0 \qquad \text{C.8}$$

Thus,

$$E(T_2) = E[E(T_2 \mid x_1)] = 0 \qquad \text{C.9}$$

To summarise the results of this section: if we wish to choose a function of X_1 with which to predict X_2, then $E(X_2 \mid x_1)$ will minimise the residual variation for each value of x_1 and will maximise the correlation between X_2 and a function of X_1.

D Linear Regression for Two Variables

How far have we come in solving our prediction problem for mathematics results? Not very far, since it is most unlikely that $E(X_2 \mid x_1)$ can be expressed in a mathematically usable form. It is very likely that its form is complex, and that we cannot determine its mathematical formula from inspection. Without such a formula, its predictive value is of limited use. Indeed, we would be confined to making predictions only for those values of X_1 which actually occurred in the population analysed.

There are two general options open to us. Firstly, we could assume that the regression function does in fact correspond to some function whose formula can be written down. In practice, we might be able to do this by inspecting a sample of results and fitting an approximate known curve to the conditional means. We assume that, in the limiting case, the known curve actually is the regression function.

A particular, but very important example of this is the case where the regression function is assumed to be linear. In this case we call the regression *unconstrained linear*.

The second option is to accept that we do not know the exact regression function, and instead to specify *in advance* what class of formulae we shall consider, and then attempt to choose the best one from that class. Many classes of function are possible, but by far the most common is again the class of linear functions. In this case we call the regression *constrained linear*.

It is important to grasp the difference between these two options. In the unconstrained linear case we assume that the regression function actually is linear. That is, we assume that

$$E(X_2 \mid x_1) = b_{21}x_1 + a_2 \qquad \text{D.1}$$

In the constrained linear case we restrict in advance the function $f(X_1)$ in equation C.2 to be linear. That is, we *demand* that

$$f(x_1) = b_{21}x_1 + a_2 \qquad \text{D.2}$$

How can we choose the best linear function in this second constrained case? Let us rewrite C.2 as

$$X_2 = b_{21}X_1 + a_2 + \xi_2 \qquad \text{D.3}$$

where ξ_2 is the residual in the case of constrained linear regression. Our task is to find a way of fixing b_{21} and a_2. This time we cannot hope to minimise the sum of squared residuals for each value of X_1 since we have only two parameters — b_{21} and a_2 — to fix. Instead, we can ask that the sum of squared residuals be minimum over all values of X_1 combined.

Thus we require to minimise $E(\xi_2^2)$ or

$$E[(X_2 - b_{21}X_1 - a_2)^2] \qquad \text{D.4}$$

The values of b_{21} and a_2 are given by *

$$b_{21} = \frac{\sigma_{12}}{\sigma_1^2} \text{ and } a_2 = \mu_2 - b_{21}\mu_1 \qquad \text{D.5}$$

It is easy to show that equations D.5 are valid in the unconstrained linear case also. From equation D.1 we have, taking expectations (over x_1),

$$\mu_2 = b_{21}\mu_1 + a_2 \qquad \text{D.6}$$

which is the second equation of D.5 in another form.

Substituting D.6 in D.1 gives

$$E(X_2 \mid x_1) - \mu_2 = b_{21}(x_1 - \mu_1)$$

or

$$E(X_2' \mid x_1') = b_{21}x_1' \qquad \text{D.7}$$

where the dashes indicate measurement from the means (i.e. μ_1 becomes the zero of X_1 and μ_2 of X_2).

Since D.7 is true for all values of X_1, we can multiply by x_1' and take expectations (over x_1) giving*

$$\sigma_{12} = b_{21}\sigma_1^2 \qquad \text{D.8}$$

which is the first equation of D.5 in another form.

This equivalence of results must not obscure the basic difference between constrained and unconstrained linear regression; only in the latter case is equation D.7 true. More importantly, if we write

$$X_2 = M(X_1) + T_2 \qquad \text{D.9}$$

and

$$X_2 = L(X_1) + \xi_2 \qquad \text{D.10}$$

where M is the conditional mean and L is the best linear function, whose coefficients are given by D.5, then we note that, from D.9, $E(T_2 \mid x_1) = 0$, so that the regression function of T_2 on X_1 is zero, and in consequence T_2 cannot be split up into a function of X_1 and some variable ϵ_2 such that the variance of ϵ_2 is less than that of T_2. On the other hand, from D.10,

$$E(\xi_2 \mid X_1) = M(X_1) - L(X_1) \qquad \text{D.11}$$

so that we have, from D.9 and D.10

$$\xi_2 = [M(X_1) - L(X_1)] + T_2 \qquad \text{D.12}$$

where the function in brackets is the regression function of ξ_2 on X_1 from D.11.

Now from the formula for a_2 in D.5 we have

$$X_2' = b_{21}X_1' + \xi_2 \qquad \text{D.13}$$

and we note that $E(\xi_2) = 0$. Multiplying D.13 by X_1' and taking expectations gives

$$\sigma_{12} = b_{21}\sigma_1^2 + E(X_1'\xi_2') \qquad \text{D.14}$$

But from D.5, $b_{21}\sigma_1^2 = \sigma_{12}$, so that

$$E(X_1'\xi_2') = 0 = \rho(X_1, \xi_2) \qquad \text{D.15}$$

Thus we see from D.15 that the pmcc between X_1 and ξ_2 is zero, whereas from D.11 the mean of ξ_2 is not independent of X_1. Finally, we note from D.12 that

$$\text{Var}(\xi_2) - \text{Var}(T_2) = E[\{M(X_1) - L(X_1)\}^2] \qquad \text{D.16}$$

We can see that the constrained linear case provides, in effect, the best linear approximation to $E(X_2 \mid x_1)$, the regression function, for we have chosen $L(X_1)$ so that $\text{Var}(\xi_2)$ is as small as possible.

Now we note that $E[L(X_1)] = \mu_2$, since $L(X_1) = b_{21}X_1' + \mu_2$. Hence, we have

$$X_2' = L'(X_1) + \xi_2 \qquad \text{D.17}$$

where $L'(X_1)$ has zero mean, i.e. $L'(X_1) = b_{21}X_1'$. In consequence, $E(L'\xi_2') = 0$ by virtue of D.15. Thus, squaring D.17 and taking expectations,

$$\text{Var}(X_2) = \text{Var}(L) + \text{Var}(\xi_2) \qquad \text{D.18}$$

Again, we have decomposed the variance of X_2 into the variance of the best linear predictor and the variance of the residuals (analogously to C.5).

Analogously with the correlation ratio we can consider the pmcc between L and X_2. Multiplying equation D.17 by L' and taking expectations, we have (by virtue of D.15)

$$\text{Cov}(X_2 L) = \text{Var}(L) \qquad \text{D.19}$$

Hence,

$$\rho^2(X_2, L) = \frac{\text{Var}(L)}{\text{Var } X_2} \qquad \text{D.20}$$

Again analogously with the general regression model, we can ask whether this value of the pmcc is the maximum possible among all linear functions. However, this question is poorly framed, since for *any* linear function $G(X_1)$ of X_1,

$$\rho(G, X_2) = \rho(X_1, X_2)^* \qquad \text{D.21}$$

We conclude that

$$\rho^2(X_1, X_2) = \frac{\text{Var } L(X_1)}{\text{Var } X_2} = 1 - \frac{\text{Var } \xi_2}{\text{Var } X_2} \qquad \text{D.22}$$

Hence ρ_{12}^2 (as $\rho^2(X_1, X_2)$ is usually written) is the proportion of the varaince in X_2 accounted for by variance in the best linear predictor of X_2 from X_1. ρ_{12} is usually referred to as the linear correlation coefficient between X_1 and X_2.

We have already seen that η_{12}^2 gives the maximum value of $\rho(X_2, f)$, f being equal to $E(X_2 \mid x_1)$, and so

$$\rho_{12}^2 \leqslant \eta_{12}^2 \leqslant 1 \qquad \text{D.23}$$

$p_{12}{}^2 = \eta_{12}{}^2$ if the regression function is linear. $\eta_{12}{}^2 = 1$ if there is no residual variation, so that $X_2 = E(X_2 \mid x_1)$ identically.

To summarise the results of this section: if we wish to constrain regression to linear functions only, Equation D.3 holds with coefficients as in D.5. If unconstrained regression is linear also, equation D.1 holds, but the coefficients are again as in D.5. In the constrained case, $E(\xi_2 \mid X_1) \neq 0$ but D.11 holds. However, D.15 holds for both cases. Finally, in the constrained case, D.22 holds, and in the unconstrained case, $\eta_{12}{}^2 = p_{12}{}^2$.

E General Regression for Three or More Variables

We have seen that even when we choose the best function of X_1 with which to predict X_2 (namely $E(X_2 \mid X_1)$), a proportion of variance $\mathrm{Var}(T_2)/\mathrm{Var}(X_2)$ remains unaccounted for by variation in X_1. Whilst this proportion may be different when we use the regression function in the future, it nevertheless gives us a guide to the precision of our predictions. It is mainly to increase this precision that we use more than one variable to make the prediction.

Let X_4 be the variable we wish to predict (which we call the response variable) and let X_1, X_2 and X_3 be the predictor variables. To fix ideas, take X_4 as the score on the public exam in mathematics and X_1 as the score on the Christmas attainment test. Take X_2 as the public exam score estimated by the teacher just prior to the attainment test (for if the estimation is made after the test this will induce a high correlation between X_1 and X_2 without any necessary increase in precision of predicting X_4). Finally, take X_3 as the candidate's own estimate of his public exam result prior to the attainment test and without knowledge of his teacher's estimate.

We write

$$X_4 = f(X_1, X_2, X_3) + T_4 \qquad \text{E.1}$$

Once again, we find that

$$E(T_4{}^2 \mid X_1, X_2, X_3) \text{ is minimised when}$$

$$f = E(X_4 \mid X_1, X_2, X_3)*$$

whence $X_4 = E(X_4 \mid X_1, X_2, X_3) + T_4$ \qquad E.2

Moreover, this value of f maximises the pmcc between X_4 and f.*

Hence, $\rho^2[(X_4, E(X_4 \mid X_1, X_2, X_3)]$ is the correlation ratio, which is written $\eta_{4(123)}{}^2$.

Moreover,*

$$\eta_{4(123)}^2 = \frac{\mathrm{Var}\,[E(X_4 \mid X_1, X_2, X_3)]}{\mathrm{Var}\,X_4}$$

$$= 1 - \frac{\mathrm{Var}\,T_4}{\mathrm{Var}\,X_4} \qquad \text{E.3}$$

Hence the correlation ratio is again a measure of the maximum variance in X_4 accounted for by the variance of a function of X_1, X_2 and X_3.

Finally, we note again that

$$E(T_4 \mid X_1, X_2, X_3) = 0 \qquad \text{E.4}$$

so that

$$E(T_4) = 0 \qquad \text{E.5}$$

All this can clearly be extended to as many variables as we wish.

F Linear Regression for Three or More Variables

We turn immediately to the linear case, since this case is most important in this book. Again we have the distinction between constrained and unconstrained regression.

In the unconstrained case we write

$$E(X_4 \mid X_1, X_2, X_3) = b_{41.23}X_1 + b_{42.13}X_2 + b_{43.12}X_3 + a_{4.123}$$
$$\text{F.1}$$

where I have used a notation for the coefficients which is common in the literature. The procedure for this notation is as follows: the first subscript is that of the variable for which a prediction is sought; the second is that of the variable to which the coefficient relates. These two are called the primary subscripts. Separated from them by a point are the subscripts of the other variables that enter the equation. These are the secondary subscripts. This notation can be cumbersome and I shall generally drop the secondary subscripts unless ambiguity arises.

In the constrained case we have

$$X_4 = b_{41}X_1 + b_{42}X_2 + b_{43}X_3 + a_4 + \xi_4 \qquad \text{F.2}$$

and our task here is to specify the coefficients.

We can ask either that $E(\xi_4^2)$ be minimised or that the pmcc between X_4 and the linear function be maximised.

If we pursue the first course we find that *

$$a_4 = \mu_4 - b_{41}\mu_1 - b_{42}\mu_2 - b_{43}\mu_3$$
$$\sigma_{14} = b_{41}\sigma_1^2 + b_{42}\sigma_{12} + b_{43}\sigma_{13}$$
$$\sigma_{24} = b_{41}\sigma_{12} + b_{42}\sigma_2^2 + b_{43}\sigma_{23}$$
$$\sigma_{34} = b_{41}\sigma_{13} + b_{42}\sigma_{23} + b_{43}\sigma_3^2$$

F.3

These equations are easily solved, though we shall not solve them here. We note, however, that F.3 implies, from F.2, that

$$E(\xi_4) = \text{Cov}(X_1\xi_4) = \text{Cov}(X_2\xi_4) = \text{Cov}(X_3\xi_4) = 0 \quad \text{F.4}$$

To show this, we rewrite F.2 as

$$X_4' = b_{41}X_1' + b_{42}X_2' + b_{43}X_3' + \xi_4 \quad \text{F.5}$$

where the dashes indicate measurement from the mean (we use the first equation of F.3 to replace a_4). If we multiply F.5 by X_1' and take expectations, then, using the second equation of F.3 we get $\text{Cov}(X_1\xi_4) = 0$; the same is true for X_2' and X_3'.

Moreover, we note that if we begin by assuming that F.4 holds, then it must follow that F.2 is the linear regression of X_4 on X_1, X_2 and X_3. This is because F.4 implies F.3, which, of course, implies that $E(\xi_4^2)$ is the minimum possible. Hence F.4 is necessary and sufficient for constrained linear regression. Note that F.4 is implied by $E(X_4 \mid X_1, X_2, X_3) = b_{41}X_1 + b_{42}X_2 + b_{43}X_3$ but does not imply this, so that F.4 is necessary but not sufficient for unconstrained linear regression.

Let us now write F.5 as

$$X_4' = L' + \xi_4 \quad \text{F.6}$$

where L' is the linear function measured from its mean (so that $L = b_{41}X_1 + b_{42}X_2 + b_{43}X_3 + a_4$). If we multiply F.6 by L' and take expectations, we have

$$\text{Cov}(X_4 L) = \text{Var}(L) \quad \text{F.7}$$

since $\text{Cov}(L\xi_4) = 0$ by virtue of F.4.

Hence, from C.1,

$$\rho^2(X_4, L) = \frac{[\text{Cov}(X_4 L)]^2}{\text{Var } L \text{ Var } X_4} = \frac{\text{Var } L}{\text{Var } X_4} \quad \text{F.8}$$

Now, squaring F.6 and taking expectations, we have (since $E(L'\xi_4) = 0$)

$$\text{Var } X_4 = \text{Var } L + \text{Var } \xi_4 \quad \text{F.9}$$

Since Var ξ_4 is the minimum possible, Var L is the maximum possible. It follows that $\rho^2(X_4, L)$ is the maximum possible (from F.8) and hence minimising $E(\xi_4{}^2)$ is equivalent to maximising the pmcc.

Combining F.8 and F.9 we see that

$$\rho^2(X_4, L) = \frac{\text{Var } L}{\text{Var } X_4} = 1 - \frac{\text{Var } \xi_4}{\text{Var } X_4} \qquad \text{F.10}$$

$\rho^2(X_4, L)$ is called the *multiple correlation coefficient* and is usually designated by $\rho_{4(123)}{}^2$ (or in a sample by $R_{4(123)}{}^2$). It measures the variance in X_4 accounted for by the joint variation of the best linear function of X_1, X_2 and X_3.

If the regression is unconstrained, Equation F.3 still holds. This can be verified by the reader by using the same technique as on p. 15. In this case, $\eta_{4(123)}{}^2 = \rho_{4(123)}{}^2$.

If the regression is constrained, then $\eta_{4(123)}{}^2 > \rho_{4(123)}{}^2$. Moreover, if we write the regression function as M we see that

$$\xi_4 = (M - L) + T_4 \qquad \text{F.11}$$

and so Var $\xi_4 = E \ [M - L]^2 \ + \text{Var } T_4$

(since $E(T_4 M) = E(T_4 L) = 0$), or

$$E[(M - L)^2] = \text{Var } \xi_4 - \text{Var } T_4 \qquad \text{F.12}$$

Since Var ξ_4 is as small as possible, we have effectively chosen L as the best linear approximation to M. (In the next section this result proves useful.)

In either the constrained or the unconstrained case it is reasonable to ask what increase in prediction is afforded by adding each variable. The Christmas test alone gives a proportion $\rho_{41}{}^2$. The Christmas test and teacher's estimate together give a proportion $\rho_{4(12)}{}^2$. $\rho_{41}{}^2$ comes from the simple two variable regression of X_4 on X_1, $\rho_{4(12)}{}^2$ from the three variable regression of X_4 on X_1 and X_2, namely

$$X_4 = b_{41.2} X_1 + b_{42.1} X_2 + a_{4.12} + \epsilon_{4.12} \qquad \text{F.13}$$

where ϵ is used to show the regression need not necessarily be constrained. (It is important to note that, in general $b_{41} \neq b_{41.2} \neq b_{41.23}$. The reasons for this are indicated below.)

The additional variance accounted for by adding X_2 is given by

$$\rho_{4(12)}{}^2 - \rho_{41}{}^2 \qquad \text{F.14}$$

This will always be positive. To see this, consider replacing X_2 in F.13

by the regression of X_2 on X_1, namely

$$X_2 = b_{21}X_1 + a_2 + \epsilon_2 \qquad \text{F.15}$$

The residual term will then be

$$b_{42.1}\epsilon_2 + \epsilon_{4.12} \qquad \text{F.16}$$

Now, multiplying F.15 (measured from its mean) by $\epsilon_{4.12}'$ shows that $\text{Cov}(\epsilon_2 \epsilon_{4.12}) = 0$. Hence,

$$\text{Var}[b_{42.1}\epsilon_2 + \epsilon_{4.12}] = b_{42.1}{}^2 \text{Var } \epsilon_2 + \text{Var } \epsilon_{4.12} \qquad \text{F.17}$$

Now when we replace X_2 in F.13 by F.15 we get a linear function in X_1 which must be the linear regression of X_4 on X_1, since the residual term F.16 is uncorrelated with X_1. (This regression equation also shows why, in general, $b_{41.2} \neq b_{41}$. In fact $b_{41} = b_{41.2} + b_{21}b_{42.1}$.) Hence, from F.17, on dividing by Var X_4,

$$1 - \rho_{41}{}^2 = b_{42.1}{}^2 \frac{\text{Var } \epsilon_2}{\text{Var } X_4} + 1 - \rho_{4(12)}{}^2$$

or

$$\rho_{4(12)}{}^2 - \rho_{41}{}^2 = b_{42.1}{}^2 \frac{\text{Var } \epsilon_2}{\text{Var } X_4} \qquad \text{F.18}$$

and the right-hand side of F.18 cannot be negative.

The proportion of variance in X_4 not accounted for by X_1, which is accounted for by the addition of X_2 is given by

$$\frac{\rho_{4(12)}{}^2 - \rho_{41}{}^2}{1 - \rho_{41}{}^2} = \rho_{42.1}{}^2, \text{ say.} \qquad \text{F.19}$$

$\rho_{42.1}{}^2$ is called the *partial correlation coefficient* of X_2 and X_4 given X_1. We can, of course, form $\rho_{4(123)}{}^2 - \rho_{4(12)}{}^2$ and then

$$\rho_{43.12}{}^2 = \frac{\rho_{4(123)}{}^2 - \rho_{4(12)}{}^2}{1 - \rho_{4(12)}{}^2} \qquad \text{F.20}$$

Let us consider what the partial correlation coefficient $\rho_{4.12}{}^2$ indicates. From F.16, we have that

$$b_{42.1}\epsilon_2 + \epsilon_{4.12} = \epsilon_{4.1} \qquad \text{F.21}$$

where $\epsilon_{4.1}$ is the residual of the regression of X_1 on X_4. Since $\text{Cov}(\epsilon_2 \epsilon_{4.12}) = 0$, F.21 is the linear regression of $\epsilon_{4.1}$ on ϵ_2.

The Theory of Causal Analysis 23

Now the pmcc between $\epsilon_{4.1}$ and ϵ_2 will be, analogously to D.21,

$$\frac{\text{Var}(b_{42.1}\epsilon_2)}{\text{Var }\epsilon_{4.1}} \text{ or } b_{42.1}{}^2 \frac{\text{Var }\epsilon_2}{\text{Var }\epsilon_{4.1}} \qquad \text{F.22}$$

From F.18 and F.19, we have that

$$\rho_{42.1}{}^2 = b_{42.1}{}^2 \frac{\text{Var }\epsilon_2}{\text{Var }X_4} \times \frac{1}{1 - \rho_{41}{}^2},$$

which simplifies to F.22.

Since ϵ_2 is the residual of X_2 after we subtract out the linear function of X_1, we see that the partial correlation coefficient is *the pmcc between the residuals of X_4 and X_2 after the linear effect of X_1 is subtracted out.* This is the reason for the term 'partial'.

Notice that, in general, a partial correlation coefficient like $\rho_{42.1}{}^2$ is *not* the pmcc between X_2 and X_4, for X_1 constant. This is only the case with some additional assumptions which are discussed in Appendix 2(II), Section 8. The definition used in F.19 is often the best interpretation to use. Thus in our 'maths test' example, $\rho_{42.1}{}^2$ is the proportion of variance unaccounted for by the Christmas test, which is accounted for by the addition of the teacher's estimate. Similarly, for $\rho_{43.12}{}^2$: the proportion of variance unaccounted for by the conjunction of the Christmas test and the teacher's estimate, which is accounted for by the pupil's own estimate.

Finally, a word should be said here about the technique of 'step-wise' regression, for assessing the importance of the predictor variables. There are two methods. One, called the forward approach, first chooses that predictor variable which correlates best with the response variable; this is step 1. Now a second predictor variable is chosen which, together with the first, correlates best; this is step 2. The process continues until some criterion measure like the increase in correlation obtained becomes small enough (or a hypothesis test based on this idea can be used), when the variables chosen are retained as predictors and the rest discarded.

The second method is the backward approach. Here we begin with the full set of predictors and then discard that one which lowers the combined correlation with the response variable by the least amount; this is step 1. Now a second predictor is discarded, which further lowers the combined correlation with the response variable by the least amount; this is step 2. The process continues until some criterion measure like the decrease in correlation obtained becomes too large (or a hypothesis test based on this idea can be used) when the variables remaining are chosen as the predictor variables, the rest being discarded.

Unfortunately, these two methods often give different subsets of predictor variables, though for various reasons most practitioners favour the backward approach. Also, it is possible to produce data where the solutions given by the methods are not optimal.

These are not the only problems with the methods, however. They are, in effect, exercises in 'data-dredging' and in the absence of any theoretical reasons for rejecting or including variables, there is no guarantee that another sample may not give entirely different results.

In general, a better approach, when considerable theoretical knowledge is available, is to test one or more specific hypotheses. (Hypothesis testing will be considered for causal analysis in Section O).

The computer, of course, makes all of this easy, but also extends the dangers of 'data-dredging'. Such procedures are best seen as exploratory only, results arising being regarded themselves as hypotheses which should be tested on other data (this is the method of replication).

More will be said on all this in the sections dealing with causal analysis, and we leave until then a detailed consideration of assessing the separate influences of variables.

G Regression and Non-cardinal Variables

The aim of regression as we have presented it here is to predict the value of one variable from one or more other variables.

If the response variable is continuous cardinal then the function of the predictor variables will always give a possible value of the variable (except in rare cases where the response variable has theoretical limits). A problem arises, however, with a discrete cardinal response variable, for in this case we are very likely to predict a value from the regression function which it is theoretically impossible for the response variable to take. As already stated, most cardinal variables can be understood to have underlying continuity, but there exist variables like 'number of children in a family' which are necessarily discrete. If we predict a value of 2.3, say, then this *must* be wrong since such a value is not possible.

This problem is solved, however, by redefining the aim of regression in this case: instead of predicting the value of the response variable, we predict its conditional mean. In the case of unconstrained regression, we are assuming that we can predict the mean precisely, for we have

$$E(X_4 \mid X_1, X_2, X_3) = M(X_1, X_2, X_3) \qquad \text{G.1}$$

where M is some function of the predictor variables which we assume we can specify. In the case of constrained linear regression, we attempt to predict the value of M, where M cannot be specified. This is seen directly from equation F.11, which can be written

$$M = L + \Lambda_4 \qquad \text{G.2}$$

where $\Lambda_4 = T_4 - \xi_4$, and from F.12

$$\text{Var } \Lambda_4 = \text{Var } \xi_4 - \text{Var } T_4 \qquad \text{G.3}$$

Since Var T_4 is fixed (by M), and since Var ξ_3 is as small as possible, L is the best linear predictor of M, as required. We will meet this problem again (in a more severe form) when we consider causal analysis.

If the response variable is not cardinal, and is not dichotomous, then we cannot take the mean. The reason for this should be clear. If the mean of a set of cardinal variables is m and we change the origin by an amount x then the mean becomes $m + x$. It thus preserves the interval level relationship of distance. Similarly, a change of scale gives sm, say, again preserving the interval level relationship of simple ratio. Hence, the mean has properties which make it invariant to exactly the same transformations as are invariant for cardinal variables (i.e. those transformations that preserve the defining characteristics of the variables). It is this that makes the use of the mean in cardinal variables mathematically valid, quite apart from whether or not it is socially meaningful. (The standard deviation does not change its value with a change of origin, but this is because it is a second order measure concerned with the distances between variables, which, of course, are independent of origin. Changes of scale, of course, are reflected in the standard deviation as they are in distances.)

The mean is not invariant to the transformations preserving the relationships on ordinal variables. As a very simple example, a variable with values 0, 1, 3 has a mean lying between 1 and 3. The same variable with new values 0, 6, 7 has a mean lying between 0 and 6. Thus order, which must remain invariant, is not preserved for the mean. In the case of nominal variables (except dichotomous) the mean is usually quite meaningless.

It follows that we cannot perform regression, in the terms we have described it, if the response variable is not cardinal. This is not contradicted by the case of dichotomous variables (taking the values 0 and 1) because it is the mean of that variable which is taken as independent, and not the variable itself. The mean is precisely the proportion taking the attribute (scored 1). In this case, we do not predict the mean as a way of specifying the variable of which it is the mean. The proportion can hardly be taken as in some way representative of the dichotomous variable: rather it is (in effect) a continuous variable in its own right. What we are doing is attempting to predict the proportion (or probability) of units having a given attribute among units who take the values x_1, x_2 and x_3, say, on X_1, X_2 and X_3.

If any predictor variable is not cardinal, a different problem arises. There is no difficulty in forming the conditional mean $E(X_4 \mid X_1, X_2, X_3)$. However, if we try to specify a function for this mean we can hardly do so unless we can specify (within a scale or origin factor, which may be accommodated by the function) the values of the variables concerned, and this we cannot do with non-cardinal variables. Hence, unconstrained regression is not available with non-cardinal predictor variables if we want to seriously attempt to give a mathematical formula for the regression function (but see below).

In the case of constrained regression there is nothing to stop us using any assigned values we like, as long as we stick to them, for non-cardinal predictor variables, and attempting to predict the response variable (or its mean). Such a course, however, is likely to be wildly inaccurate, and we would probably be better off just guessing; using regression in this way would simply be a form of obfuscation.

The solution in both the unconstrained and constrained cases is to partition the population into sub-populations taking the various categories of the non-cardinal predictor variable or variables and then to run separate regressions on each sub-population. In the unconstrained linear case we would assume a linear form in each sub-population, but that the values of the regression coefficients would vary from sub-population to sub-population.

A very popular alternative to this in the linear case is to use dummy variables. To understand this idea, consider first a simple dichotomous variable, say X_c. We include in the regression equation a term $b_{4c}X_c$. If $X_c = 0$ there is no 'effect'; if $X_c = 1$ the 'effect' is b_{4c}. If X_c is, instead, polytomous (with three or more categories) we simply use 'dummies'. Hence, if X_c has categories A, B, C, D we form $X_A : A \mid \text{not } A; X_B : B \mid \text{not } B$; and $X_C : C \mid \text{not } C$. Scores on these variables are not independent, of course: only one can score 1; and if none score 1, we have category D.

In cases where we mix cardinal and non-cardinal variables this method makes a large assumption, namely that only the constant term and not the regression coefficients is affected by the category taken. In order to incorporate change in regression coefficients many interactive terms (like $cX_A X_1$) would be needed. Such interaction models are complex and can pose estimation problems. Hence the use of dummy variables in 'mixed' regression is not always to be recommended. In the case of only non-cardinal variables, however, the idea is very sound, but is usually presented differently, under the rubric 'analysis of variance'.

H Estimating Regression Coefficients: The Method of Least Squares

In general, our observable data will be a sample from some target population, as we have already discussed. Our problem is to estimate the value of the regression coefficients in the population from our sample data. We will look only very briefly at the problem here, since the important results will be considered after we have considered causal analysis.

Consider first constrained regression. In the four variable case we have

$$X_4 = b_{41}X_1 + b_{42}X_2 + b_{43}X_3 + a_4 + \xi_4 \qquad \text{H.1}$$

where, *in the population*, $E(\xi_4^2)$ is minimum. The analogy to $E(\xi_4^2)$ in the sample is $\Sigma_N \xi_{4i}^2$ where Σ_N represents a sum over the sample of size N, and where ξ_{4i} is the value of ξ_4 for unit of analysis i.

Now, in general, the value of $\Sigma_N \xi_{4i}^2$ will *not* be the minimum possible, given the *population* values of the regression coefficients. The most intuitive approach to estimation, however, is to estimate the population values by minimising the sum of the residuals in the sample. That is, we have

$$X_4 = \hat{b}_{41}X_1 + \hat{b}_{42}X_2 + \hat{b}_{43}X_3 + \hat{a}_4 + e_4 \qquad \text{H.2}$$

where Σe_4^2 is the minimum possible for the sample, and $\hat{b}_{41}, \hat{b}_{42}, \hat{b}_{43}$ and $\hat{a}_4$ are the corresponding values of the coefficients for this minimum. We note that e_4 is not the same as ξ_4 since the sample regression coefficients will not, in general, have the same value as the population regression coefficients.

What we have done here, in effect, is to apply constrained linear regression to the sample. The line obtained is taken as an estimate of the population line.

Now, in the unconstrained case, by analogy, it seems we should choose the estimate by minimising the residuals for each set of values of X_1, X_2 and X_3. Unfortunately, however, it is most unlikely that we will get the same values of the regression coefficients for each set of values of X_1, X_2 and X_3. The situation is the same as that encountered with constrained linear regression in the population: we have too few parameters to maintain a minimum value of Σe_4^2 for each set of X_1, X_2 and X_3 values in the sample. What we do in the unconstrained case, therefore, is to use the same method as the constrained case. This method is called, for obvious reasons, *the method of least squares*.

28 An Introduction to Causal Analysis in Sociology

Since we have effectively applied constrained regression to the sample, all the results already obtained for a population will carry through to this case by replacing population measures by their corresponding sample measures. Hence, from F.3

$$\hat{a}_4 = \bar{x}_4 - \hat{b}_{41}\bar{x}_1 - \hat{b}_{42}\bar{x}_2 - \hat{b}_{43}\bar{x}_3$$
$$s_{14} = \hat{b}_{41}s_1^2 + \hat{b}_{42}s_{12} + \hat{b}_{43}s_{13}$$
$$s_{24} = \hat{b}_{41}s_{12} + \hat{b}_{42}s_2^2 + \hat{b}_{43}s_{23}$$
$$s_{34} = \hat{b}_{41}s_{13} + \hat{b}_{42}s_{23} + \hat{b}_{43}s_3^2 \qquad \text{H.3}$$

Similarly,

$$\text{cov}(X_1 e_4) = \text{cov}(X_2 e_4) = \text{cov}(X_3 e_4) = 0 \qquad \text{H.4}$$

where the small c indicates a sample covariation. From F.8,

$$r^2(X_4, L) = \frac{\text{var } L}{s_4^2} \qquad \text{H.5}$$

and so

$$R_{4(123)}^2 = 1 - \frac{\text{var } e_4}{s_4^2} \qquad \text{H.6}$$

Finally, from F.20

$$r_{43.12}^2 = \frac{R_{4(123)}^2 - R_{4(12)}^2}{1 - R_{4(12)}^2} \qquad \text{H.7}$$

Now we can ask how good the regression estimates are. Two criteria are generally taken as important here. Firstly, that the conditional average of each estimate equals the population value. That is, we would like, for instance

$$E(\hat{b}_{41} \mid x_1, x_2, x_3) = b_{41} \qquad \text{H.8}$$

where the expectation is taken over all possible samples when $X_1 = x_1$, $X_2 = x_2$ and $X_3 = x_3$. If this is the case we say that b_{41} is (conditionally) *unbiased*. To ensure this we need to assume that

$$E(\xi_4 \mid X_1, X_2, X_3) = 0 \qquad \text{H.9}$$

Hence we need to assume unconstrained regression to ensure unbiasedness; in the constrained case we normally have biased estimates (in the sense defined here).

Secondly, we would like the variance of our estimates to be as small as possible so that they tend to cluster close to the population value (assuming unbiasedness). To ensure this we need to assume the homoscedasticity of ξ_4 on X_1, X_2 and X_3, that is:

$$\text{Var}(\xi_4 \mid X_1, X_2, X_3) = \text{constant} \qquad \text{H.10}$$

This assumption is additional to that involved in unconstrained regression.

If we give X_1, X_2 and X_3 probability distributions, then we can express the resultant unbiasedness and minimum variance unconditionally. This depends upon the values of X_1, X_2 and X_3 in the sample being chosen at random from the population; this is not always practicable, however.

It is worth noting that if, in addition, we assume that ξ_4 is conditionally normal, then so is e_4, and moreover the converse also holds. Indeed, equations H.9 and H.10 can be expressed in terms of e_4 instead of ξ_4, regardless of the normality assumption, the observed values, e_4, being a kind of weighted average of the unobserved values ξ_4. (See also p. 158.)

There is nothing to stop us using least squares, of course, without these assumptions, but when we do, we know that the estimates are not the best possible in the terms so defined. Unfortunately, this is usually a theoretical point, since we do not know which *are* the best estimates nor how to obtain them in a simple practical way. Thus, least squares is used anyway because it is the most convenient and intuitively reasonable.

The behaviour of the correlation coefficients is not so easy to discuss, however, and in general they are not unbiased. Again, attempting to correct this is quite complex, and it is usual to make do with the sample estimates anyway, unless we wish to make statistical tests.

If we make an assumption about the distribution of e_4 — namely that it is normal for each set of values of X_1, X_2 and X_3 — then we can make statistical tests. We shall not discuss this here, however, since the important statistical tests we require will be discussed after our discussion of causal analysis.

The fact that least squares is used even when we cannot make assumptions to ensure that the estimates obtained are best should not be viewed as an invalid procedure. Rather, it is best to view the procedure as constrained regression on a sample, the sample being understood as a sort of random sub-population. Then inferences from the sample to the wider population are rather like that from a population to unobserved population (see Section B), and the generalisation involved is to some extent extra-statistical, depending for instance on the representativeness of the observations according to theoretical considerations. When we consider causal analysis, however, we will find that this view is not applicable; and it is to causal analysis that we now turn.

I Causal Analysis

Earlier, we saw how to best predict X_4 from X_1, X_2 and X_3. In our analysis we did not need to make any causal assumptions about these variables — our aim was simply that of prediction. Of course, our choice of X_1, X_2 and X_3 was guided both by convenience and by our theoretical preconceptions: convenience, because we generally try to choose independent variables which are relatively easy to measure; theoretical preconceptions, because we try to choose variables which we feel have a strong association with the variable we wish to predict. In many cases, convenience includes the idea of temporal priority, since the predicted value is often hard to measure, in the sense that it is relatively inaccessible at a given time, whereas the independent variables chosen are relatively easily accessible at that time. Moreover, our theoretical considerations often involve ideas about causality, for it is with the imagery of causality that we often assess strength of association. Nevertheless, whilst temporal priority and our theoretical considerations implicitly involve ideas of causality, these ideas are not taken into account explicitly in the treatment of regression.

Let us suppose, however, that we are willing to assume explicitly — for whatever reasons — that X_1, X_2 and X_3 have causal priority over X_4. By this we mean that X_4 may be causally dependent (and not just functionally dependent) on the independent variables. We assume, then, that X_1, X_2 and X_3 are potential causes of X_4. Given this assumption, can we use regression to help us assess the causal effect of X_1, X_2 and X_3 on X_4?

Consider the values of X_4 when X_1, X_2 and X_3 are held constant. We will expect to see variation in this case, but since the independent variables are constant, this variation must be due to units of analysis taking various values on causal variables other than X_1, X_2 and X_3. Let us call these latter variables implicit causes, in contrast to X_1, X_2 and X_3 which we call explicit causes.

Now the size of the effect that X_1, X_2 and X_3 have on X_4 may differ for different units of analysis, this being so if the size of the effect is dependent on the values taken by some implicit causes. Let us assume, however, that this effect is constant for all units. Then we can write this effect as a function of X_1, X_2 and X_3 only, say $\phi(X_1, X_2, X_3)$, and this function has the same form for all units.

Hence we can write,

$$X_4 = \phi_4(X_1, X_2, X_3) + \Lambda_4 \qquad \text{I.1}$$

where Λ_4 represents the effect on X_4 of other causes of X_4 — the implicit causes — giving us what we might call the implicit effect.

Now we may feel able to specify the mathematical form of ϕ_4 (and indeed, as we shall see, we usually assume it to be linear). In order to identify the parameters of ϕ_4, however, we shall need to assume something about Λ_4. We can assume that Λ_4 is uncorrelated with X_1, X_2 and X_3, whence we have constrained regression, and in the linear case, constrained linear regression. In this case the parameters of ϕ are identifiable.

What substantive assumption about the implicit causes do we need to make in order to guarantee this lack of correlation? It is difficult to find a convincing and meaningful assumption which can be based on theoretical considerations other than what we might call the assumption of causal independence. This is that the implicit causes are neither causes of, nor effects of, nor have causes in common with X_1, X_2 and X_3. Of course, we could just say that there exists no linear combination of implicit causes which will account for any part of X_1, X_2 or X_3 (and thus no linear combination of X_1, X_2 and X_3 which will account for any part of any implicit cause), but then this begs the question as to why this is so and soon we must return to causal independence.

Causal independence, however, implies more than just lack of correlation between Λ_4 and X_1, X_2 and X_3; it implies their statistical independence. It is easy to see this. If X_1, X_2 and X_3 are held constant, all the causes of the implicit variables will be expected to vary in just the same way as if X_1, X_2 and X_3 were not constant. Moreover, none of the implicit variables will be constrained in value by the holding constant of X_1, X_2 and X_3 since none are causes of X_1, X_2 or X_3. Hence, the distribution of Λ_4 will be the same for all values of X_1, X_2 and X_3, which is statistical independence.

Now, apart from there being no other convincing assumption other than causal independence to account for lack of correlation, we shall see later that, for the purposes of hypothesis testing, we need indeed to assume that Λ_4 is statistically independent of X_1, X_2 and X_3. Even if we do not require to make hypothesis tests, for optimum estimates we need to assume the constancy over X_1, X_2 and X_3 of the mean and variance of Λ_4 (as we have already seen in the last section). We cannot rely here on extrastatistical generalisation from a random sub-population (as was advocated in the last section when dealing with prediction) since the form of ϕ_4 constitutes a theoretical model, and we wish to use statistical inference to best estimate the parameters of that model. No finite data set will exhibit these parameters precisely, because their estimation rests on an assumption of causal independence, the statistical consequences of which only hold at a theoretical level. (For a much more extensive analysis of this see Birnbaum (1979).)

The implication of causal independence is that none of X_1, X_2 or X_3

have any common causes with X_4 (apart from another variable from the explicit set X_1, X_2 and X_3), that X_4 is not a cause of any of X_1, X_2 or X_3 (but see Appendix 1) and that the effect of X_1, X_2 and X_3 as measured by ϕ_4 includes indirect effects through other non-explicit variables (since these cannot, by assumption, be included in Λ_4). The latter implication is really a definition of causal effect as measured by ϕ_4, but the former implication is really substantive. If we suspect an implicit variable which is a common cause of one or more of the explicit variables and X_4, then we *must* include it explicitly. Equivalently, we must have theoretical reasons for supposing that the implicit variables are, at worst, negligibly associated with the explicit ones so that we do not need to include them explicitly. To be sure, we may well be in error, but the best we can do is to attempt to minimise error whilst at the same time not including so many variables that we cannot cope with the implications theoretically or practically (though computers make this latter seemingly unimportant). To practise causal analysis convincingly, we need sound theories which will guide our model-building. This will become even more of a necessity when we specify ϕ_4 and when we causally order the explicit variables themselves. To these points we now turn.

J Linear Causal Models: The Regression Coefficient Interpretation

It is very usual to assume that the causal effect of X_1, X_2 and X_3 is linear. Then we have

$$X_4 = b_{41}X_1 + b_{42}X_2 + b_{43}X_3 + U_4 \qquad \text{J.1}$$

where U_4 represents the effects of implicit causes. Causal independence implies that the regression is unconstrained linear, the constant term being $E(U_4)$.

Since J.1 holds for every unit of analysis, it follows that b_{41} is the effect on X_4 of a one unit change in X_1 with X_2, X_3 and implicit (non-intervening) effects constant. It is valid to imagine this admittedly hypothetical change being at least theoretically possible even if X_1 is a cause of X_2 and of X_3. For the tendency of X_2 to change due to a change in X_1 can be offset by changing other causes of X_2 which, by the causal independence assumption cannot be causes of X_4 and so cannot affect the change in value of X_4. The causal independence assumption therefore gives theoretical grounds for considering such hypothetical changes as meaningful (albeit impossible to perform in practice). Similar arguments apply to the causes responsible for changing X_1, since none of these can be causes of X_4.

The Theory of Causal Analysis   33

b_{41} is called the *direct effect of X_1 on X_4* in the context of X_2 and X_3, often abbreviated to direct effect of X_1. Similarly for b_{42} and b_{43}. The context is important, since it stresses those potentially intervening variables which we can hold constant (recall that implicit intervening variables will vary with X_1 by virtue of the definition of ϕ_4 implied by causal independence).

The direct effect is, in the linear model, quite independent of other explicit (and implicit) variables. We need theoretical reasons to assume this. If our theory leads us to strongly suspect this assumption, then we will need to use terms like cX_1X_2; cX_2 is the direct effect of X_1 which depends for its size on which value X_2 has. In this book, however, only linear models will be considered. Interactive models (as models with such terms as cX_1X_2 are called) can be incorporated in the linear case by defining Y_1, say, as X_1X_2. It must be stressed, however, that problems may occur in estimation due to the effect known as multi-collinearity where the linear regression equation *in the sample* of at least one of the explicit variables on the rest accounts for a very high proportion of the variance in that variable. If we have terms in Y_1, X_1 and this may well happen, and thus care must be taken with interactive models. In any case, some care needs to be taken with linear models too, though it is often difficult to deal with in practice, and we must then be aware of the drop of precision in estimation implied. Actually, in the cross-sectional data that characterise much of the causal analysis described here, the situation is relatively rare, for typically there is considerable residual variation.

The coefficients b_{41}, b_{42} and b_{43} are, of course, just regression coefficients but the causal interpretation we have been able to give them depends on the additional causal assumptions specified above. In this case, the coefficients are often referred to as structural coefficients, and the regression equation is called a structural equation.

Notice that there has been no need to make any causal ordering amongst X_1, X_2 and X_3 themselves. If we are content with this, and thus with equation J.1 only, then we say that X_1, X_2 and X_3 are all *exogenous variables*, because none of them is accounted for in any way by any other explicit variable in the system. By contrast, X_4, which is so accounted for, is called an *endogenous variable*.

It is usual, however, to want to investigate what are called indirect effects, and to this end further orderings are made. Let us suppose, then, that X_1 and X_2 are causally prior to X_3. Assuming linearity, we have

$$X_3 = b_{31}X_1 + b_{32}X_2 + U_3 \qquad \text{J.2}$$

where we assume the causal independence of U_3 with X_1 and X_2.

With both equations J.1 and J.2, X_1 and X_2 are exogenous, X_3 and X_4 endogenous. Since X_1, X_2 and X_3 are all causally independent of U_4, so must be U_3 of U_4, which implies that X_3 and X_4 have no common causes except X_1 and X_2, a point we have already noted above.

If we substitute J.2 in J.1 we get

$$X_4 = (b_{41} + b_{43}b_{31})X_1 + (b_{42} + b_{43}b_{32})X_2 + (b_{43}u_3 + u_4) \quad \text{J.3}$$

Now, a change of one unit in X_1 with X_2 and non-intervening implicit effects constant gives an effect $(b_{41} + b_{43}b_{31})$ on X_4. The size of the regression coefficient has changed (and could indeed now be zero) because X_3 has become an intervening explicit variable which cannot be controlled for in this equation. This explains why we often wish to make explicit, variables which are implicit — intervening — if we suspect they have important effects then their inclusion can greatly elucidate the effect of the other explicit variables. We note here that X_3 has been allowed to change only to the extent that its change is due to X_1, since U_3 is held constant. Hence $b_{43}b_{31}$ is the *indirect effect of X_1 on X_4 through X_3* with X_2 and implicit effects constant. Similarly, $b_{43}b_{32}$ is the indirect effect of X_2 on X_4 through X_3.

This can be represented very concisely by the use of what are called *path diagrams*. It can be seen that we need only multiply the coefficients of the 'paths' in this diagram to get the desired results:

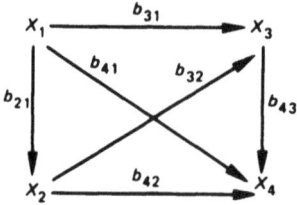

In the context of this diagram, the structural coefficients are often referred to as path regression coefficients. Such diagrams will recur often in future chapters of this book, and are very easy to interpret.

The double-headed arrow between X_1 and X_2 serves to indicate that X_1 and X_2 may be causally related, but in an unspecified way. However, we may also want to assume that X_1 is causally prior to X_2. We then have, assuming linearity,

$$X_2 = b_{21}X_1 + U_2 \quad \text{J.4}$$

where U_2 is causally independent of X_1. Again, U_2 is causally independent of both U_3 and U_4, so, in addition, X_2 and X_4 have no common causes outside X_1, and, of course, X_1 and X_4 have no common causes at all.

If we substitute J.4 in J.3 we get

$$X_4 = (b_{41} + b_{43}b_{31} + b_{42}b_{21} + b_{43}b_{32}b_{21})X_1$$
$$+ [(b_{42} + b_{43}b_{32})U_2 + b_{43}U_3 + U_4] \qquad \text{J.5}$$

The new term, $b_{43}b_{32}b_{21}$ is the indirect effect of X_1 on X_4 through X_2 and X_3. Again we can use a path diagram, which is

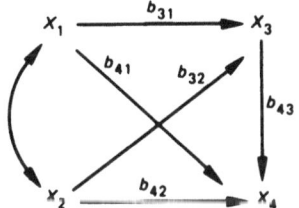

and again multiplication of coefficients along paths give the required effects.

Equations J.1, J.2 and J.4 together constitute what is called a *fully recursive system* with one exogenous variable (X_1); J.1 and J.2 constitute a fully recursive system with two exogenous variables $(X_1$ and $X_2)$. Such systems are characterised by a lack of bicausality on endogenous variables, so that X_4 cannot be a cause of X_1, X_2 or X_3 (see also Appendix 1). In the two exogenous case, X_1 and X_2 can be bicausally related; in the three exogenous case (i.e. Equation J.1 alone) X_1, X_2 and X_3 can be bicausally related.

So far we have included every lower numbered variable in every equation for a higher numbered variable. Sometimes it is possible, however, to have enough theory to specify that one (or more) of the lower numbered variables is not a direct cause (and, of course, not an effect) of some higher numbered one. In such a case we have an *a-priori-trimmed recursive system*.

For instance, let us retain J.4 but rewrite J.1 as

$$X_4 = b_{41}X_1 + b_{43}X_3 + U_4 \qquad \text{J.6}$$

and J.2 as

$$X_3 = b_{32}X_2 + U_3 \qquad \text{J.7}$$

We have assumed here that X_2 is not a direct cause of X_4 and that X_1 is not a direct cause of X_3.

It is clear now that we no longer need to assume that X_2 and U_4 are causally independent — so that U_2 and U_4 may be causally dependent, and thus X_2 and X_4 may have common causes other than X_1. Furthermore, X_1 and U_3 are not necessarily causally independent, so X_1 and X_3 may have common causes.

It is possible, however, to begin with a fully recursive system and to test for $b_{42} = 0$ and $b_{31} = 0$ (see later). We would then arrive at a *tested-a-priori-trimmed recursive system*. However, in this case we would need to assume the causal independence of X_2 and U_4 and of X_1 and U_3, and so, while this is sometimes the better approach, since it makes no untested a priori assumption about the causal effects, it does need more causal independence assumptions than the former case. These and related issues will be taken up again later.

The path diagrams as we have shown them would look identical in these two cases, but there is a difference due to causal independence assumptions. It is usual, therefore, also to include the effects of the implicit causes on path diagrams. In the a priori case this would give

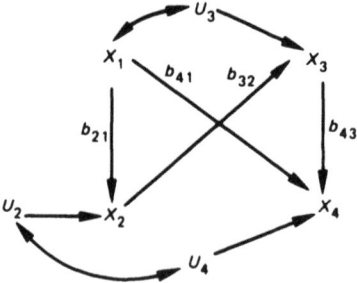

and in the tested a priori case

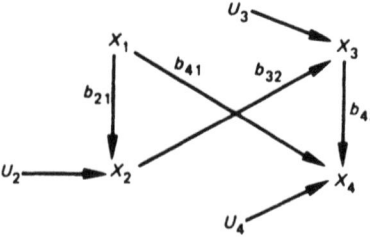

Notice the double-headed arrow between U_2 and U_4 and between U_3 and X_1 in the a priori case — the tested a priori case assumes causal independence between these variables.

There is a third category, which we may call the *a-posteriori-trimmed recursive system*. In this case, we begin with a full system, and then apply an algorithm which systematically reduces the number of coefficients until a criterion value is exceeded. This is discussed in Section O below, along with a priori tests. The diagram for the a posteriori case will be like that for the tested a priori case, since causal independence is assumed, but the cases are, from a substantive point of view, very different.

Equations similar to J.6 and J.7, where variables are missing, occur also in *block recursive* systems. In such cases it is not the case that a direct effect is assumed to be zero; rather the effects between two or more variables are simply unspecified. More will be said on block recursivity in the introduction to Chapter 2 of Part II, p. 86. For now, we can note that equation J.6 would still be valid if the direct effect of X_2 on X_4 was not zero. In that case, some of the correlation between U_2 and U_4 would be due to that direct effect. Whilst the analysis would be correct, however, the interpretation would be faulty, since the entire correlation between U_2 and U_4 would be attributed to other causes if the direct effect is posited to be zero. In general, it is quite pointless to leave out the direct effect if we suspect it to be non-zero.

Sometimes the implicit effect U_1 is shown on a path diagram (so that in the a priori case U_1 and U_3 would have a double-headed arrow). The equation is $X_1 = U_1$, which is really a pseudo-equation expressing X_1 as an exogenous variable. It is not necessary, however, to include such equations in the system.

The results and methods discussed here can, of course, be generalised without difficulty to any number of variables.

K Linear Causal Models: The Variance Interpretation

Thus far, our interpretation of the parameters of the linear causal model has been in terms of a hypothetical experiment concerned with changing one or more of the explicit variables and holding the others and the implicit effects constant. This experiment is based upon the usual idea of causality, whereby manipulation of a cause produces a change or an effect. We are now going to consider a different interpretation, one which is quite popular in the literature.

We begin by standardising our variables; this is achieved by measuring from the mean, a change of origin, and by using units of standard deviation, a change of scale. Thus, associated with X_1 we define $Y_1 = (X_1 - \mu_1)/\sigma_1$, and similarly with X_2, X_3 and X_4. Note that $Y_1 = 0$ when $X_1 = \mu_1$ and one unit of Y_1 is σ_1 in X_1 as required. We now write

$$Y_4 = p_{41}Y_1 + p_{42}Y_2 + p_{43}Y_3 + p_{4v}V_4 \qquad \text{K.1}$$

where we define p_{4v} so that $\mathrm{Var}(V_4) = 1$. (Note that in regression theory, the p's are often written as β-coefficients, and called *standardised regression coefficients*.)

What is the relationship between K.1 and J.1? Taking the mean value of J.1 and subtracting from J.1 we have

$$X_4' = b_{41}X_1' + b_{42}X_2' + b_{43}X_3' + U_4' \qquad \text{K.2}$$

where the dashes indicate measurement from the mean (in fact $U_4' = U_4$ since $E(U_4) = 0$).

Now define

$$p_{41} = \frac{\sigma_1}{\sigma_4} b_{41},\, p_{42} = \frac{\sigma_2}{\sigma_4} b_{42},\, p_{43} = \frac{\sigma_3}{\sigma_4} b_{43}$$

and $\qquad p_{4v} = \dfrac{\sigma_{u4}}{\sigma_4} \qquad$ K.3

Replacing the equivalent value of b_{41}, b_{42}, b_{43} from K.3 in K.2 gives

$$X_4' = \sigma_4 \left(p_{41}\frac{X_1'}{\sigma_1} + p_{42}\frac{X_2'}{\sigma_2} + p_{43}\frac{X_3'}{\sigma_3} + p_{4v}\frac{U_4'}{\sigma_{u4}} \right) \qquad \text{K.4}$$

which is equivalent to K.1 if $V_4 = U_4/\sigma_{u4}$, and so V_4 is causally independent of X_1, X_2 and X_3 and so of Y_1, Y_2 and Y_3, by definition.

In order to interpret the p coefficients, which we call *path coefficients*, we proceed as follows, confining our attention to p_{41}.

Take the conditional expectation of J.1, with X_2, X_3 and U_4 constant. This gives

$$E(X_4 \mid X_2, X_3, U_4) = b_{41}E(X_1 \mid X_2, X_3, U_4)$$
$$+ b_{42}X_2 + b_{43}X_3 + U_4 \qquad \text{K.5}$$

Subtract K.5 from J.1, square, and take conditional expectations with X_2, X_3 and U_4 constant to give

$$\sigma_{4.23u}^2 = b_{41}^2 \sigma_{1.23u}^2 \qquad \text{K.6}$$

where $\sigma_{4.23u}^2 = \mathrm{Var}(X_4 \mid X_2, X_3, U_4)$ and $\sigma_{1.23u}^2 = \mathrm{Var}(X_1 \mid X_2, X_3, U_4)$. Now replace b_{41} by p_{41} in K.6 and rearrange to give

$$p_{41}^2 = \frac{\sigma_1^2}{\sigma_{1.23u}^2} \times \frac{\sigma_{4.23u}^2}{\sigma_4^2} \qquad \text{K.7}$$

or, in terms of standard deviation,

$$p_{41} = \frac{\sigma_1}{\sigma_{1.23u}} \times \frac{\sigma_{4.23u}}{\sigma_4} \qquad \text{K.8}$$

The second term on the right of K.7 is the ratio of the variance of X_4 when X_2, X_3 and U_4 are held constant, to the variance of X_4 when these variables are allowed to vary. Now, in general, this term will depend on the value at which X_2, X_3 and U_4 are held constant. Nevertheless, at whatever value they are so held, the variance of X_1 will be decreased (unless X_1 be causally independent of X_2 and X_3 — we know it is causally independent of U_4), and consequently the variance of X_4 due to X_1 when X_2, X_3 and U_4 are held constant, namely $\sigma_{4.23u}^2$, will be an undervaluation of the variance of X_4 which *would be* due to X_1 with X_2, X_3 and U_4 constant if X_1 varied to the extent that it did unconstrained. This undervaluation is important since σ_4^2 is precisely the variance due to X_1 unconstrained, as well as due to X_2, X_3 and U_4. Hence, the first term is a correction factor which upgrades $\sigma_{4.23u}^2$ to the value it would be expected to take if X_1 could vary to the same extent that it does unconstrained. We note with this correction factor that the value at which X_2, X_3 and U_4 are held does not affect the value of the corrected ratio, for p_{41}^2 is a constant. Hence,

$p_{41}^2 =$ Variance of X_4 with X_2, X_3 and U_4 constant, which would occur if X_1 varied to the extent that it does unconstrained in the population *as a proportion of* Variance of X_4 due to X_1, X_2, X_3 and U_4 all varying

It follows that p_{41}^2 is the proportion of variance in X_4 directly due to X_1. It is worth noting that p_{41}^2 can be greater than 1. This is explained by saying that X_1 has a propensity to cause X_4 to vary more than X_4 actually did, this propensity being damped down by the effects of X_2, X_3 and U_4 in the population.

This interpretation of p_{41}^2 in terms of variance (or of p_{41} in terms of standard deviation) is claimed to establish the path coefficients as measuring the direct causal effect of X_1 on X_4. There is, however, an important objection to this.

From K.6 we see that $b_{41}^2 = \sigma_{4.23u}^2/\sigma_{1.23u}^2$. Thus b_{41}^2 is independent of the variance of X_2, X_3 or U_4 in the population. Moreover, as the denominator $\sigma_{1.23u}^2$ increases or decreases in the population, so will the numerator $\sigma_{4.23u}^2$, which depends only on X_1. It follows that if we compare the value of b_{41} in two populations, then the comparison is quite independent of the variance of any implicit causes in the two populations. Similarly, if we consider the ratio b_{41}/b_{42}, which gives the causal effect of X_1 relative to X_2, and compare this ratio in two populations then again this comparison does not depend on the variance of implicit causes in the two populations. This is just what we require of a causal parameter: its interpretation is population-independent.

Now $p_{41}^2 = (\sigma_1^2/\sigma_4^2) b_{41}^2$. σ_4^2 depends in part for its value on the variation in U_4, which σ_1^2 does not. Further, X_2 and X_3 affect the variance of X_1 in a different way from the variance of X_4. It follows that the ratio σ_1^2/σ_4^2 is population-specific. Hence, comparing p_{41}^2 in two populations depends in part on the variance of implicit causes in each of the two populations. Similarly, the ratio p_{41}^2/p_{42}^2 depends on σ_1^2/σ_2^2, and the same objection arises. σ_2^2 depends in part on the variance of U_2, whereas σ_1^2 does not. Furthermore, X_3 and X_4 have differential 'effects' on the variance of X_1 and X_2. Thus again, if we compare the ratio p_{41}^2/p_{42}^2 over two populations, we contaminate the causal effects with variance of implicit causes in each population.

Conceivably then, not only can the *same* causal effect have different values in two populations, but also the same *relative* causal effect of one variable to another can have different values in two populations. This makes the *interpretation* of the path coefficients as causal parameters undeniably population-specific.

This is a very serious onjection and it is not possible to cope with it using the variance interpretation. Paradoxically, however, if we return to the hypothetical experiment interpretation then it is possible to rescue these parameters as causal measures and to dissolve the objection.

L   Standardised Linear Models

Let us confine our attention initially to a single population. If we look at Equation K.1, we see that p_{41}, for instance, can be interpreted as the number of σ_4's by which X_4 will change for a change of σ_1 in X_1, all other causes constant. Hence, p_{41}, p_{42} and p_{43} are standardised path regression coefficients. What is the point of standardising, however?

To see this, we must return to the basic problems of measurement. Measurement of any quantity can only take place against some standard. Consider, for instance, the old CGS system in physics. Length has the standard of the centimetre, and this gives standards for area and volume too. Time has the standard of the second, and together with length we get standards for velocity and acceleration. Temperature has the standard of the Centigrade scale which is calibrated with respect to the properties of water

(0°C for freezing point and 100°C for boiling point, both at 760mm of mercury). Mass is then also calibrated with respect to water — the gram is the mass of 1 cm^3 of water at 4°C. Hence we see that units are defined to interrelate to other units and also to relate to the properties of the most common element, water. Furthermore, choices of unit are often made to simplify the use of theory, thus being defined in the light of theory. For instance, Newton's Second Law states that force equals the product of mass and acceleration (or at least implies this in normal circumstances). If we use grams and cm/sec^2 for these latter two, then it is natural to define force according to the law. Indeed, 1 dyne is defined as the force producing an acceleration of 1 cm/sec^2 in a mass of 1 gram. And so we could go on.

In sociology, we have few laws (if any) and we have few scientifically accepted standards. Problems of measurement are severe. We usually measure variables according to some accessible criteria — often those used by the 'man in the street' in society — and we then search for laws using these measurements, guided by some theory. This, however, can lead to problems of interpretation.

Consider the path regression coefficients $b_{41} = 0.1$ and $b_{42} = 3.69$. It would seem reasonable, at first sight, to conclude here that X_2 has a far greater effect on X_4 than does X_1. But is this really a reasonable conclusion? We may be inadvertently choosing units of measurement for X_1 which are relatively much smaller than those for X_2. By relatively much smaller, we mean that, say, a change of 50 units in X_1 is about as commonplace empirically as a change in X_2 of 1 unit. If we redefined our units for X_1 we would then find that b_{41} is about 5, actually greater than b_{42}. It is as if we inadvertently defined a gram as the mass of 1000 cm^3 of water at 4°C (this would actually be the kilogram), but left length defined in centimetres. We would then find that laws concerning concepts connected with mass and concepts connected with length gave coefficients for mass which were considerably smaller, relatively, than those for length. Of course, in CGS the definitions are deliberately linked, so that 1 cm^3 and not 1000 cm^3 is used in the definition of mass.

Again, suppose $b_{41} = 25$, $b_{42} = 27$ and $b_{43} = 30$. Huge effects we might say, compared to these same variables' effect on another variable X_5, say, where $b_{51} = 0.8$, $b_{52} = 0.6$ and $b_{53} = 0.9$. Yet it may be that the units we have chosen for X_4 are relatively much smaller than those for X_5.

Hence our problem is to choose scales which allow us to compare meaningfully different effects in a population. Standardisation is one attempt to solve this problem. The reasoning is as follows.

Let P_1 and Q_1 be measures of a concept where the measures differ only by origin and scale. Then we have $P_1 = cQ_1 + d$, so that when Q_1 is zero P_1

is equal to d (i.e. the origin of Q_1 is the value d of P_1) and when Q_1 changes by one unit, P_1 changes by c units (i.e. each unit of the scale of Q_1 is c times each unit of the scale of P_1).

We have, for any given population, $\mu_{P_1} = c\mu_{Q_1} + d$ and $\sigma_{P_1}{}^2 = c^2 \sigma_{Q_1}{}^2$. Hence,

$$\frac{P_1 - \mu_{P_1}}{\sigma_{P_1}} = \frac{(cQ_1 + d) - (c\mu_{Q_1} + d)}{c\sigma_{Q_1}} = \frac{Q_1 - \mu_{Q_1}}{\sigma_{Q_1}} \qquad \text{L.1}$$

Thus, on standardisation, all measures of a concept which differ by origin and by scale reduce to an equivalent measure in a given population. The scale of the equivalent measure will depend upon the variability of the concept measured in the given population.

The objection of the last section does not apply here, since we use variance to solve a measurement problem and not as an index of causal strength. In the last section, variance was used to *interpret* the parameters as causal parameters, and it was this that made the objection a telling one. In the approach of this section, the parameters are interpreted as causal parameters through the ideas of the hypothetical experiment. The distinction between the two approaches is crucial. We know that regression coefficients like b_{41} depend for their size on the units of measurements used, but their interpretation as causal parameters is determined independently of these units. On standardisation, it happens that the units of measurement have their scale fixed by variance. The objection to using p_{41} etc. as causal parameters now has no force, however, since their interpretation as causal parameters does not depend upon variance — indeed, from the point of view of the hypothetical experiment they are no different from b_{41} etc.

Of course, standardisation does not solve all our measurement problems, since we use variance as an index of scale distortion, and it may well be that in our particular population the concept measured varies untypically compared to others. Such variation is due to variation in implicit factors in the population affecting the values taken by the concept, and these factors are beyond our control.

This brings us to the problem of what to do when we have two or more empirical populations. It seems obvious that we should standardise based on the information in all the populations at our disposal. For the point of standardisation is to use variance as an indicator of relative scale size, not in any one population, but in general. Of course, if we have one only population then this is what we must use. With more than one, however, we should combine variances over populations for each variable estimating this, if necessary, from sample variances and means — see Section 11, Appendix 2(II), p. 149.

This conclusion is not generally recognised in the literature, but it seems to follow from this discussion of standardisation. Of course, if we always standardise over all available populations where we have measurements of all the variables of interest then we run into no problems when we compare regression coefficients over these populations, since the units of measurement are the same for all the populations — this is essential for any comparison of effects between populations.

It should be clear that the variance interpretation of path coefficients cannot allow for such a combining of variance over two or more populations, without sacrificing comparison of effects between the two populations. This is a further reason why the variance interpretation obfuscates the real benefit of standardisation: variance in the former case is used as a standard for assessment of causal effect; in the regression interpretation it is used as a standard for scale distortion. These uses are entirely different, although, in the case of a single population, the quantitative results are the same.

We must conclude, then, that standardisation has its uses, and hence that path coefficients interpreted as path regression coefficients have their uses as causal parameters. The variance interpretation of path coefficients, however, is not to be recommended.

M   Using Discrete Variables in Causal Analysis

If an exogenous variable is discrete cardinal then the discussion is just as in Section G and no problem arises. Again, if an exogenous variable is non-cardinal the discussion in Section G applies, with the conclusion that we should generally make an analysis in terms of sub-populations for each category of the non-cardinal variable.

A conceptual problem arises, however, if an endogenous variable is discrete cardinal and one or more of the determining variables is continuous. Suppose, for example, that X_4 is discrete and X_1 continuous. We write the causal effect of X_1, X_2 and X_3 on X_4 as $\phi(X_1, X_2, X_3)$. Now ϕ cannot be a continuous function of X_1, since for X_2, X_3 and U_4 constant, ϕ will give infinitely many values which it is impossible for X_4 to take. We cannot solve this by taking ϕ as the causal effect on $E(X_4 | X_1, X_2, X_3)$, since, conceptually, this effect must be precisely the same as the effect on X_4 itself, for we are assuming this effect to be the same for all units of analysis who take the same values on X_1, X_2 and X_3. Clearly, ϕ must be a step function of X_1, making discontinuous jumps as X_1 passes a critical point. Indeed, it is obvious that a small enough change in X_1 will not affect X_4, so that there will always be a range of values of X_1 when X_4 is constant.

Fortunately, most of the variables we use in causal analysis can be conceived as continuous. Nevertheless, it is as well to consider the problems involved when we wish to explain causally a variable that is intrinsically discrete. Often the best course, if possible, is to form some continuous index to replace the discrete variable; this will not usually involve any change of theory, rather a change of indicator for a theoretical concept. An alternative is to use methods where ϕ is not assumed constant over units of analysis (see Appendix 1).

N Estimating Path Regression Coefficients

(Note: This section is mathematically more difficult than the rest.)

As already indicated above (p. 31), since the statistical qualities of causal independence hold only at a theoretical level and any finite data set will deviate from the implied statistical independence, we need to estimate the parameters using statistical inference.

One way of doing this is to use the method of least squares on each structural equation. Causal independence implies that the mean and variance of U is independent of the explicit variables in that equation, and hence our estimates will be 'best' in the sense already described, which we may call linear minimum variance unbiased (linear MV unbiased).

However, we can improve this notion of 'best' by assuming further than U is normally distributed for each set of values of the explicit variables in the equation. For, without this assumption, the least squares estimates are 'best' only amongst those estimators which are formed by a linear combination of the values of the response variable (these being called linear estimates), and indeed they are rarely 'best' (i.e. MV unbiased) in the set of all possible estimators. If U is conditionally normal, however, then they are indeed MV unbiased overall.

This is not the only reason for assuming U normal, however; if we wish to make hypothesis tests, then this assumption is necessary. The assumption is not as arbitrary as it seems, and the interested reader is referred to Birnbaum (1979) for the theory underlying the assumption of normality.

Now, given this normality, we can use a method of estimation which in many ways is more intuitively convincing than least squares, and which is certainly more general. This method is called *maximum likelihood*, and it has the advantage here of leading on directly to hypothesis testing. In the case of linear regression, as here, the estimates obtained are exactly the same as those obtained using least squares. The method gives estimators which have certain optimum properties in large samples. Firstly, as the sample size increases so does the probability that the estimator is 'very close' to the true value — this very desirable property is called *consistency*. Secondly, as the sample size becomes very large the variance of the estimator is the minimum possible — this MV property in infinitely large samples is called *efficiency*. This second property is only approximate for finite samples, but a sample size of 100 usually gives a sufficient approximation. In the case of linear regression, however, the MV property is exact for any sample size. Maximum likelihood estimators (ML estimators) are not generally unbiased in small samples, though they are in infinite samples (so-called asymptotic unbiasedness) and again a large sample will give reasonably approximate results. This fact about ML estimators not generally being unbiased is taken by some to be a criticism more of the notion of unbiasedness than of the ML method. Indeed, this tendency to bias is far outweighed, in my opinion, by a very desirable property of ML estimators. If $\hat{\theta}_1, \hat{\theta}_2, \ldots, \hat{\theta}_t$ are the ML estimators of $\theta_1, \theta_2, \ldots, \theta_t$, then if θ is any function of any subset of the parameters then the ML estimator of θ, $\hat{\theta}$, is that *same* function of the same subset of the ML estimates. This is an intuitively reasonable property of estimators, but the restriction of unbiasedness generally makes it impossible to achieve using other methods (for if $\hat{\theta}_1$ is unbiased for θ_1, $f(\hat{\theta}_1)$ is not generally unbiased for $f(\theta_1)$).

Having briefly considered the merit of the ML estimators, let us now look at the method. Let a variable X depend on t parameters $\theta_1, \theta_2, \ldots, \theta_t$ so that the probability of X taking a value x is $p(x \mid \theta_1, \theta_2, \ldots, \theta_t)$; that is, the probability is dependent on the values of the parameters. Now for a *fixed* observation x, we can regard $p(x \mid \theta_1, \theta_2, \ldots, \theta_t)$ as a function of the t parameters (whereas for a non-fixed X and fixed, true parameter values it is a function of X). It is intuitively reasonable, since $X = x$ has indeed been observed, to choose those values of $\theta_1, \ldots, \theta_t$ which maximise the probability of X being x. This is the method of maximum likelihood. For computational purposes, it is usual to take the natural logarithm of $p(x \mid \theta_1, \theta_2, \ldots, \theta_t)$ and then to ignore additive constants since these do not affect the maximisation process. We call this logarithm the *log-likelihood*, $L(\theta_1, \theta_2, \ldots, \theta_t)$ so that

$$L(\theta_1, \theta_2, \ldots, \theta_t) = \log_e [p(x \mid \theta_1, \theta_2, \ldots, \theta_t)]. \quad \text{N.1}$$

Now, if observations $x_{a1}, x_{a2}, x_{a3}, \ldots, x_{an}$ are made on a variable X_a, and these observations are statistically independent, then the probability of all these observations occurring is given by the product of the probabilities.

Since the log of a product is a sum, it follows that the log-likelihood of the sample of observations on X_a is given by the sum of the separate log-likelihoods, namely;

$$L^{(1)}(\theta_1, \theta_2, \ldots, \theta_t) + L^{(2)}(\theta_1, \theta_2, \ldots, \theta_t)$$
$$+ \cdots + L^{(n)}(\theta_1, \theta_2, \ldots, \theta_t) \quad \text{N.2}$$

where the bracketed superscript $^{(i)}$ indicates the observation $X_a = x_{ai}$.

Let us now apply the method of maximum likelihood to the path regression coefficients.

Consider the general structural equation

$$X_k = \sum_{i=1}^{k-1} b_{ki} X_i + U_k \quad \text{N.3}$$

We know that

$$E(X_k | X_1, \ldots, X_{k-1}) = \sum_{i=1}^{k-1} b_{ki} X_i + c_k,$$

where $c_k = E(U_k)$, a constant. Note that c_k consists of the effect of explicit variables when they are zero plus the average effect of implicit variables. We assume that for every configuration of $X_1, \ldots, X_{k-1}$, U_k is normally distributed with the same mean, c_k, and the same variance, which will be $\text{Var}(U_k)$. It follows that for each configuration of $X_1, \ldots, X_{k-1}$, X_k is normally distributed with mean

$$\sum_{i=1}^{k-1} b_{ki} X_i + c_k \text{ and variance } \text{Var}(U_k).$$

Thus, for a particular unit of analysis j, the probability that the value taken on X_k is x_{kj} given that the values on $X_1, \ldots, X_{k-1}$ are $x_{1j}, \ldots, x_{k-1j}$ is the frequency function of the normal distribution with mean $\sum_{i=1}^{k-1} b_{ki} X_i + c_k$ and variance $\text{Var}(U_k)$, i.e.

$$\frac{1}{\sqrt{2\pi \text{Var}(U_k)}} \exp - \frac{\left(x_{kj} - \sum_{i=1}^{k-1} b_{ki} x_{ij} - c_k \right)^2}{2 \text{Var}(U_k)} \quad \text{N.4}$$

There are $(k+1)$ parameters here, $b_{k1}, \ldots, b_{kk-1}, c_k$ and $\text{Var}(U_k)$ all pertaining to X_k. Let us write these parameters as θ_k, for short. Then the log-likelihood, conditional on the values of $X_1, \ldots, X_{k-1}$, for unit j (omitting additive constants) is

$$L^{(j)}(\theta_k) = -\frac{\left(x_{kj} - \sum_{i=1}^{k-1} b_{ki}x_{ij} - c_k\right)^2}{2\,\text{Var}(U_k)} - \frac{1}{2}\log \text{Var}(U_k) \qquad \text{N.5}$$

(since for any value T, $\log \exp(T) = T$, when the log is natural).

Now suppose we have m variables altogether in our recursive system, $X_1, \ldots, X_m$. Assume, without any loss of generality, that only X_1 is exogenous. Then X_1 has no parameters on which it depends, and no parameters to estimate. Let us consider then $P_{\theta m,2}(X_2, \ldots, X_m \mid X_1)$, which is the conditional probability of $X_2, \ldots, X_m$ given X_1 over all parameters $\theta_2, \theta_3, \ldots, \theta_m$ which we write as $\theta_{m,2}$.

Now,

$$P_{\theta m,2}(X_2, \ldots, X_m \mid X_1) = P_{\theta m,3}(X_3, \ldots, X_m \mid X_1, X_2)P_{\theta 2}(X_2 \mid X_1)$$

N.6

where $\theta_{m,3}$ is the parameter set $\theta_3, \ldots, \theta_m$. We can continue with equation N.6, ending up finally with

$$P_{\theta m,2}(X_2, \ldots, X_m \mid X_1) =$$
$$P_{\theta m}(X_m \mid X_1, \ldots X_{m-1})\, P_{\theta m-1}(X_{m-1} \mid X_1, \ldots, X_{m-2}) \cdots P_{\theta 2}(X_2 \mid X_1)$$

N.7

Hence the log-likelihood of the term on the left can be written as the sum of the log-likelihoods of those on the right.

Each log-likelihood has the form N.5. So from N.7

$$L^{(j)}(\theta) = L^{(j)}(\theta_m) + L^{(j)}(\theta_{m-1}) + \cdots + L^{(j)}(\theta_2) \qquad \text{N.8}$$

and from N.5 and N.8

$$L^{(j)}(\theta) = -\sum_{k=2}^{m}\left[\frac{\left(x_{kj} - \sum_{i=1}^{k-1} b_{ki}x_{ij} - c_k\right)^2}{2\,\text{Var}(U_k)}\right] - \frac{1}{2}\sum_{k=2}^{m}\log \text{Var}(U_k) \qquad \text{N.9}$$

This is the log-likelihood for the jth unit of analysis over the entire recursive system.

Now assuming that the n units of analysis are observed in an independent fashion, so that the observations on one do not affect those on another, we can use N.2 on N.8 to give

$$L(\theta) = \sum_{j=1}^{n} L^{(j)}(\theta_m) + \sum_{j=1}^{n} L^{(j)}(\theta_{m-1}) + \cdots + \sum_{j=1}^{n} L^{(j)}(\theta_2) \quad \text{N.10}$$

or

$$L(\theta) = \sum_{j=1}^{n} \sum_{k=2}^{m} L^{(j)}(\theta_k) \quad \text{N.11}$$

where $L(\theta)$ is the log-likelihood for the entire sample over the entire recursive system. Thus from N.9.

$$L(\theta) = -\sum_{j=1}^{n} \sum_{k=2}^{m} \left[\frac{\left(x_{kj} - \sum_{i=1}^{k-1} b_{ki} x_{ij} - c_k\right)^2}{2 \operatorname{Var}(U_k)} \right]$$

$$- \frac{n}{2} \sum_{k=2}^{m} \log \operatorname{Var}(U_k) \quad \text{N.12}$$

Note that with s exogenous variables $X_1, \ldots, X_s$, instead of just one, k would run from $s + 1$ to m and not from 2 to m.

Our problem is now to maximise N.12. This may seem a formidable task but, assuming that we do not know anything about the relationship between any of the parameters, it is relatively easy. We can treat each item on the right-hand side of N.10 separately, since the parameters therein have no known connection with parameters in the other terms. This means that we can concentrate quite generally on

$$L(\theta_k) = - \frac{\sum_{j=1}^{n} \left(x_{kj} - \sum_{i=1}^{k-1} b_{ki} x_{ij} - c_k\right)^2}{2 \operatorname{Var}(U_k)} - \frac{n}{2} \log \operatorname{Var}(U_k) \quad \text{N.13}$$

and maximise this. For those acquainted with calculus, the results are derived in Appendix 2(II). For the entire parameter set θ we have,

$$c_k = \bar{x}_k - \sum_{i=1}^{k-1} b_{ki} \bar{x}_i \qquad k = 2 \text{ to } m \quad \text{N.14}$$

$$\widehat{\operatorname{Var}}(U_k) = \frac{1}{n} \left[\sum_{j=1}^{n} x_{kj}' - \sum_{i=1}^{k-1} b_{ki} x_{ij} \right]^2 \quad \text{N.15}$$

(dashes indicate measurement from sample mean)

and for each value of k (2 to m) we get $k-1$ equations of the form

$$s_{lk} = \sum_{i=1}^{k-1} b_{ki} s_{il} \quad l = 1 \text{ to } k-1 \qquad \text{N.16}$$

These results are precisely those of least squares. The beauty of this method, however, is that we can make estimates when we constrain certain parameters to be equal to one another, which we cannot so easily do with least squares. Moreover, as will be seen in the next section, we can also make hypothesis tests including comparisons across populations.

If we have just one population and standardise, we have $p_{ki} = (\sigma_i/\sigma_k) b_{ki}$ and we estimate p_{ki} by $\hat{p}_{ki}$ where

$$\hat{p}_{ki} = \frac{s_i}{s_k} \hat{b}_{ki} \qquad \text{N.17}$$

Hence, from N.16 and N.17

$$s_{lk} = \sum_{i=1}^{k-1} \frac{p_{ki} s_{il} s_k}{s_i} \text{ or } \frac{s_{lk}}{s_l s_k} = \sum_{i=1}^{k-1} p_{ki} \frac{s_{il}}{s_i s_l}$$

And so,

$$r_{lk} = \sum_{i=1}^{k-1} \hat{p}_{ki} r_{il} \quad l = 1 \text{ to } k-1 \qquad \text{N.18}$$

Equations N.16 are called the *normal equations* for the path regression coefficients, and equations N.18 the normal equations for the standardised path regression coefficients (or path coefficients). We note from N.18 that the simple correlation coefficients are all that are required for estimation of the path coefficients, and in N.16 similarly only the covariations are required. It should be observed that N.16 can be obtained from equation N.3, and N.18 from its standardised equivalent, by treating the *sample* covariance (or correlation) between U_k and the explicit variables as zero. This can be used as a rule of thumb to obtain the normal equations.

Now N.15 can be simplified using N.16 to *

$$\hat{\text{Var}}(U_k) = s_k^2 - \sum_{i=1}^{k-1} \hat{b}_{ki} s_{ik} \qquad \text{N.19}$$

Then if we estimate p_{ku}^2 by $\hat{\text{Var}}(U_k)/s_k^2$ we have from N.17 and N.19

$$\hat{p}_{ku}^2 = 1 - \sum_{i=1}^{k-1} \hat{p}_{ki} r_{ik} \qquad \text{N.20}$$

50 An Introduction to Causal Analysis in Sociology

Now it can be shown that the variance of b_{ki} conditional on the sample values taken by the explicit variables $X_1, \ldots, X_{k-1}$ is

$$\text{Var}(\hat{b}_{ki} \mid \text{sample}) = \frac{\text{Var}(U_k)}{ns_i^2 [1 - R_i^2(1, \ldots, i-1, i+1, \ldots, k-1)]} \quad \text{N.21}$$

where $R_i^2(1, \ldots, i-1, i+1, \ldots, k-1)$ is the *sample* multiple regression coefficient of X_i on $X_1, \ldots, X_{i-1}, X_{i+1}, \ldots, X_{k-1}$. The issue of multicollinearity mentioned earlier (p. 33) becomes more clear here, for the conditional precision of b_{ki} is the smaller the larger is R^2 in the sample.

It is usual to choose an unbiased estimator of N.21 and this is obtained by estimating $\text{Var}(U_k)$ by $s^2(U_k)$ where

$$s^2(U_k) = \frac{n}{n-k} \widehat{\text{Var}}(U_k) \quad \text{N.22}$$

giving an unbiased estimate of N.21 as

$$\widehat{\text{Var}}(\hat{b}_{ki} \mid \text{sample}) = \frac{s_k^2}{(n-k)s_i^2} \times \frac{1 - \sum_{i=1}^{k-1} p_{ki} r_{ik}}{1 - R_i^2(1, 2, \ldots, i-1, i+1, \ldots, k-1)} \quad \text{N.23}$$

using N.20, N.21 and N.22.

N.23 is also an unbiased estimate of the unconditional variance of $\hat{b}_{ki}$ — e. the variance over all possible samples, $\text{Var}(\hat{b}_{ki})$.

Given the sample values taken by $X_1, \ldots, X_{k-1}$,

$$\frac{\hat{b}_{ki} - b_{ki}}{\sqrt{\widehat{\text{Var}}(\hat{b}_{ki} \mid \text{sample})}},$$

is distributed as Student's t, with $n - k$ degrees of freedom. This enables us to form confidence intervals, if we wish, but it must be noted that if each one is 95 per cent then taken over all the parameters of the model simultaneously, the percentage is lower than this. It is probably better to just use $\sqrt{\widehat{\text{Var}}(\hat{b}_{ki})}$ (given by N.23) as an index of precision, this being an estimate of the so-called standard error of $\hat{b}_{ki}$.

From N.23 we see that an estimate of the variance of p_{ki} is given by

$$\frac{1 - \sum_{j=1}^{k-1} \hat{p}_{kj} r_{jk}}{(n-k)(1 - R_i^2(1, \ldots, i-1, i+1, \ldots, k-1))} \quad \text{N.24}$$

where we have estimated

$$\text{Var}\left(\frac{s_i}{s_k} b_{ki} \mid \text{sample}\right) \text{ by } \frac{s_i^2}{s_k^2} \hat{\text{Var}}(\hat{b}_{ki} \mid \text{sample}).$$

Now $1 - \hat{p}_{ku}^2 \left(= \sum_{i=1}^{k-1} \hat{p}_{ki} r_{ik}\right)$ can be used as an estimate of the degree to which the causal variables account for the variance of X_k, and whilst this is not relevant to the causal effect of the variables — the regression coefficients measure this — it is an indication of the predictive value of the set of variables in a given population.

A more important use of $\hat{p}_{ku}^2$, however, is in N.23 or N.24 — it is an index of the precision of the causal parameter estimates.

Note that if we standardise over two or more populations but estimate effects in each separately (as suggested in Section L), then N.18 does not hold since in this expression s_i and s_k are taken over both populations (as in N.17) but s_{ik} and s_{il} are specific to each population. Similarly N.20, N.23 and N.24 do not hold. These will have to be derived from the non-standardised equations (N.16 and N.19). Note that in N.19 s_k^2, and in N.21 s_i^2 and R^2, are still taken over the separate populations.

O Testing Hypotheses in Causal Analysis

Given N.14 and N.15, N.13 simplifies greatly. If we make the substitutions we get the maximum value of $L(\theta_k)$, and we have

$$L_{\max}(\theta_k) = -\frac{n}{2} - \frac{n}{2} \log \hat{\text{Var}}(U_k) \qquad \text{O.1}$$

Since $\hat{\text{Var}}(U_k) = s_k^2 \hat{p}_{ku}^2$, we have

$$L_{\max}(\theta_k) = -\frac{n}{2} - \frac{n}{2} \log s_k^2 \hat{p}_{ku}^2$$

$$= -\frac{n}{2}(1 + \log s_k^2) - \frac{n}{2} \log \hat{p}_{ku}^2 \qquad \text{O.2}$$

$$L_{\max}(\theta) \text{ is simply } \sum_{k=2}^{m} L_{\max}(\theta_k) \qquad \text{O.3}$$

We may now look at various cases, in every one of which we use the method of the likelihood ratio test, described below.

52 An Introduction to Causal Analysis in Sociology

Case 1: Testing an *a-priori*-trimmed model

We hypothesise, on the basis of theory, and perhaps earlier empirical results, that certain direct effect parameters are zero in the fully recursive system. We wish to use the data to examine whether, for this *a priori* hypothesis (*a priori* to inspecting the data, that is), evidence exists to reject it. The logic of hypothesis testing does not allow us to investigate whether the data supports the hypothesis, except insofar as it is a form of support for the data not to make a rejection.

We begin with a fully recursive system, with all the causal independence assumptions, and compute the maximum value of the log-likelihood. This is O.3, with each term being taken from O.2, but where, for reasons which will become obvious in a moment, we may ignore $-(n/2)(1 + \log s_k^2)$. Hence we need only compute

$$L_{\max}(\theta) = -\frac{n}{2} \sum_{k=2}^{m} \log \hat{p}_{ku}^2 \qquad \text{O.4}$$

where $\hat{p}_{ku}^2$ is given by N.20.

We then re-estimate the parameters given the constraint that the direct effects hypothesised as zero are indeed zero. We do this as follows. In N.13 all those b_{ki} assumed zero are put to zero. In N.14 and N.15 we put the relevant $\hat{b}_{ki}$ to zero. This means that the maximum value again has the form O.4 (again ignoring the term $-(n/2)(1 + \log s_k^2)$), but $\hat{p}_{ku}^2$ will be estimated differently.

In N.18 we again put relevant $\hat{p}_{ki}$ to zero, but we also delete those equations where (lk) corresponds to a b_{kl} hypothesised as zero. Hence we delete as many equations as there are hypothesised zero coefficients. The remaining equations will estimate the non-zero $\hat{p}_{ki}$, and then N.20, with the relevant $\hat{p}_{ki}$ as zero, will give the value of $\hat{p}_{ku}^2$. Notice that we use standardised coefficients, even if we are testing a non-standardised model — this makes the computations easier.

The first log-likelihood is called the unconstrained maximum log-likelihood — say L_u — and the second the constrained maximum log-likelihood — say L_c. It is clear that $L_u - L_c$ will be positive or zero, and intuitively if $(L_u - L_c)$ is 'too large' we will be inclined to reject the hypothesis, otherwise not. How much is 'too large'? Now it happens that $2(L_u - L_c)$ is approximately distributed in large samples as a chi-square statistic with degrees of freedom equal to the number of coefficients hypothesised as zero. The fact that we consider $L_u - L_c$ shows why we can ignore $-(n/2)(1 + \log s_k^2)$, for it is the same in both L_u and L_c. Moreover, if,

The Theory of Causal Analysis 53

in certain structural equations, no parameters are assumed zero, we need not calculate $L_{\max}(\theta_k)$ for these equations since this value will be the same for L_u and L_c, and will subtract out. This can greatly simplify the calculations.

Now, depending on our theoretical and other empirical support for the hypotheses, we choose a significance level α (often 0.05) and then reject the hypothesis if

$$2(L_u - L_c) \geqslant c_\alpha$$

where c_α is such that the probability that $\chi^2(s) \geqslant c_\alpha$ is 100α per cent, where s is the number of assumed zero coefficients. For example, at the 5 per cent level with four restrictions, $c_\alpha = 9.49$.

We have already pointed out that the total value of $2(L_u - L_c)$ is equal to the sum of the separate values of $2(L_u - L_c)$ for each equation, assuming that we postulate no functional relationship between parameters in different equations. Now, two possibilities can arise, which lead to important problems.

Firstly, on the basis of the total value we may be led to reject the hypothesis, whereas on the basis of separate values we may be led not to reject some of the hypotheses concerning the separate equations. This presents no logical problem unless every separate value would lead to a non-rejection. This is certainly possible. For example, consider 4.6 with 2 d.f. and 7.5 with 3 d.f., both of which are not significant at 5 per cent. Their sum is 12.1 with 5 d.f., which is significant at 5 per cent. This seems to be a contradiction.

Secondly, on the basis of the total value we may be led not to reject the hypothesis whereas one or more of the separate values would lead to a rejection. Again this is possible. Consider 4.1 with 3 d.f. and 9.7 with 4 d.f., the second leading to a rejection. Their sum is 13.8 with 7 d.f., which would not lead to a rejection. Again, this seems to be contradictory.

Although both cases are rare, the problems they raise are important. The important thing to understand here is that a test of a hypothesis is a test of a theory. The theory predicts a given statistical hypothesis, and rejecting the hypothesis amounts to rejecting the theory. Now, while the statistical hypothesis can easily be separated into various parts, the theory which predicts it may not be capable of separation into parts, each part of which corresponds to the parts in the statistical hypothesis. Thus, if the theory must be taken as a whole, the hypothesis must be tested as a whole. In the first case above, the statistical test tells us that whilst there is not enough evidence to support replacing each part of the hypothesis *separately* by an alternative hypothesis, nevertheless there is evidence to support replacing the *joint* hypothesis by another joint hypothesis. This is no contradiction. Each separate test tests for one set of parameters zero in one equation when the parameters in the rest of the equations are allowed to take values which reproduce the correlations pertaining to those equations exactly. Only when all equations are constrained simultaneously is this a test of the theory as a whole.

The second case cannot be dealt with in this way. If there is evidence to support the rejection of one part of the hypothesis separately, then we must conclude that there is evidence supporting rejection of the theory regardless of the results of the overall test. What happens here is that some parts of the joint hypothesis are so well supported that in the overall test they nullify the lack of support that the other parts would otherwise have.

Now it must follow from this that we should only not reject the theory if the overall statistic and the separate statistics for each equation are not significant. We do not need to extend this to individual coefficients, since if the statistic for an equation is not significant it can be shown that the statistics for individual coefficients are not significant also.

The procedure for testing is as follows, therefore. We first form the overall statistic, and if this is significant we reject the theory. Otherwise, we make tests on each individual equation, and reject the theory if any of these are significant. Since the first test affects the probabilities associated with the other tests, if we use 5 per cent for the overall test then we should use, say, 2½ per cent for the individual equations, and not 5 per cent.

Now, if the theory can be separated into quite distinct parts, whereby different subsections of the original hypothesis apply to each part, then it is reasonable to test each part separately. The criterion guiding how many coefficients we test at once must be their link with the theory under test. By linking hypothesis testing to theory in this way, we circumscribe a distinct set of coefficients which we must test jointly: theory thus provides us with a natural criterion for choosing which area of reality we should focus upon at one time.

If we do decide to reject the model and the theory along with it we have effectively two alternatives. One is to modify our theory in the light of competing theoretical and other empirical results, and reduce the number of zero coefficients in the light of these considerations and make a re-test. In this case we have a theory to back up the resulting model and we use the data at hand to test that model. The other alternative is very different from this. In this case we adopt a strategy, described fully in Case II below, where we use the data to give us the best and most parsimonious fit. Here, we usually have no theory to account for the results. We shall have more to say about this below, but it should be clear that if the first alternative is possible, it is by far the best one to take.

If we do not reject the theory we must remember to present the path diagram as on p. 36 — the tested a priori case — since we have needed all the causal independence assumptions to make the test.

Case II: Obtaining an a posteriori-trimmed model

In this case we often begin with no a priori restrictions, but sometimes on the basis of what we might call low-level theoretical assumptions (i.e. assumptions which do not constitute a theory but which are based on some insights of a theoretical nature) we begin with some restrictions, which normally we do not test. In either case, the process is the same. We reduce the number of coefficients (i.e. increase the number of zero coefficients) one by one in such a way that at each stage $(L_u - L_c)$ increases by as small an amount as possible over its previous value, stopping the process when $2(L_u - L_c)$ exceeds the 5 per cent c_α level with the given degrees of freedom. For example, with a four variable model, and so six parameters, the sequence of c_α values is 3.84, 5.99, 7.81, 9.49, 11.07 and 12.59, these spanning from 1 d.f. (i.e. just one parameter zero) to 6 d.f. (all parameters zero).

The limitations of this procedure must be understood, and they are similar to the 'step-wise' regression we discussed on p. 23. Since there is no theory to account for the reduced model with which we end the process, the procedure cannot be called one of theory trimming, a term in common use, for there is no real theory to trim. Rather, the motivation is one of parsimony in a given model, which is a perfectly respectable aim. However, there is no assurance whatsoever that new data would give similar results, and so, as in the case of step-wise regression, the result should be treated as a hypothesis to be tested on other data. Moreover, if there exists a theory which predicts values different from those obtained by this procedure, it does not follow that the data will reject this theory, for a hypothesis test is essentially conservative with respect to the null hypothesis. Hence, results from such reduction techniques cannot be used to assess the validity of theories; the methods discussed in Case I (above) must be used for this. In general, it is far better to have a theory to test, as in Case I, rather than using the 'data-dredging' techniques discussed in this section. For exploratory purposes, however, analysis of possible configurations of zero parameters using techniques like this can be useful in formulating a

56 An Introduction to Causal Analysis in Sociology

theory; once formulated, however, the theory should be tested on new data using the methods described in Case I, above.

Occasionally in the literature one observes a piecemeal procedure whereby each parameter is separately tested, using a Student's t-test, or the equivalent, at the 5 per cent level of significance. There are two problems with this. Firstly, it is clear that we must re-estimate the other parameters every time we take one parameter as zero before making a test on the next parameter. Unfortunately, the order in which we test the parameters is critical, for by changing the order of testing we can end up with a different set of zero parameters. In the approach described above, this problem does not arise, since the order is fixed by the criterion that the inflation of $2(L_u - L_c)$ be minimised. Secondly, the overall level of significance for the model as a whole will not be 5 per cent in this piecemeal procedure, but will be rather more, depending on how many parameters are tested and on the interdependence between them. Again, in the overall testing procedure this problem does not arise, and we must conclude that the piecemeal approach is not to be recommended.

Case III: Comparing Causal Parameters Over Two (or More) Populations

We may have a theory which not only predicts that certain parameters are zero in a given population, but also that in another population precisely the same model holds, with exactly the same parameter values. What this amounts to is that the criteria which serve to differentiate the two populations have no effect whatsoever on the relationship between the variables. We can test this by using the likelihood ratio test.

We first estimate the parameters in each separate population, with no constraints whatsoever, giving us $L_u^{(1)} + L_u^{(2)}$, the superfixes indicating populations 1 and 2 respectively, where we are assuming that sample values in the first population are chosen independently of those in the second. We then apply the constraints that the same s parameters are zero in each population, and that the other $(r - s)$ in one population are equal to the corresponding $(r - s)$ in the other, there being r parameters altogether in each population. We then calculate the constrained log-likelihood $L_c^{(12)}$ taken over the combined data of both samples. Then $2(L_u^{(1)} + L_u^{(2)} - L_c^{(12)})$ is distributed as chi-square with $(r + s)$ degrees of freedom. (The same process can be used if we make no assumptions about zero parameters, merely wishing to test a lower level theory which predicts that the criteria differentiating the populations have no effect, regardless of the relationship between the variables, and then we have r degrees of freedom.) If required, the test can be generalised to M populations, giving $(M-1)r + s$ d.f.

If we reject this theory, it may be that we have another theory which predicts that the same parameters will be zero, but that the remaining parameters will not be equal. If we can split this theory into two parts, one for each population, then we can make separate tests on each population, computing $2(L_u^{(1)} - L_c^{(1)})$ and $2(L_u^{(2)} - L_c^{(2)})$. If, on the other hand, the theory must be taken as a whole, then we must compute also $2(L_u^{(1)} + L_u^{(2)} - L_c^{(1)} - L_c^{(2)})$, which will have twice the degrees of freedom of the separate statistics. (Again this can be generalised to M populations.) This procedure is in line with our recommendations discussed in Case I above: we do not reject the hypothesis only if none of the three statistics are significant.

It ought to be noted that, letting d be the degrees of freedom, the statistic $2[(n-d)/n](L_u - L_c)$ is, when either n is small or d is large, or both, a better approximation to chi-square than $2(L_u - L_c)$. The difference is usually negligible, but in the comparison test above, where d is likely to be quite large, the correction factor $(n-d)/n$ should be applied, especially if n is relatively small.

This concludes our survey of hypothesis testing. In the next section, hypothetical data is used to illustrate the analysis in earlier sections, thus bringing together most of the ideas on causal analysis we have discussed.

P An Example with Hypothetical Data

Imagine that a random sample of 200 trades union members are chosen, and that the following four variables are measured for each member:

X_1 : educational background,

X_2 : occupational status,

X_3 : degree of job satisfaction,

X_4 : degree of disagreement with union aims.

We shall suppose that all variables are measured as indices and are continuous. Also we shall ignore measurement error (see Appendix 1). All variables are standardised over the given sample.

58 An Introduction to Causal Analysis in Sociology

We take the full causal model for these variables to be

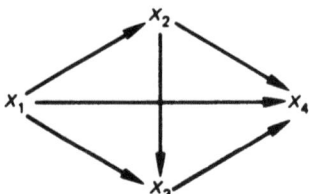

We assume also that X_1 and X_2 have no common causes; X_2 and X_3 have no common causes other than X_1; X_2 and X_4 have no common causes other than X_1; and X_3 and X_4 have no common causes other than X_1 and X_2.

On the basis of some theory, we shall suppose that p_{31}, p_{41} and p_{42} are zero and test this theory. If the theory is rejected, we have additional theory which implies that p_{42} is not zero, and we can then make a retest with with only p_{31} and p_{41} zero.

The data is as follows (it is purely hypothetical):

	1	2	3	4
1	1	0.65	0.60	−0.12
2	X	1	0.90	−0.20
3	X	X	1	0.05
4	X	X	X	1

this being a correlation matrix. So for example, $r_{12} = 0.65$ and $r_{23} = 0.90$. Since $r_{11} = r_{22} = r_{33} = r_{44} = 1$, by definition, we have a diagonal of 1's. Also, since $r_{12} = r_{21}$ etc., we do not need to fill in the lower triangular half of the matrix. All correlation coefficients are given correct to two decimal places.

Now, the equations for the full model are:

$$X_4 = p_{41}X_1 + p_{42}X_2 + p_{43}X_3 + p_{4u}U_4 \qquad \text{P.1}$$

$$X_3 = p_{31}X_1 + p_{32}X_2 + p_{3u}U_3 \qquad \text{P.2}$$

$$X_2 = p_{21}X_1 + p_{2u}U_2 \qquad \text{P.3}$$

The normal equations associated with these are:

$$r_{14} = \hat{p}_{41} + \hat{p}_{42}r_{12} + \hat{p}_{43}r_{13}$$
$$r_{24} = \hat{p}_{41}r_{12} + \hat{p}_{42} + \hat{p}_{43}r_{23} \quad \quad \text{A}$$
$$r_{34} = \hat{p}_{41}r_{13} + \hat{p}_{42}r_{23} + \hat{p}_{43}$$

$$r_{13} = \hat{p}_{31} + \hat{p}_{32}r_{12}$$
$$r_{23} = \hat{p}_{31}r_{12} + \hat{p}_{32} \quad \quad \text{B}$$

$$r_{12} = \hat{p}_{21} \quad \quad \text{C}$$

where A is derived from P.1, B from P.2 and C from P.3. These all follow from N.18 (where $r_{ii} = 1$ and $r_{ij} = r_{ji}$, of course) or, alternatively, by operating on the equation as if the *sample* correlations between U_4 and each of X_1, X_2 and X_3, U_3 and each of X_1 and X_2, and U_2 with X_1 are all zero (see p. 49).

The calculations which follow are usually performed by the computer, but it is instructive to set them out in full here.

From A,

$$\hat{p}_{41} = \frac{r_{14}(1 - r_{23}^2) + r_{24}(r_{13}r_{23} - r_{12}) + r_{34}(r_{12}r_{23} - r_{13})}{\Delta}$$

$$\hat{p}_{42} = \frac{r_{24}(1 - r_{13}^2) + r_{14}(r_{13}r_{23} - r_{12}) + r_{34}(r_{12}r_{13} - r_{23})}{\Delta}$$

$$\hat{p}_{43} = \frac{r_{34}(1 - r_{12}^2) + r_{14}(r_{12}r_{23} - r_{13}) + r_{24}(r_{12}r_{13} - r_{23})}{\Delta}$$

where $\Delta = 1 + 2r_{12}r_{13}r_{23} - (r_{12}^2 + r_{13}^2 + r_{23}^2)$.

These give

$$\hat{p}_{41} = -0.0141553, \quad \hat{p}_{42} = -1.2812785, \quad \hat{p}_{43} = 1.2116438.$$

(We have given these results correct to seven decimal places. This is because we require to perform further arithmetic on them. For purposes of interpretation, two decimal places only should be used, since the correlation coefficients were given only to this degree of accuracy.)

From B,

$$\hat{p}_{31} = \frac{r_{13} - r_{12}r_{23}}{1 - r_{12}^2} \text{ and } \hat{p}_{32} = \frac{r_{23} - r_{12}r_{13}}{1 - r_{12}^2}$$

60 An Introduction to Causal Analysis in Sociology

These give

$$\hat{p}_{31} = 0.0259740 \text{ and } \hat{p}_{32} = 0.8831169.$$

Finally,

$$\hat{p}_{21} = 0.65.$$

Now, in the constrained case the equations are

$$X_4 = q_{43}X_3 + q_{4u}U_4 \qquad \text{P.4}$$
$$X_3 = q_{32}X_2 + q_{3u}U_3 \qquad \text{P.5}$$
$$X_2 = q_{21}X_1 + q_{2u}U_2 \qquad \text{P.6}$$

where we have used q instead of p in order to avoid confusion with the earlier coefficients. Of course, $q_{21} = p_{21}$ and $q_{2u} = p_{2u}$, since P.6 is formally identical with P.3.

The normal equations are $r_{34} = \hat{q}_{43}, r_{23} = \hat{q}_{32}$ and $r_{12} = \hat{q}_{21}$. Hence,

$$q_{43} = 0.05, \hat{q}_{32} = 0.90 \text{ and } \hat{q}_{21} = 0.65$$

whilst,

$$\hat{q}_{42} = \hat{q}_{41} = \hat{q}_{31} = 0, \text{ by hypothesis.}$$

Now, from O.4,

$$L_u = -\frac{n}{2} \sum_{k=2}^{4} \log \hat{p}_{ku}^2$$

where L_u is the unconstrained maximum likelihood and

$$L_c = -\frac{n}{2} \sum_{k=2}^{4} \log \hat{q}_{ku}^2$$

where L_c is the constrained maximum likelihood and the $\hat{q}_{ku}$'s are associated with the q's in P.4, P.5 and P.6.

Now, from N.20,

$$\hat{p}_{2u}^2 = 1 - \hat{p}_{21}r_{12}$$
$$\hat{p}_{3u}^2 = 1 - \hat{p}_{31}r_{13} - \hat{p}_{32}r_{23}$$
$$\hat{p}_{4u}^2 = 1 - \hat{p}_{41}r_{14} - \hat{p}_{42}r_{24} - \hat{p}_{43}r_{34}$$

Similarly,

$$\hat{q}_{2u}^2 = 1 - \hat{q}_{21}r_{12}$$
$$\hat{q}_{3u}^2 = 1 - \hat{q}_{32}r_{23}$$
$$\hat{q}_{4u}^2 = 1 - \hat{q}_{43}r_{34}$$

the other terms being zero by hypothesis.

We need to consider $2(L_u - L_c)$ (see p. 52). Since $\hat{p}_{2u}^2 = \hat{q}_{2u}^2$, this gives,

$$-2 \times \frac{n}{2} [(\log \hat{p}_{3u}^2 - \log \hat{q}_{3u}^2) + (\log \hat{p}_{4u}^2 - \log \hat{q}_{4u}^2)] \quad \text{P.7}$$

Now, $n = 100$, $\hat{p}_{3u}^2 = 0.1896104$, $\hat{p}_{4u}^2 = 0.6814635$, $\hat{q}_{3u}^2 = 0.19$, $\hat{q}_{4u}^2 = 0.9975$. Hence $2(L_u - L_c) = 0.41052 + 76.201892 = 76.61$ to two decimal places. This is far greater than $c_{5\%}$, which, with three degrees of freedom, is 7.81. (Indeed it is far greater than $c_{0.1\%}$, which is 16.27.)

It is clear that the problem lies with the term $\log \hat{p}_{4u}^2 - \log \hat{q}_{4u}^2$, and indeed with the assumption $p_{42} = 0$ since $\hat{p}_{42} = -1.28$. We said *a priori* that further theory would predict a non-zero p_{42}.

If we assume then that q_{42} is not zero, then P.5 and P.6 stay the same but R.4 becomes

$$X_4 = q_{43}X_3 + q_{42}X_2 + q_{4u}U_4 \quad \text{P.8}$$

The normal equations from P.8 are

$$r_{24} = \hat{q}_{42} + \hat{q}_{43}r_{23}$$
$$r_{34} = \hat{q}_{42}r_{23} + \hat{q}_{43}$$

Therefore

$$\hat{q}_{42} = \frac{r_{24} - r_{34}r_{23}}{1 - r_{23}^2} \text{ and } \hat{q}_{43} = \frac{r_{34} - r_{24}r_{23}}{1 - r_{23}^2}$$

Hence,

$$\hat{q}_{42} = -1.2894737 \text{ and } \hat{q}_{43} = 1.2105263.$$

$\hat{q}_{3u}^2$ remains the same, but $\hat{q}_{4u}^2$ becomes $1 - \hat{q}_{42}r_{24} - \hat{q}_{43}r_{34}$ which equals 0.6815789.

Hence $2(L_u - L_c) = 0.41052 + 0.0338811$

$$= 0.44 \text{ to two decimal places.}$$

Since $c_{5\%} = 5.99$ with two degrees of freedom, we have no evidence to reject the modified hypothesis. Moreover, examining equations independently, we have $c_{5\%} = 3.84$ for X_3 and $c_{5\%} = 3.84$ for X_4, and again there is no evidence against the modified hypothesis.

Hence our model is $\hat{p}_{21} = 0.65$, $\hat{p}_{31} = 0$, $\hat{p}_{32} = 0.90$, $\hat{p}_{41} = 0$, $\hat{p}_{42} = -1.29$ and $\hat{p}_{43} = 1.21$. Also, $\hat{p}_{2u}^2 = 0.58$, $\hat{p}_{3u}^2 = 0.19$ and $\hat{p}_{4u}^2 = 0.68$.

Using N.24, we can now compute estimates of the standard deviations of the estimates of the non-zero coefficients.

$$\sqrt{\widehat{\text{Var}}\,\hat{p}_{21}} = \sqrt{\frac{\hat{p}_{2u}^2}{n-2}} = \sqrt{\frac{0.65}{198}} = 0.06$$

$$\sqrt{\widehat{\text{Var}}\,\hat{p}_{32}} = \sqrt{\frac{\hat{p}_{3u}^2}{(n-3)(1-r_{12}^2)}} = \sqrt{\frac{0.19}{197 \times 0.5775}} = 0.04$$

$$\sqrt{\widehat{\text{Var}}\,\hat{p}_{42}} = \sqrt{\frac{\hat{p}_{4u}^2}{(n-4)(1-R_{2(13)}^2)}} = \sqrt{\frac{0.68}{196 \times 0.1711}} = 0.14$$

and $\sqrt{\widehat{\text{Var}}\,\hat{p}_{43}} = \sqrt{\dfrac{p_{4u}^2}{(n-4)(1-R_{3(12)}^2)}} = \sqrt{\dfrac{0.68}{196 \times 0.1896}} = 0.13$

where for $R_{i(jk)}^2$ we have used the formula

$$R_{i(jk)}^2 = \frac{r_{ij}^2 + r_{ik}^2 - 2r_{ij}r_{jk}r_{ik}}{1-r_{jk}^2} \text{ or } 1 - \frac{\Delta}{1-r_{jk}^2}$$

where Δ is defined as on p. 59.

The S.D.'s of $\hat{p}_{42}$ and $\hat{p}_{43}$ are quite large, but since $\hat{p}_{42}$ and $\hat{p}_{43}$ are themselves so sizeable, this does not matter. We can say that it is likely that both $\hat{p}_{42}$ and $\hat{p}_{43}$ have an effect of at least about one standardised unit.

Even though our data is hypothetical, this model might be reasonable. In particular, an increase in one's occupational status causes an individual to be more in agreement with union aims, but an increase in job satisfaction causes an individual to be more in disagreement with those aims. The total effect of X_2 on X_4 is $\hat{p}_{42} + \hat{p}_{43}\hat{p}_{32}$ which is -0.2. Hence a model lacking X_3 would give quite misleading results. Similarly, the total effect of X_1 on X_4 is $p_{21}p_{32}p_{43} + p_{21}p_{42}$, which is -0.13, again a very misleading result.

Finally, notice how misleading also is the original correlation matrix: $r_{34} = 0.05$, which might seem to indicate that X_3 has hardly any effect on X_4, yet $p_{43} = 1.21$, a very sizeable effect in fact. Again, $r_{24} = -0.2$, yet $p_{42} = -1.29$, the true effect being masked. (Of course, r_{24} is the total effect of X_2 on X_4, since $p_{41} = 0$.) It is clear, then, that causal analysis

The Theory of Causal Analysis 63

helps us to disentangle the separate effects of variables in the context of a causal model.

Q Time and Causal Analysis

The reader will have noticed that thus far we have had very little to say about time.

From the point of view of our interpretation of a causal model in terms of the hypothetical experiment, time has been implicit. To say that if we change X_1 then X_4 changes by so much assumes that this latter change, the effect of X_1, will take some time to occur after the initiating cause. It is possible to conceptualise the cause and effect as being instantaneous, but this is in no way implied by the model. Indeed, in most applications in sociology, instantaneous change is unlikely to be a reasonable approximation to reality.

In the model itself we need not make time explicit. The parameters are defined in terms of the final change in the effect variable due to a change in the cause variable; so the intermediate results, at intervening times, are not relevant to the interpretation of the model. This is why the variables are defined without reference to time.

(For readers who know calculus, the following formulation will make the time independence clear. We can write the four variable equation, for instance, as the outcome of the three partial differential equations:

$$\frac{\partial X_4}{\partial X_1} = b_{41}; \frac{\partial X_4}{\partial X_2} = b_{42}; \frac{\partial X_4}{\partial X_3} = b_{43}.$$

In each case, the differentiation is made holding the other two variables constant. In the solution to these equations (see Q.1 below) U_4 is functionally independent of X_1, X_2 and X_3. It can be seen that time has been eliminated.)

Time has to be made explicit, however, when we wish to estimate the value of the parameters. We estimate the value of the parameters, not by attempting to perform the hypothetical experiment, but rather by recording, for each unit of analysis, the value of the causes and their corresponding effect. It is as if each unit represents the resultant of an already performed experiment; thus by comparing units against one another, we can estimate the parameters without experimenting with each unit.

Consider the model

$$X_4 = b_{41}X_1 + b_{42}X_2 + b_{43}X_3 + U_4 \qquad \text{Q.1}$$

and its corresponding realisation for unit i,

$$x_{4i} = b_{41}x_{1i} + b_{42}x_{2i} + b_{43}x_{3i} + u_{4i} \qquad \text{Q.2}$$

If Q.2 is to be the final result of the experiment embodied in the interpretation of Q.1, then it is clear that x_{4i} must be the *final* value in X_4 caused by whatever change in values in X_1, X_2, X_3 and U_4 occurred prior to their taking the values x_{1i}, x_{2i}, x_{3i} and u_{4i}.

If we measure X_1, X_2 and X_3 at the same point in time, say at time t, at what time should we measure X_4? Measuring X_4 at different times in this case corresponds to indirectly attempting to measure U_4 at different times, and only for some of these times will measured values of U_4 be statistically independent of the values of X_1, X_2 and X_3 at the specified point of time t. This is not in contradiction to the theoretical assumption that U_4 be causally independent of X_1, X_2 and X_3. For only in a certain range of times is the measured value of U_4 uncontaminated with earlier or later values of X_1, X_2 and X_3 measured at time t. If X_4 is measured too early, then it is values of at least one of X_1, X_2 or X_3 at an earlier time than t that are responsible, and these will be incorporated in the measurement of U_4. Similarly, if X_4 is measured too late, then the measured value of U_4 contains at least one of X_1, X_2 or X_3 at a later time than t.

It is clearly very difficult indeed to pinpoint the exact time at which X_4 should be measured. Very often, however, all variables in a recursive system are measured at the same time (so-called cross-sectional data). How can this be justified?

Basically, we assume that the values of X_1, X_2 and X_3 taken at the respective times at which they are responsible for X_4 at time t are no different from the values they take at time t. This effectively assumes that the system is stable, and that by time t it has settled down. In terms of the full recursive model, if X_1, X_2 and X_3 cause X_4 at time t at respective times t_1, t_2 and t_3, then necessarily t_1 must be earlier than t_2, and t_2 earlier than t_3. Moreover, if X_1 causes the value of X_2 at time t_2 (and so at time t) at a time t_0, then we assume that X_1 at time t must be at the same value of X_1 at time t_0. Similar assumptions apply to X_1 and X_2 as causes of X_3.

We can account for the constancy of the system only by assuming that the exogenous variables and the implicit effects remain constant at and around time t. Reasons should be provided for this assumption, of course, but often it is the nature of the variables themselves that provide a basis for believing it to be at least approximately correct. However, if there are strong suspicions that this is not so, then it may be necessary to lag the variables at different points of time. This can present new problems, however, since it is not usually clear at what time the measurements should be taken. Generally, therefore, the cross-sectional approach might be used even when the approximation is expected not to be particularly close.

In the hypothetical data example of the last section, it would seem reasonable to assume stability on the basis of the essentially stable variables involved. However, measurement should not be taken at a time where an event which would be expected to affect the variables has recently occurred (for example, a strike).

In Part II of the book, three articles from research journals are reproduced. All three contain causal models, and the reader should consider whether stability assumptions are required, and if so whether they can reasonably be expected to apply.

Part II Causal Analysis in Action

General Introduction to Part Two

This part contains three research papers reprinted from academic journals. The first two papers make direct use of path analysis; the third deals with an application of regression analysis.

The papers have been chosen to illustrate the diverse uses to which causal analysis can be put. In the preceding pages, the theory underlying causal analysis has been examined and a simple hypothetical example has been discussed. The purpose of the subsequent three chapters is to show how this theory can be put to real practical use.

None of the papers makes use of the likelihood method of hypothesis testing, illustrated in the example presented in the last section of Part I. This is because, to date, real examples of the use of this technique are rare. The reader is urged to examine in which respects the use of the likelihood test would benefit the analysis in each of these papers — in this way he will greatly increase his understanding of the theory and its practical implications.

The fact that these papers do not use the more sophisticated methods of statistical inference discussed in Part I should in no way detract from their merits. In each one, careful consideration is given to measurement and to specification problems, and a careful analysis is made of the theoretical implications of the quantitative results. Imaginative use is made of causal analysis, and, in many ways, this far outweighs the absence of the more sophisticated inferential techniques. If these papers go some way to teaching the reader how to use causal analysis creatively then this knowledge, coupled with the theoretical skills gained in Part I, should allow him to make the best use of causal analysis in whatever fields of research he wishes to pursue.

1 Causal Models for the Study of Prevalence

Editor's Introduction and Commentary

The methodological interest of this article is that it uses causal analysis to take account of the incidence, prevalence and duration of a behavior or state. The prevalence is the number of units of analysis engaging in the behaviour or having the state in a given time interval. The duration is the average length of time the state or behaviour persists. The incidence is the number of units of analysis engaging in the behaviour or having the state, per unit time (the units of time being those in which prevalence is measured). Hence, the three concepts are connected by:

Prevalence = Incidence x Duration   or $P = I \times D$.

These concepts are clearly important. The prevalence gives us the scale of the behaviour or state; and by distinguishing between incidence and duration, we can separate out the causal factors responsible for the conception of a state and the longevity of that state. Eaton here applies these concepts to psychiatric illness.

Cross-sectional data are not appropriate for this type of study; rather, longitudinal data are required in the form of a cohort. A cohort is a group of units of analysis studied and measured over time (either continuously or, more usually, at several points of time). Eaton uses discrete time cohort data, and a useful appendix to his article explains how this data was transformed for analytical purposes.

The structural equations used are of some interest in that the system is not fully recursive so that certain implicit variable terms are allowed to correlate. With reference to Figures 2 and 3 we see that

$$X_3 = p_{31}X_1 + p_{32}X_2 + p_{3B}B \qquad 1$$

$$X_4 = p_{41}X_1 + p_{42}X_2 + p_{4A}A \qquad 2$$

$$X_5 = p_{53}X_3 + p_{54}X_4 \qquad 3$$

Equation 3 is not a causal equation as such, but rather one based on the definition of the concepts involved. For, by definition, $P = I \times D$ so that

$$\log P = \log I + \log D.$$

Now, letting X_3, X_4 and X_5 be, respectively, the standardised form of $\log I$, $\log D$ and $\log P$ (e.g. $X_3 = (\log I - \overline{\log I})/\sqrt{\text{var}(\log I)}$), we have Equation 3, where

$$p_{53} = \frac{\text{var}(\log I)}{\text{var}(\log P)} \text{ and } p_{54} = \frac{\text{var}(\log D)}{\text{var}(\log P)}.$$

Notice that there is no implicit factor term in Equation 3.

These expressions for p_{53} and p_{54} can be calculated from sample correlation coefficients by $(r_{35} - r_{34}r_{45})/(1 - r_{34}^2)$ and $(r_{45} - r_{34}r_{35})/(1 - r_{34}^2)$, respectively, obtained by multiplying Equation 3 by X_3, and then taking the average, for the first, and by X_4 and then taking the average for the second. This is not a process of estimation, for the expressions are exactly the same as the 'true' values above.

The other coefficients do need to be estimated, and, as usual, this is most simply done by operating as if the *sample* correlations between A and X_1 or X_2 and between B and X_1 or X_2 are zero (see p. 49).

In particular, there will be a correlation between A and B, the implicit factors for X_3 and X_4, since X_3 and X_4, though not causes of each other, are nevertheless associated — this is allowable by virtue of the discussion on p. 35. Their association, ρ_{AB}, will be estimated by r_{AB}, and r_{AB} is found as follows.

Multiplying 2 by B and taking averages gives

$$r_{4B} = p_{4A}r_{AB}.$$

To find r_{4B}, which is unobserved, multiply 1 by X_4 to give

$$r_{34} = p_{31}r_{14} + p_{32}r_{24} + p_{3B}r_{4B}$$

Hence,

$$r_{AB} = \frac{r_{34} - p_{31}r_{14} - p_{32}r_{24}}{p_{3B}p_{4A}}$$

The p's are estimated by the other normal equations obtained in the way outlined above.

In an addendum to the article, Eaton presents a similar analysis for the concept of chronicity, rather than prevalence, with components of recurrence (the pattern of repetition) and duration. No doubt readers will think of other concepts which can be usefully decomposed in this way.

Article 1.

Causal Models for the Study of Prevalence[1]

WILLIAM W. EATON, *Jewish General Hospital and McGill University*

Sociologists often study the causes of behaviours or attitudes by comparing the characteristics of individuals engaging in the behaviour or holding the attitudes with characteristics of the general population. In some cases two populations are compared — one with many, the other with few who engage in behaviour. A difference between the two populations for a characteristic is described as an 'association' or 'relationship' between the given characteristic and the behaviour under study. Causal inferences are made from such associations under certain conditions.

In the field of social epidemiology causal inferences are sought also. But here, the method just described is considered naive, or at least, incomplete. Social epidemiologists have learned the importance of distinguishing between the prevalence, incidence, and duration of a behaviour. The purpose of this paper is to stress the importance of this distinction in sociological research, and to offer some new causal models for studying prevalence.

Take the behaviour, rioting, as an example. One might hear the report: 'For two weeks there were hundreds of people rioting in city X.' This bit of data could have two divergent interpretations. It could be that about 250 individuals rioted for two weeks each. If this were true, one might conclude that there was a small cadre of rioters, and that the behaviour was not widespread. In this interpretation one might be led to minimise the importance of the riot. A second interpretation is that 250 individuals rioted each day, but that a new group began each day, and and no one engaged in rioting for more than one day. Under the first interpretation, one might conclude that there was a small, ideologically committed elite, whereas the second interpretation might indicate more general unrest.

Another example, from epidemiology, is schizophrenia. Very few people ever become schizophrenic, yet at any one time, over one-quarter of the hospital beds in this country are occupied by schizophrenics (Jackson, 1960). Schizophrenia is a major health problem mainly because it entails long periods of chronicity. The opposite pole for illness might be appendicitis, which many persons contract, but which lasts a very short while. The dynamics of the two illnesses are different.

Prevalence, Incidence and Duration

Epidemiologists have made the distinction between prevalence, incidence and duration of illness which allows one to distinguish accurately the two interpretations of rioting above (Kramer, 1957). The statement 'For two weeks there were hundreds of people rioting' is an interval prevalence estimate. Prevalence is defined as the number of persons having an illness at any given time (point prevalence) or during any given period (interval prevalence). It is generally expressed as a rate (i.e. divided by the total population), and has been widely used in demography, where it indicates the number or proportion engaging in a given behaviour. Incidence is defined as the number of people falling ill (or initiating a behaviour) during a given period, and can be expressed as a rate also. Duration is defined as the length of time the illness lasts.

The three concepts are related according to the formula: $P = I \times D$ (prevalence equals incidence times duration). The formula expresses a simple model for the process of the behaviour under study. If the incidence of rioting is 250 per day, and the duration one day for each person (as under the second interpretation above), the prevalence is 250. If the first interpretation (above) applies, the incidence is 250/14 per day (about 18), with duration 14 days. The first interpretation is a behaviour with low incidence and high duration, the second having high incidence and low duration. A third interpretation might be the following. At the start no one is rioting. Suddenly the incidence of rioting is at 50 per day, with duration of 5 days. The first day there are 50 rioters, the next day 100, the third day 150, and so on, up to the fifth day on which 250 persons riot. On the sixth day, 50 begin to riot, but 50 stop (who began five days ago). On the following days, there are 250 rioters. The prevalence has thus stabilised at 250. Notice that the prevalence stabilises at 250 under all three divergent interpretations. The concept of prevalence–stabilisation is not new to epidemiologists (Kramer, 1957).[2]

These concepts are important for practical and theoretical reasons. Practically speaking, it is important to know the 'size' of the behaviour in terms of its prevalence, so that facilities can be planned to accommodate the behaviour if necessary. Also, it may be important to know how many persons have ever engaged in a behaviour or experienced an illness. Theoretically *it is important to distinguish between the inception of behaviours and their longevity.* The distinction is particularly important when studying the causes of behaviours. In many cases causal influences on the initiation and duration of behaviours will not be identical. It is difficult to make a general statement, but it may be true that for some behaviours the causes of the initiation are less likely to be situational or social-psychological, and more likely to be coincidental or random, than the causal influences on the duration of the behaviours.

The defect noted above can be more explicitly stated now. It consists in basing causal statements solely on estimates of prevalence. Without a knowledge of the dynamics of the inception and continuance of a given behaviour, causal statements based on comparisons of 'more prevalent' with 'less prevalent' populations (comparisons such as those mentioned in the first paragraph of this paper) may be incorrect. An assumed causal inference may be unjustified or, where a true causal link exists, it may be hidden, and the researcher may incorrectly conclude that no cause is present.

Path Models for the Decomposition of Prevalence

The methods of path analysis have recently come to the attention of sociologists (Duncan, 1966). The technique of decomposition, first used by Winsborough, is an important advantage of path analysis. When a variable is the sum of other variables, the decomposition technique allows one to examine the effects of each component (each addend) on the sum. If a variable is multiplicatively determined by other variables, logarithmic transformations can be applied so that the relationship is consistent with the additive assumptions of path analysis.[3]

In the present case, prevalence is multiplicatively determined by incidence and duration, as in the formula in the last section. A regression equation, showing the joint dependence of prevalence on incidence and duration, can be set up (in standardised form) as follows:

$$\log P = b_1 \log I + b_2 \log D.$$

In this regression, the observations are aggregates, or groupings according to causal variables of interest.[4] The prevalence figure is constructed for each observation from the incidence rate and the mean duration for each group (observation). Thus the prevalence figure, in this case, is constrained to be totally determined by its two components.

In a similar manner, each component can be regressed onto n causal variables separately, e.g.

$$\log I = b_1 X_1 + b_2 X_2 + \cdots + b_n X_n + b_{n+1} U.$$

In this case, '$\log I$' is not totally determined by the causal 'X' variables, and thus 'U' is a source of unexplained variation. Sources of unexplained variation in the determination of the components '*I*' and '*D*' may be allowed to correlate (Duncan, 1966).

The three regressions (with log *I*, log *D*, and log *P* as the three dependent variables) may legitimately be combined in a path model, under certain restrictive assumptions (Heise 1969). The reader may want to refer ahead to the example in Figure 2 for an illustration of such a model with two independent variables. The model allows one to assess easily the major determinant of prevalence. Also, the effect of a causal variable on prevalence may be examined as it operates through either incidence or duration. An estimate of this effect will be the product of the path from the causal variable to the log of incidence, and the path from the log of incidence to prevalence.[5] Comparison of these effects may provide valuable information.

An Example

Data are presented below which suggest that the formula for prevalence describes the process operating for the prevalence of mental disorder. The specific question is then: How do variables affect the prevalence of mental disorder? Unfortunately, data in the social sciences are rarely collected in a form amenable to this sort of analysis. A cohort study is needed, and one by Malzberg (1958) is used here. He published data on five cohorts of individuals admitted for the first time to New York state mental hospitals during the years 1943–8. The cohorts were classified by date of admission, age, sex, and the percentage being released or dying each year. From these data on the 1950 census, age and sex-specific incidence[6] rates were estimated, along with a mean duration for each age–sex group. An Appendix to this paper explains the transformations necessary to fit Malzberg's data into the present model.

In the following analyses the prevalence figure is constructed from the cohort data, using the formula. A prevalence was constructed for each age–sex category, using the mean duration and incidence for each. The total prevalence is the sum of these category prevalences, figured at 85,126. In another publication, Malzberg (1967) gives a prevalence of 86,365 for the same institutions for a point five years after the cohort measurements. It appears that the actual process is approximated, at least, by the formula.

The presentation of these two figures is not designed to invite statistical test: it is only meant to suggest that the model approximates the real process.[7] There are grave deficiencies in the data which preclude accurate estimation of true prevalence. For instance, there is no information on recidivists in Malzberg's cohort data, yet these recurrent admissions will enter into the (second) prevalence figure. Also, there is no information on the prevalence at the beginning of the cohort study. Finally, there are no data on the fluctuation of the incidence rate or duration over this time period.

Age and sex are two variables that are frequently studied in psychiatric epidemiology. Although there are several reviews of the literature, the most recent and complete review is by Dohrenwend and Dohrenwend (1969). They conclude that there is 'no consistent pattern' of relationships between age or sex and the prevalence of psychological disorder. Malzberg's data can be set up in a path model as in Figure 1 to reveal the relationship between age, sex, and the prevalence of mental disorder.

Since the model in Figure 1 is relatively simple, the structural equations for it have been omitted. (They have been included in the model for Figure 2, however). The variable sex is dichotomised, with males receiving a score of one and females zero. The value of the variable age is the mean age of Malzberg's groupings and therefore the correlation of age and sex is constrained to be zero.

The model in Figure 1 reveals a weak relationship for sex and a strong relationship for age and the prevalence of pshychological disorder. One can see that the path from sex to prevalence is rather small (0.018 while the path from age to prevalence is sizeable (0.415).

Prevalence can be decomposed into its components, incidence and duration. Figure 2 presents this decomposed model. The variables incidence, duration, and prevalence are in logarithmic form since the relationships must be additive to meet the assumptions of path analysis. The residual paths to incidence and duration are allowed to have freely correlated residuals, because there is no attempt to order them causally. There is no residual path to prevalence, since it is totally determined by incidence and duration. Structural equations for the model in Figure 2 are presented in Figure 3.

The model in Figure 2 is different from that in Figure 1. Again, sex has

Figure 1

little effect. But the effects of age on prevalence are large and contradictory. Age is positively associated with the logarithm of incidence; the older one is, the higher the probability that he will enter a hospital (the path coefficient, p, is 0.803). But age is negatively associated with the duration of stay; the older one is, the shorter his duration of stay at the hospital ($p = -0.797$). Since both incidence and duration affect prevalence in the same positive manner, the effect of age on prevalence is masked in the reduced form in Figure 1. It is interesting to note, however, that incidence has a much greater effect on prevalence than does duration ($p = 0.645$). Clearly, the dynamics of the process are exposed more fully in Figure 2.

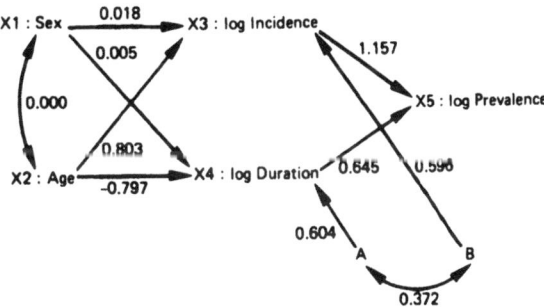

Figure 2

Figure 2 implies an important recommendation for those who would decompose prevalence in this manner. Age must be included as a causal variable in the study of any behaviour with sizeable duration. Older people have less time left in their lives to spend in any behaviour. The high negative path from age to duration is not surprising. This path suggests that mortality be taken into account in the model. For there are two ways of discountinuing to be mentally ill: becoming mentally healthy, or dying. In both cases, one leaves the hospital. Perhaps the effect of age on duration would not be so great if the persons who died were removed from the model. Or to put it another way, perhaps the duration of stay in the hospital for those who die is different from the duration for those who become healthy again. This line of reasoning suggests separate models for those who move out of the hospital and those who stay in until they die. A further decomposition which presents the separation of the 'movers' from the 'stayers' is presented in Figure 3.

78   An Introduction to Causal Analysis in Sociology

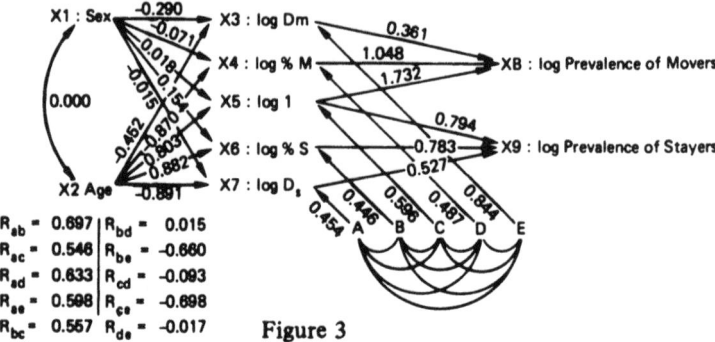

Figure 3

The model in Figure 3 assumes that sex and age can affect the total incidence of mental illness, as in the previous models. It also assumes that sex and age can affect the probability that one will get out of the hospital alive (percentage move) and the probability that one will not get out of the hospital (percentage stay). Further, it assumes that sex and age can independently affect the duration of those who move and the duration of those who stay in.

This model has two prevalence figures, the prevalence of movers and the prevalence of stayers. The prevalences decompose in a manner similar to the general model above. In this case, the analogy for incidence is: total incidence x probability of moving; or, total incidence x probability of staying. The formula for movers is thus:

$$P_{movers} = I \times M \times D_m$$

and the formula for stayers:

$$P_{stayers} = I \times S \times D_s.$$

Both prevalences stabilise, as does the general prevalence figure. The prevalence of movers and the prevalence of stayers sum to form the general prevalence figure (discussed below in reference to Figure 4).

The effects of age are still strong. It has the same effect on total incidence as earlier ($p = 0.803$). The large positive effect of age on the chance of staying ($p = 0.882$) indicates that age is strongly associated with the incidence of stayers, whereas it seems clear that age has no strong relationship with the incidence of movers—the positive association with total incidence is counteracted by the negative association with probability of moving ($p = -0.870$). The effect of age on duration of movers is largely reduced ($p = -0.452$), as expected. This path is puzzling, however, because

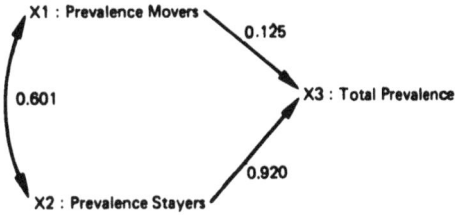

Figure 4

it is still negative and sizeable; it was predicted to be reduced to nothing when the effects of mortality in the hospital were removed. It may be that removal to a general hospital for serious illness (possible resulting in death) is more probable for older persons.

Notice that for the first time in the decomposition sex has a noticeable effect. Apparently women who move through the hospital tend to stay longer ($p = -0.290$). Otherwise the effect of sex is still trivial.

The effects of prevalence of movers and prevalence of stayers on total prevalence is shown in Figure 4. It is impossible to combine a multiplicative decomposition with an additive one in a path analysis because the assumptions are strictly additive; therefore this model is presented separately. It is clear that the major force in determining the total prevalence is the prevalence of stayers ($p = 0.920$).

The decomposition of prevalence has revealed effects that were masked in the reduced form in Figure 1. The effect of age on prevalence in that model was $p = 0.415$. In the first stage of decomposition (Figure 2), this effect was decomposed into a strong positive effect operating through incidence ($0.803 \times 1.157 = 0.0929$) and a somewhat less strong negative effect operating through duration ($-0.797 \times 0.645 = -0.514$). Further decomposition into 'movers' and 'stayers' revealed that the positive effect of age on incidence was limited to the incidence of stayers (Figure 3), and that the prevalence of stayers was a most important determinant of the total prevalence.

Summarising the models, it is clear that the major determinant of prevalence is age, and that it operates through increased incidence of persons who remain in the hospital until death.

Another type of decomposition which might prove fruitful is an alternative to the second stage presented above (Figures 3 and 4). Instead of decomposing into movers and stayers, one might want to decompose into incident and recurrent admissions. Above it was suggested that the causes of the inception of behaviour may be different from the causes of their continuance. This distinction implies that the causes of a first initiation of a given behaviour (a recurrence), and that the influences on the duration of first and repetitive occurrences are distinct.

This logic and the techniques of decomposition are applicable to many areas of sociology. Any chronic behaviour fits this scheme. Unemployment is an example: the reasons one loses one's job are different from the reasons one stays unemployed. A causal study of the prevalence of unemployment might benefit from an analysis such as the one above. Political activism might be another example. Sometimes brief, accidental occurrences can induce an individual to some form of political activity. Whether he (or she) continues to be politically active over an extended period depends on a variety of factors such as personal background, present values, reference groups, and so forth. It seems reasonable to suppose that two sets of causal factors, one set for incidence and one set for continuance, are operative.

Addendum (1977)[8]

Above, I described the application of a decomposition technique from path analysis to the study of prevalence. Because of the rarity of comprehensive longitudinal data, I was forced to use aggregate level data in the application. I would like now to demonstrate how this conceptualisation applies to the study of chronic behaviours with individual-level data.

The dictionary defines chronic as 'ever-present or recurring'. The word is derived from Chronus, the god of time, and has no inherent pejorative connotation, although often used with bad behaviours to yield combinations like chronic delinquency, chronic illness, or chronic alcoholism.

Duration and recurrence may be thought of as two components of chronicity. They fit precisely into the dictionary definition: duration refers to the ever-present nature of a chronic behaviour, and recurrence to the pattern of repetition. But duration and recurrence are not just components in a verbal sense: they are mathematical components also. For a given population, duration and recurrence combine to form the total time engaged in the behaviour for each individual, according to the formula:

$$TT = \bar{D} \times R$$

(total time equals mean duration multiplied by number of recurrences).

The formula is conceived at the individual level but is useful for studying the pattern of chronicity of an entire population. It is analogous to the epidemiological queuing formula I discussed earlier: $P = I \times D$ (prevalence equals incidence times duration). Regressing the components, recurrence and duration, onto total time reveals a measure of their relative importance. Logarithms must be taken to meet the additive assumptions of multiple regression, giving the equation (in standardised form):

$$\log TT = b_1 \log D + b_2 \log R$$

There is no residual because total time is completely determined by recurrence and duration. In a similar manner, causal variables can be regressed onto the two components individually.

It may be important to discover if two components have distinct causes. Causes connected to the social situation (as opposed to causes connected to the personality configuration of the individual) are especially likely to differ, because the social situation itself is usually different. For instance, prior to rehospitalisation an individual is located in his own social network or community, and his probability of being rehospitalized is affected by events and persons in that community. After hospitalisation, his situation is changed: he is in the hospital with a new social network and a reformulated view of himself as sick. The behaviours that precipitated entry into the hospital may not be the same as those that keep him there. Not all behaviours involve such radical changes in social situations and self-image as hospitalisation but, by definition, commencement of a behaviour changes one's situations and/or self-image, and causes of recurrence and duration are likely to be distinct in important ways for many behaviours. This decomposition technique was first used by Winsborough to study the components of regional growth, and is common to path analysis.

As path analytic model, using data on the chronicity of schizophrenia from the Maryland Psychiatric Case Register, is presented in Figure 5. Clearly in this case duration is the more important component of the total time engaged in the chronic behaviour. However, education and age have little effect on either component of chronicity.

Reprinted from Social Forces (54(2), December, 1975)
Copyright © University of North Carolina Press.

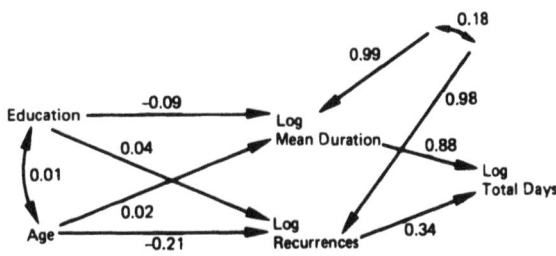

Figure 5

Notes

[1] This research was supported by a National Institute of Mental Health Grant (MH 07413). Many people have given helpful comments, but I would like to thank particularly William Sewell, Hal Winsborough and Duane Alwin. Of course, they are in no way responsible for the final content.

[2] The formula is an example of the general queueing formula: $L = \lambda \times W$. L, the length of the waiting line, is the analogue to prevalence. λ is the rate of arrival, or incidence. W is the waiting time, or duration. The formula has been mathematically derived in various ways, involving various assumptions (Cooper, 1972; or Jewell, 1967). The assumptions are not restrictive and the formula holds for numerous types of waiting-line models. W and λ must be finite averages, and the system must be allowed a little time to stabilise. The system can be stochastic or deterministic, and no assumptions are necessary about the independence or inter-arrival intervals, the number of service channels, or the capacity of the system.

[3] Fortunately the logarithmic transformation is often consistent with the nature of the data. See Bartlett (1947) for a general consideration of this transformation.

[4] There are many difficulties involved in making inferences from grouped data of this sort. See Blalock (1964), Goodman (1953), Hammond (1973), and Hannan (1970) for discussions of these problems.

[5] This product gives an estimate of the direct effect. Other effects can be estimated also, according to Duncan (1966).

[6] The figures used here are *not* true, untreated incidence or prevalence figures, but first admission rates and resident population rates of mental hospitals in New York. The summarising statement given by the Dohrenwends' concerns untreated prevalence, and is not, strictly speaking, applicable here. Nevertheless, the model of analysis here can be applied to untreated or treated rates.

[7] In fact, the prevalence of mental disorder was fluctuating over this time period, and this particular year gives a good fit. However, lack of close fit does not detract from the logic of analysis below.

[8] Reprinted from Social Forces (56(2), December 1977).

APPENDIX

Conversion of Cohort Data for Causal Model

Data are rarely published or even collected in a form amenable to the type of analysis presented here. Longitudinal data are required. The followup can be continuous, as in a case register, or at several points in time, as in Maltzberg's cohort study (or as in panel studies with several followups). Where followup is not continuous, average durations must be estimated in a manner described below. Where followup stops before all durations have terminated, a further survival-extrapolation is necessary, also described below.

Malzberg's data were published as in Table A.1. For the sake of brevity, this table considers only males, and merges the table of first admission figures with the table concerning discharge percentages. Malzberg included an identical analysis for females which were used in the causal models here. He also included an analysis of deaths occurring in the hospital. The format of presentation for deaths was precisely like that for discharges. Thus, should the reader with to reproduce the data set used in the present analysis, he could construct three tables beyond Table A.1: one for admission and discharge percentages of females (Malzberg, a: Table 3; Table 5); a second for death percentages for males (Malzberg, 1958; Table 11); and a third for females (Malzberg, 1958: Table 11). Malzberg presents a synthesized cohort of first admission. The admission period was identical to the follow-up period (1943–8), and thus follow-up for the later-admitted cohorts is much shorter than for the cohort admitted first (1943–4). The lack of follow-up for later-admitted cohorts does not bias the discharge or death percentages, because these figures are calculated using as base only persons actually being followed. But the lack of follow-up for later-admitted cohorts does make some of the percentages less reliable than others. For instance, the percentages discharged during the fifth year are calculated using only the first (1943–4) cohort, while the percentages discharged during the first three months are calculated using the entire five-year cohort of admission. Therefore, early discharge and death percentages, based on a larger population, are more stable.

About 75 per cent of the cohorts died or were discharged within five years. (Not a single sex–age group fell below 70 per cent and for many groups more than 80 per cent either dies or were discharged). Times of discharge and times of death had to be estimated for the remaining 25 per cent (or so) for each sex–age group. This estimation was performed as in a multiple-decrement life table. For deaths, the average decrement of the fourth and fifth years was used. (A two-year average was used to increase the population base and thus stabilise the figure.) For discharge, the survival was assumed to proceed exponentially, using the ratio of the fourth to the fifth year percentage as the rate of decrement. The exponential assumption was not tenable for deaths because occasionally more people died in the fifth year than in the fourth. For each year after the fifth, both decrements were calculated, until the population was depleted. About ten years of extrapolation was necessary.

Averages could be computed once 100 per cent of each age–sex cohort had been accounted for. The total number of months spent in the hospital by each age–sex cohort was calculated by multiplying the percentage depleted during any given period by the length of the period and summing. Dividing by the total group size yielded a (weighted) average duration.

The effect of these estimating procedures is probably to bias the durations slightly. For instance, it is assumed that all persons discharged during a period are discharged at the end of the period, yielding an upward bias. But the exponential assumption for discharge has a slight downward biasing effect, since it is likely that survival curves for mental hospitals are flatter than the exponential. The effect of the method of extrapolation of death also has a downward bias, more so than the exponential. The biases are small and roughly equivalent for all the age–sex groupings, and the analysis via causal modeling therefore seems to be justified.

Table A.2 contains the converted and death data for males. These data, accompanied by age–sex specific first admission rates, form the basic data for the causal analysis. The correlation matrices for the primary and secondary decompositions are presented in Tables A.3 and A.4, respectively.

Table A.1. Male Cohort Admission and Discharge Data: First Admissions to New York Civil State Hospitals, Fiscal Years 1943–4 to 1947–8 inclusive

Age	Number*	Per cent discharged† within:							
		1st 3 Mos.	2nd 3 Mos.	3rd 3 Mos.	4th 3 Year	2nd Year	3rd Year	4th Year	5th Year
under 15	592	15.0	9.0	7.1	2.2	16.0	9.9	4.8	3.3
15–19	1346	15.6	5.3	3.6	2.5	37.3	8.9	2.9	1.2
20–24	1789	15.8	6.5	2.6	2.2	34.1	6.9	3.5	1.7
25–29	1786	17.5	4.8	3.0	1.6	34.7	6.2	2.2	1.3
30–34	1895	16.6	4.0	2.0	1.7	36.2	6.7	3.1	1.6
35–39	1989	15.9	3.3	1.5	1.6	34.3	5.9	2.4	1.1
40–44	2083	14.8	3.4	1.1	1.1	34.0	5.3	2.1	1.2
45–49	2003	12.8	2.9	1.2	0.9	30.9	5.8	1.9	0.8
50–54	2082	10.1	2.3	1.0	0.7	26.9	4.5	0.9	0.5
55–59	2243	8.3	1.8	1.0	0.6	23.8	3.9	1.6	0.2
60–64	2372	5.2	1.1	0.9	0.6	16.3	2.1	1.4	0.2
65–69	2396	4.4	0.3	0.4	0.4	11.8	1.9	1.2	–
70 or over	7650	2.2	0.4	0.3	0.3	4.0	0.4	0.3	0.1

*From Malzberg (1958: Table 3).
†From Malzberg (1958: Table 5).

Causal Models for the Study of Prevalence 85

Table A.2. Converted Discharge and Death Data for Males: First Admission to New York Civil State Hospitals, Fiscal Years 1943–4 to 1947–8 inclusive

Age	Est. % Ever Discharged (alive)	Est. Mean Duration (months)	Est. Mean Duration for Those Discharged Alive (months)	Est. Mean Duration For Those Dying in Hospital (months)
under 15	74.2	177.4	27.2	629
15–19	78.1	137.9	20.8	553
20–24	74.8	142.6	20.1	510
25–29	73.1	134.0	20.8	440
30–34	73.5	112.3	21.8	370
35–39	66.8	107.6	20.7	284
40–44	64.4	97.2	20.2	234
45–49	57.8	89.0	20.9	183
50–54	47.5	79.8	26.5	129
55–59	41.8	65.1	20.6	96
60–64	27.8	52.0	21.0	64
65–70	25.5	35.6	27.1	38
70 or over	8.1	21.7	18.0	22

Table A.3. Correlation Matrix for Primary Decomposition

	X_1	X_2	X_3	X_4	X_5
X_1					
X_2	0.000				
X_3	0.018	0.803			
X_4	−0.005	−0.797	−0.506		
X_5	0.018	0.415	0.831	0.061	

Table A.4. Correlation Matrix for Secondary Decomposition

	X_1	X_2	X_3	X_4	X_5	X_6	X_7	X_8	X_9
X_1									
X_2	0.000								
X_3	−0.290	−0.452							
X_4	−0.071	−0.870	0.409						
X_5	0.018	0.803	−0.719	−0.727					
X_6	0.154	0.882	−0.691	−0.775	0.859				
X_7	−0.015	−0.891	0.178	0.916	−0.568	−0.647			
X_8	−0.147	0.315	−0.455	−0.064	0.711	0.426	0.041		
X_9	0.084	0.404	−0.795	−0.268	0.802	0.821	−0.008	0.821	

2 Religious Identification and its Ethnic Correlates

Editor's Introduction and Commentary

This article is rather complex but very instructive. The author specifies eight variables, or dimensions as he calls them, and seeks among other things to find interrelationships between them using causal analysis. The variables refer to those attributes which seem important in providing and maintaining religious identification in Jews and Protestants. The variables are described both conceptually and operationally; the latter consists of those measurements likely to tap the content of the former.

The model is presented in block recursive format. In general, this means that variables are arranged in blocks, no variable being in more than one block. The blocks are so arranged that no variable in a lower numbered block can be a cause of one in a higher numbered one. If we can specify the causal relationships in a given block, then all those variables in higher numbered blocks are effectively exogenous variables for the given block. This means that if the given block consists of one-way causal connections (that is, if the model in that block is recursive, as are all the models discussed in Part I) then the relationship between variables in higher number blocks is not relevant to the analysis of the given block. We can perform path analysis on the given block with higher numbered blocks as exogenous variables.

Moreover, even if we leave unspecified the relationships within the given block, recursive analysis is still possible. For instance, this diagram is effectively block recursive:

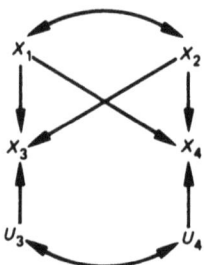

X_1 and X_2 constitute one block; X_3 and X_4 another, lower numbered block. The equations are

$$X_3 = P_{31}X_1 + P_{32}X_2 + U_3$$

$$X_4 = P_{41}X_1 + P_{42}X_2 + U_4$$

We do not need to assume that U_3 and X_4, U_4 and X_3 are causally independent to be able to analyse these equations. Similarly to the case discussed on p. 35, we can use normal estimation techniques even though U_3 and U_4 are causally related. Note, however, that whilst the case on p. 35 resulted from our assuming that a direct effect was zero, our analysis here shows that the converse of this is not necessarily true. That is, the fact that U_3 and U_4 are correlated and no arrow is drawn from X_3 to X_4 does not imply that the direct effect is zero. For all we know, X_3 and X_4 might be bicausally related – it does not matter.

The diagram on p. 36 is not block recursive, however, since X_2 and X_4 cannot constitute a block. This is because X_2 is a cause of X_3, so X_2 must be in a higher block than X_3; and X_3 is a cuase of X_4, so X_4 must be in a lower block than X_3. It is clear in this diagram that X_2 and X_4 cannot be bicausally related, so that the absence of an arrow from X_2 to X_4 must be construed as an assumption of zero direct effect.

In Lazerwitz's article, block 3 is recursive but blocks 1 and 2 do not have their internal relationships specified. The purpose of blocks 1 and 2 is to act as controls, so that the effects of age, sex, generation, education, occupation and income on the other blocks are effectively 'filtered out'.

Blocks 3 and 4 are the mainparts of the model. The reason for separating these blocks is to make the presentation more manageable both from the point of view of exposition and analysis. Blocks 3 and 4 could be combined, since each is itself recursive in structure, but they relate to different concepts. Moreover, the hypothesised effects from block 3 to block 4 come only from the 'middle' of block 3, and the block format makes starkly clear the essentially separate nature of the interrelationships between the two sets of variables.

Two analyses are presented, one for Jews and the other for Protestants. This serves both to provide additional empirical evidence for the models as well as helping to pinpoint deficiencies by the existence of differences between the religious groups. Indeed, this leads the author to hypothesise two new and more elaborate models which better fit the evidence.

Finally, mention should be made of the Automatic Interaction Detection (AID) and Multiple Classification Analysis (MCA) computer packages used by the author. Both packages require variables in nominal form, and cardinal variables must be rendered nominal by some more or less arbitrary categorisation. The general idea of AID is to split up the population into groups in a binary fashion with respect to the variables chosen, repeating the process until one of a number of conditions is satisfied. Asymmetry in the branching process with respect to any variable at a given level of splitting may well imply some interaction. MCA, a companion to AID, is a sort of multiple regression equivalent for non-cardinal variables.

When applied to cardinal variables, both methods suffer from the problems associated with turning these variables into non-cardinal form, but the author's use of the packages seems sensible and their careful use is bound to be beneficial to any analysis.

In this case, the author discovered using AID that the control variables in blocks 1 and 2 probably interact with those in block 3 on liberalness for Jews only. MCA returned results comparable to the regression analysis (though necessarily not as precise) and thus doubts about the measurement levels of the variables were resolved, at least for practical purposes.

ARTICLE 2.

Religious Identification and Its Ethnic Correlates: A Multivariate Model*

BERNARD LAZERWITZ, *University of Missouri*

Research on the persistence of religious and ethnic groups in the United States has typically fixed on the traits of people displaying varying degrees of religious and ethnic involvement. But a review of this research confronts one with differing sets of definitions, concepts, and measurement procedures. One set has emerged from studies of Christians, primarily Protestants; another set has come from numerous studies of United States Jews.

Some of the outstanding Jewish studies have been those by Sklare and Greenblum (1967), Goldstein and Goldscheider (1968), Rothman (1965), Axelrod *et al.*, (1967), and the earlier insightful essays by Lewin (1948). Christian religious orientations have been investigated by Glock and Stark (1965), and Stark and Glock (1968); Fukuyama (1961) has looked at Protestant church members; and King (1967) has factor analyzed Methodist church membership in Dallas. Lenski (1961) has studied Protestants and

Catholics in Detroit. Fichter (1954), and Greeley and Rossi (1966) have studied Catholics.[1] To advance their research, students of Jewish identification have developed measures of: (1) religious behaviour; (2) Jewish education; (3) activities in and contributions to Jewish organisations; (4) type of Jewish ideology; (5) attitudes toward Israel; (6) concentration of courtship and friendships among Jews; (7) the Jewish rearing of one's children; (8) Jewish home background when a child; and (9) encounters with anti-Semitism and anxieties over social interaction with Christians.[2]

Greeley and Rossi (1966), inquiring into the consequences of Catholic education, work with measures of adult religious behaviour, Catholic education, activity in Catholic organisations, doctrinal and religious knowledge, friendship and courtship concentration among Catholics, and parental religiousness.

From work on Christian identity, Glock and Stark (1965: 18–66) and Lenski (1961: 21–4) have evolved these three equivalent and two different dimensions.

Glock

(1) Experimental—the feeling of some degree of communion with the divine.
(2) Ideological—the degree of acceptance of a faith's belief system.
(3) Ritualistic—the performance of various religious rituals and attendance at church services.
(4) Intellectual—knowledge about a faith's belief system and sacred literature.
(5) Not included.

Lenski

Devotionalism—a private, personal communion with God.

Doctrinal orthodoxy—stresses intellectual assent to prescribed doctrines.

Associational involvement—frequency of attendance at church services.

Not specifically included.

Communal involvement—the degree to which marriage, relatives, and friends are limited to one's own ethnic community.

Then Glock includes another measure of the effects of his prior four dimensions upon other aspects of behaviour and attitudes. Lenski proceeds to study the relations between his dimensions and a large variety of measures on civil liberties, civil rights, social mobility, attitudes toward work, and child-rearing methods.

90 *An Introduction to Causal Analysis in Sociology*

A Unifying Conceptual Scheme and Causal Model

A detailed review of these streams of research on Jews and Christians indicates that they can be united by eight identity dimensions and their associated operational measures. They are:

Dimension

(1) Religious Behaviour—This is akin to Lenski's associational involvement and the Glock ritualistic dimension.

(2) Pietism—This is equivalent to Lenski's devotionalism concept and to the Glock experiential dimension.

(3) Religious education—Same as the Glock intellectual dimensio dimension.

(4) Activity in religious and ethnic voluntary associations and charities.

Operational measure

Attendance at weekly religious services and at annual religious holidays. Sklare and Greenblum (1967) also use home religious observances. Usually, a simple summary index of religious behaviour is formed as in Demerath (1965).

Questions typically cover private prayer, observance of religious fasts, concern with God's will. Again, researchers add together the several items in this area to form a summary index or to classify respondents as high, moderate, or low (see Lenski, 1961:52).

Formal religious education and tests of religious knowledge have customarily been employed by researchers. For example, Greeley and Rossi (1966) group respondents by amount of Catholic education received and also form a religious knowledge index.

Researchers have developed Chapin scale scores from activities in religious and ethnic organisations and Sklare and Greenblum (1967) work with extent of activity in Jewish organisations.

(5) Ideological—Equivalent to Glock ideological dimension and covers Lenski's orthodoxy. Sometimes, subdivisions are made into traditional (orthodox) beliefs and those beliefs now current among the better educated and informed members of a religious group.

(6) The ethnic communal involvement dimension—The extent of intragroup friendships and courtships. This is akin to Lenski's communal involvement index.

(7) Family socialization—This covers what parents do to socialise children into their religious and ethnic community. It can be broken into two parts. One part concerns what one's parents do to socialise him in childhood. The other part focuses upon what one does, as an adult, to socialise his children.

(8) Beliefs about and concern for co-religionists in the rest of the world.

Researchers have employed a variety of questions for this area such as belief in Genesis as actually describing the creation of the world, strong emphasis upon a Hell, or the sinfulness of smoking. Greeley and Rossi (1966:62) and Lenski (1961:51) develop orthodoxy indices for their respondents.

Usually questions are asked about the religious and ethnic backgrounds of respondents' best friends, spouses, and relatives. Lenski (1961: 21) groups respondents into high and low on his index of communal involvement.

Typically covered by questions about childhood religious memories and childhood religious and ethnic activities. Sklare and Greenblum (1967:87, 296) contrast mean home religious observances and years of Jewish education for respondents and their parents. The later parental roll has most frequently been covered by questions about religious education expectations and goals for one's children and by questions on children's memberships in ethnic organisations. Sklare and Greenblum (1967) employ measures such as amount of Jewish education received by respondent's children and attitudes toward intermarriage.

Most frequently employed to ascertain involvement with Israel (Zionism) and Russian Jewry. Herman (1971) forms respondent groups and scales from Israeli attitudes toward World Jewry.

In the research literature cited we find little about how the dimensions are related. Lenski does devote some effort to establishing relationships. In his *Religious Factor* (1961), he maintains that ethnic life has two major facets. The first has to do with a group's religious institutions and covers religious behaviour, pietism, and traditional beliefs. The second bears on the communal, non-religious, life of the group. Lenski (1961:22) found little, or no, statistical communal life. He (1961:52) did find a limited association between his measures of pietism and traditional beliefs.

Sklare and Greenblum (1967:263) reach pretty much the same conclusion when they find that Jewish organisational life in Lakeview provides a secular alternative for a sizeable portion of Jews who have little religious involvement.

The major conclusion to be drawn from these two studies is this: we must attend especially to those dimensions which tap ethnic group life, but fall outside of religious institutions. Here, such dimensions are those of ethnic communal involvement, activities in ethnic organisations, and traditional beliefs. One might suspect that traditional (orthodox) beliefs are more the result of a respondent's life within his ethnic community than they are of his religious involvement.

Given this basic split into communal and religious branches, the causal models of Chart 1 readily follow. Both the Jewish and Protestant models are four-part recursive block systems.[3] As Blalock (1969:71–4) points out, regardless of the internal causal connections of a particular block, it has a one-way causal connection with succeeding variables. Here, nothing is said about the relationships among the variables of the biosocial or socioeconomic blocks 1 and 2. They function as model control variables so that one can determine other variable effects above and beyond those of age, sex, generation, education, occupation and income. The variables of blocks 1 and 2 are considered external to the interrelated variables of blocks 3 and 4.

The third recursive block is composed of the religious and ethnic dimensions. It starts with childhood home background and then the religious education of respondents. It is maintained that childhood socialisation background is an influential variable which effects religious education, religious behaviour, and ethnic communal involvement. After religious behaviour is influenced by childhood background and religious education, it influences pietism and religious education for one's children. For Jews, there is a simple, chain relationship from pietism to children's religious education to Zionism. Zionism is at the end because it is thought that interest in Israel (or in other sectors of World Jewry) flows from the other identity dimensions.

For Jews, the communal branch begins with ethnic communal involvement, goes forward into traditional beliefs, and then into Jewish organisation activities. The two branches meet at children's religious education. For Protestants, it is hypothesised that Protestant organisation activities form the meeting point of the religious institution and communal branches.[4]

The fourth part of these models consists of the three consequence variables of general community organisation activities, anomie, and liberalness which are hypothesised to be related in the indicated causal chain. Thus greater activity in general communal voluntary associations results in lessened anomie which, in turn, results in greater liberalness.

The most difficult task is to relate the identity and consequence variables. Certainly, the social science literature is contradictory on such relationships. Lenski (1961:185–6, 220) maintains that pietism is associated with voluntaristic humanitarianism, but that the more clearly such humanitarianism is linked with governmental solutions the more those high in pietism shy away from the liberal position. He also finds that traditional beliefs have neutral or negative effects on political and economic issues. Again, Lenski (1961:173–4) points out that his data support the view that ethnic communal involvement is associated with a conservative position on public issues while there seems to be some, usually not very strong, association between religious behaviour and a more liberal orientation.

Other investigators debate the results of being a more or less involved Jew, Protestant, or Catholic. For example, Fuchs (1956) points out how liberal, and strongly Democratic, Jews have been. Indeed, his limited data on 1952 Boston Jewish areas show small differences on these variables for different amounts of Jewish education, different United States generations or identification with different Jewish subgroups. Berelson et al. (1954) disagree with Fuchs by finding in their Elmira, NY. research that the more Jewishly identified are more Democratic than the less identified. The Allinsmiths (1948) show that Jews differ relatively little by status ranks on either economic or civil liberty issues, while Protestants and Catholics do so differ. Rothman (1965) finds no relationship between degree of Jewish identification among teenagers and their attitudes toward non-Jewish groups.

Johnson (1962, 1964) has studied the political consequences of Protestant theology and denomination affiliation. He points out that frequency of attendance at theologically conservative churches is directly associated with preference and voting for the Republican party, while frequency of attendance at theologically liberal churches produces an inverse relationship.

Glock and Stark (1966), investigating the connection between Christian beliefs and anti-Semitism find that fundamentalist Christian positions, coupled with a view of Christianity as the only true religion, are strongly associated with anti-Semitism. Allen and Spilka (1967), in their thorough review of the literature, point out that a large block of research maintains that church members or frequent attenders are less tolerant people than non-members or irregular attenders. Another major group of their cited studies reveals little or no association between these same variables. A third set of research articles finds that those who are highly involved in their faith are distinctively less prejudiced than the less involved.

Glock *et al.* (1967), in a study of Episcopalian church members, find no relationship between respondents' church involvement and their social ideology. In their study of American Catholics, Greeley and Rossi (1966) find weak associations between Catholic education and liberal attitudes toward other minorities and current social issues.

These initial causal models accept Lenski's position: pietism will display a moderate, positive association and ethnic communal involvement a moderate negative association with liberalness.

It is expected that both models will show sizeable path coefficients among the variables connected by arrows in Chart 1. It is also expected that such path coefficients for childhood background, religious behaviour, and pietism will usually be considerably larger than the ones for ethnicity, traditional beliefs, and ethnic community organisation activities.

Apart from these specifications, we anticipate that the remaining relations will be weak ones. For these models, a strong relationship is considered to be any direct, or indirect, path coefficient with a value of 0.25 or more. Moderate and weak relationships are defined by magnitudes of *0.10* to *0.24* and *0.09*, or less, respectively.

Source of Data

The data to test these models were obtained from a 1966 survey tapping factors affecting religious and ethnic identification and their relations to fertility. Pertinent characteristics of the study are the following:

(a) The survey was restricted to Cook and south-eastern Lake counties in Illinois, covering most of the population of the Chicago SMSA.
(b) The sample was disproportionately stratified to obtain a large number of Jewish interviews and used multistage area probability sampling.
(c) Interviewing time was held to about one hour.

Religious Identification and its Ethnic Correlates 95

A. For Jews

Control Block 1: Bio-Social
a. Age
b. Sex
c. U.S. Gen.

Control Block 2: Socio-Economic
a. Educ.
b. Occup.
c. Income

Block 3: Religious and Ethnic

Block 4: Consequence Variables

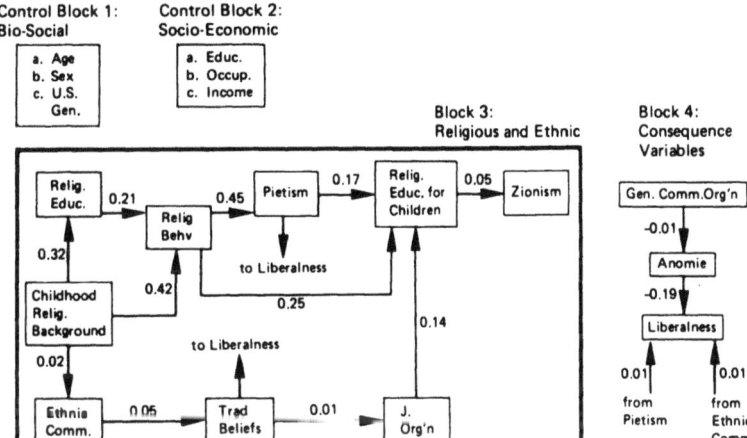

B. For Protestants

Control Block 1: Bio-Social
a. Age
b. Sex
c. Gen. Urb.

Control Block 2: Socio-Economic
a. Educ.
b. Occup.
c. Income

Block 4: Consequence Variables

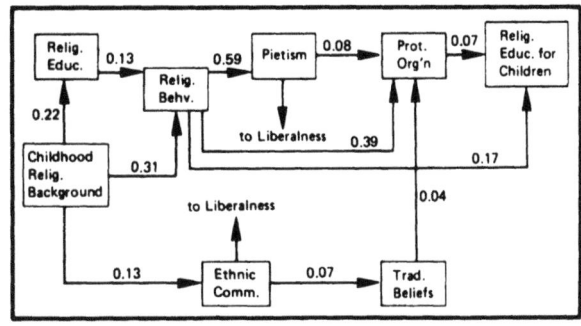
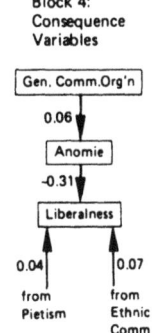

(d) Questions stressed readily ascertained behaviour and attitudes.
(e) Questions concentrated on the acceptance of traditional beliefs and confined concern about co-religionists in the rest of the world to Jewish attitudes toward and involvement with Israel.[5]

The survey yielded 572 Jewish interviews with adults 20 years or older at a 66 per cent response rate, and 464, white Protestant interviews with adults 20 years or older at a 64 per cent response rate.[6] Clearly, one must treat these data in full awarness of their response limitations. Nevertheless, the quality of the data should be adequate for developing identification models.

Operational Measurement of Dimensions

To recapitulate, briefly, the aim of this study is to develop a model from these several dimensions of religious and ethnic identification and to determine the effects of these dimensions upon some 'consequence' variables. The identity dimensions are derived from those used in a number of studies of Jewish and Christian identification and involvement. The questions and the operational measures of these dimensions are the same as, or equivalent to, those cited above in the list of eight dimensions.

Questions pertaining to the various identity dimensions were grouped together. Next, the code categories of each question were ranked in order of decreasing behavioural involvement or attitude acceptance and scored according to rank. Finally, the several question scores for each dimension were added to establish a dimension score. The score for ethnic organisational involvement was a Chapin scale applied to the questions on this dimension. Similarly, scores were assigned to the education, occupation, and income codes. Age was scored in number of years.[7]

A 'liberalness' score was formed from a series of questions on:

(1) economic help to poor nations;
(2) the federal poverty programme;
(3) attitudes about a black person moving on one's block;
(4) attitudes about a black person joining one's church or a Jewish community centre;
(5) federal aid to public education;
(6) reasons why people are poor.

Respondents were scored one point for each liberal response on these questions. Additional consequence variable scores were developed through use of the Chaplin scale on activities in general community voluntary associations and Srole's (1956) anomie scale.

This use of simple summary indices to form variable scores is not being defended as the best way to measure the components of religious and ethnic identification. Instead, this method is used here to replicate the typical manner in which research has been operationalised in this area. Having organised and scored survey data in such an equivalent way, it is then possible to explore the gains to be derived from model building with the common variety of measures of identification.[8]

Model Statistics

The basic statistical tool for model formation will be path coefficients generated by a recursive series of multiple regression equations. Since such regression equations are linear additive models, it was thought best to check each one of them for any sizeable interactions among the set of variables. When such interactions are detected, their variable combinations ought to be incorporated in their respective regression equations or used as additional control variables. Such an interaction search was done by the automatic interaction detection (AID) computer system developed by Sonquist and Morgan (1964).

Only one equation revealed solid evidence of interaction and this was handled by introducing a control for variable level. Of course, the failure to find clear indications of other interaction effects does not rule out their existence. Nevertheless, it does seem quite probable that for these equations (but one) any interactions have quite limited impact and can be ignored (if they have gone undetected).

Besides the issue of interaction of variables, there remain two additional problems with the use of multiple regression techniques. First, this method requires interval scale measures; second, it imposes a linear model on the data. The use of typical (one might say traditional) simple summary indices to create dimension scores that are 'pseudo-interval scales' is a slippery (but commonplace) sociological procedure. Then, too, although there is little theoretical support for the assumption of linearity, the existing research literature either assumes linearity or ignores the issue.

Because of this, it was decided to repeat all multiple regression equation relationships with the technique known as multiple classification analysis (MCA) presented by Andrews *et al.* (1969). This technique is a variation of dummy variable multiple regression that does not require the assumption of linearity. It also permits regression equation independent variables to enter calculations as nominal (dummy variable) scales. However, an MCA equation's dependent variable must still be an interval one (or a pseudo-

98 An Introduction to Causal Analysis in Sociology

interval scale). This considerably reduces, but does not fully eliminate, the difficulties of working with pseudo-interval scales.[9]

This use of two different analysis techniques has the added advantage of distinguishing between those findings common to both the regression and the MCA procedures and those that differ. Fortunately, specific results were quite similar for both methods and overall conclusions were the same. Hence, data presentation will be limited to the regression system.[10]

The Jewish Identity Model

The recursive system equations for the Jewish identity model are packed into Table 1, which lists the sixteen variables by name and number and provides the matrix of their total correlations. For example, between the score for the Jewish religious behaviour dimension, which is variable number 7, and the score for the Jewish background of a respondent's childhood home, variable number 5, there is a total (Pearsonian) correlation of 0.46. These sixteen variables are introduced by name and number in their recursive system order. In other words, variable number 1 is age; then comes education (number 2), etc., down through liberalness, variable 16. The table margin gives the dependent variable for each regression equation; the table column headings give the variable numbers for all the independent variables of each regression equation. For example, when the Jewish religious behaviour score appears as a dependent variable (horizontal number 7), it is part of a regression equation whose independen variables are respondent's age (number 1) and education score (number 2), family head's occupation score (number 3), total family income score (number 4), the score for the Jewish background of a respondent's Jewish education (number 6). The multiple correlations for each equation are given in the last column of Table 1.

The total indirect effect of any independent variable on any dependent variable can be obtained by subtracting their direct effect 'p' coefficient of Chart 1 (or given in the text) from their total correlation of Table 1. For example, the total indirect effect of childhood home background upon Jewish religious behaviour is equal to their total correlation of 0.46 minus their direct effect p coefficient of 0.42 or 0.04.

Chart 1 indicates by arrows the predicted relationships and gives their actual path coefficients. Now, let us connect hypotheses with actual data.[11]

1. Childhood home Jewish religious background does not have all its expected effects. While having sizeable influence on Jewish religious

Table 1. Total and Multiple Correlations Among Jewish Model Recursive System Variables

Dependent Variables		Independent Variable Numbers															Multiple
Name	No.	1	2	3	4	5	6	7	8	9	10	11	12	13	14	15	Correlation
Age	1																
Education	2	−0.46															
Head's occupation	3	−0.33	0.39														
Family income	4	−0.13	0.35	0.40													
Jewish bkgrd. of childhood	5	0.44	−0.30	−0.20	−0.17												0.44
Jewish education	6	0.13	−0.01	0.07	−0.02	0.31											0.31
Relig. behaviour	7	0.19	−0.03	0.12	0.04	0.46	0.36										0.55
Pietism	8	0.28	−0.25	−0.13	−0.22	0.58	0.30	0.59									0.71
Ethnic communal	9	0.09	−0.06	0.12	−0.02	0.18	0.10	0.38	0.23								0.40
Trad. beliefs	10	−0.02	−0.22	−0.16	−0.20	0.28	0.05	0.30	0.46	0.15							0.55
J. org. activity	11	0.17	0.05	0.19	0.13	0.18	0.21	0.37	0.27	0.20	0.06						0.46
J. educ. for children	12	0.07	−0.05	0.17	0.05	0.23	0.24	0.47	0.37	0.31	0.16	0.32					0.54
Zionism	13	0.05	0	0.04	0	0.19	0.22	0.25	0.23	0.12	0.13	0.19	0.19				0.32
General com. org. activity	14	−0.07	0.30	0.10	0.26	−0.08	−0.03	0.06	−0.08	0.13	−0.05	0.18	0.05	−0.07			0.43
Anomie	15	0.20	−0.34	−0.28	−0.25	0.24	0.02	−0.03	0.18	−0.04	0.22	−0.10	−0.04	0.05	−0.15		0.45
Liberalness	16	−0.26	0.29	0.29	0.23	−0.16	−0.01	0.01	−0.14	0.02	−0.22	0.04	0.04	0.09	0.08	−0.32	0.46

education and religious behaviour, it fails to have an effect on ethnic communal involvement. Then, contrary to what was expected, it also has path coefficients of 0.30 with pietism and 0.14 with anomie. All its other (not presented) path coefficients range from 0.07 to −0.04.

2. Religious education also comes up with a surprise by having an unexpected relation of 0.13 with Zionism. Its other, not reported, values range from 0.07 to −0.09.

3. Jewish religious behaviour is even more powerful than predicted. Besides its relations and values shown in Chart 1A, it also has a path coefficient value of 0.37 with ethnic communal involvement; 0.13 with traditional beliefs; 0.19 with Jewish organisational activities; and −0.13 with anomie. Its other (unreported) values range from 0.06 to 0.03.

4. Pietism, too, has more direct effects than given by Chart 1 and displays a value of 0.38 with traditional beliefs and 0.15 with Jewish organisations. Its other (unreported) values range from 0.07 to −0.06.

5. Ethnic communal involvement does not have its expected Chart 1 relationship with traditional beliefs. Instead, it relates to Jewish education for one's children with a value of 0.14 and to general community organisation activity with a value of 0.15. Its other unreported values range from 0.07 to −0.04.

6. 'Traditional beliefs' fails to have its expected Chart 1A direct effect. In fact it only has a direct effect upon anomie with a −0.14 value and upon liberalness with a −0.18 value. Its other values range from 0.05 to −0.01.

7. Jewish organisational activities also relates to general community, organization activities with direct effect of 0.16. Its other unreported values range from 0.09 to −0.06.

8. When it is an independent variable, Jewish education for one's children has low direct effects with range from a high of 0.05 to a low of 0.01.

9. On the other hand, Zionism has a direct effect of −0.10 on general community organisation activities and of 0.11 on liberalness.

10. General community organisation has the low relationship of 0.01 to both anomie and liberalness.

11. Anomie behaves as expected.

On the whole these detailed findings indicate:

1. There is no separation of religion from Jewish communal life contrary to the positions of both Sklare and Lenski. The Jewish ethnic communal dimension is closely related to religious behaviour by a strong beta of 0.38. Traditional beliefs are moderately affected by religious behaviour and strongly affected by pietism. Jewish organisations, the third variable of the supposedly separated communal branch, is moderately affected by both religious behaviour and pietism.

2. There does exist a mainstream of Jewish identity which flows from Jewish childhood background to Jewish education to religious behaviour to pietism to Jewish organisation activity to Jewish education for one's children. Ethnic communal involvement, traditional beliefs, and Zionism seem to be identity model bypaths.
3. Both Jewish education and, to a lesser extent, Jewish background operate through their indirect effects. Unlike religious behaviour, which has lots of both kinds of effects, these two usually display either direct or indirect effects. Only on pietism does Jewish background show substantial direct and indirect effects, and only with religious behaviour does Jewish education combine substantial amounts of both types of effects.[12]
4. First Jewish childhood home background and, then, religious behaviour dominate the identity block.[13] As hypothesised, their path coefficients, and those of pietism, are almost always larger than those of the other identification variables. Automatic interaction detection analysis presented differing relationships between the identity components and liberalness with social status change. To handle this interaction, three new

Table 2. Standardised Regression Components of Liberalness Controlling for Occupation and Age

	I*	II†	III‡
Age	−0.18	−0.04	−⁜
J. bkgrd.	0	0.15	0.15
J. educ.	−0.07	−0.02	0
Rel. behav.	−0.03	−0.10	0.02
Pietism	0.06	−0.12	−0.13
Ethnic	−0.10	0.23	0.18
Trad. beliefs	−0.21	−0.02	0.02
J. org.	0	0.09	0.14
J. Educ. for Chldr.	0.02	0.08	0.12
Zionism	0.08	0.27	0.21
Gen. Com. Org.	−0.01	−0.06	−0.08
Anomie	−0.27	−0.02	−0.01
Mean Liberal Score	5.1	4.1	4.0
Mean Anomie Score	3.0	6.0	5.3

 * Jewish Rs ranking high or moderate on family head's occupation.
 † Jewish Rs ranking low on family head's occupation.
 ‡ Jewish Rs 20 to 59 years old ranking low on family head's occupation.
 ⁜ Age omitted because of respondent age restriction.

102 An Introduction to Causal Analysis in Sociology

regression equations, controlling for high-moderate and low occupational levels, were computed and are given in Table 2.[14] Now for high-moderate status Jews, both traditional beliefs and ethnic communal involvement have moderate, negative, impacts on liberalness.
The two low-status equations both show pietism with a negative impact on liberalness. Traditional beliefs have almost no impact. But, now, Jewish background, Jewish organisations, Jewish education of one's children, ethnic communal involvement, and Zionism all have moderate, positive, effects on liberalness. Among low-status Jews, those identity variables representing involvement with the communal and non-religious aspects of Jewish life display a positive effect on liberalness.[15]

The Protestant Identity Model

The Protestant data indicate:

1. Protestant childhood home background has considerably greater direct impact than expected. Besides those direct effects given in Chart 1B, it has direct effects of 0.19 on pietism; 0.20 on traditional beliefs; −0.14 on Protestant organisations; 0.12 on Protestant education for one's children; and −0.11 on liberalness. It has effects of just −0.02 on general community organisations and −0.03 on anomie.
2. Protestant education turns up with the additional direct effect of 0.32 on Protestant organisations and 0.17 on anomie. Otherwise, its other, not reported, direct effects run from a high of 0.09 to a low of −0.04.
3. Protestant religious behaviour also has a direct effect of 0.20 on traditional beliefs and −0.11 on anomie. Its other unreported direct effects run from a high of 0.05 to a low of 0.01.
4. Pietism does not have a sizeable direct effect on Protestant organisations, contrary to what was predicted. However, it does have sizeable, unexpected, direct effects of 0.27 on traditional beliefs, of 0.10 on Protestant religious education for one's children, and of −0.10 on anomie. Its remaining direct effects are in the range of 0.04 and 0.03.
5. Ethnic communal involvement does not have the expected sizeable relation with traditional beliefs but has a 0.11 direct effect on Protestant organisation activity for its largest impact. Its remaining effects range from 0.09 to 0.06.
6. Traditional beliefs do not relate to Protestant organizations but do relate to anomie with a direct effect of 0.15. It has a value of 0.01 for

Protestant education for one's children; −0.03 for general community organisations, and −0.09 for liberalness.
7. Protestant organisational activities do not relate as strongly as expected to Protestant religious education for one's children. It does have a direct effect of 0.13 on general community organisational activities, −0.16 on anomie, and 0.02 on liberalness.
8. Protestant religious education for one's children has a 0.12 direct effect on general community activities, −0.06 on liberalness, and zero on anomie.
9. General community organisation activities also have a −0.06 impact on liberalness.

In summary, then:

1. For Protestants we do get that Lenski pattern. Protestant childhood background has a moderate impact on ethnic communal involvement which has weak relations with Protestant education, religious behaviour, and pietism, but some effect upon Protestant organisation activities.

Our hypothesized change of inserting traditional beliefs as a linkage between the ethnic communal and Protestant organisations is unsupported. Traditional beliefs are related to Protestant background, religious behaviour, and pietism but to none of the other identity variables.
2. The mainstream of Protestant identity does flow from Protestant background to religious education to religious behaviour to pietism.
3. All but one of the relations between the identity variables and liberalness are weak ones—including the hoped-for stronger associations for pietism and ethnic communal involvement. Only for Protestant background does a relationship as large as 0.11 appear.
4. It was predicted that all relations among the identity variables and general community activities and anomie would be weak ones. Often this does happen. However, there are noticeable impacts from religious education of one's children and Protestant organisations on general community organisations. Protestant education and traditonal beliefs, have moderate, positive effects; religious behaviour, pietism, and Protestant organisations have moderate, negative effects on anomie.

Extended Models

The MCA equations back-stopping the calculations for the Jewish and Protestant recursive systems were extended by expanding age into a full biosocial recursive block of age, sex, and generations in the United States, for Jews; or generations urban, for Protestants. Also, present denomin-

Table 3. Total and Multiple Correlations Among Protestant Model Recursive System Variables

Dependent Variables Name	No.	Independent Variable Numbers													Multiple Correlation
		1	2	3	4	5	6	7	8	9	10	11	12	13	14	
Age	1															
Education	2	−0.25														
Head's occupation	3	−0.20	0.50													
Family Income	4	−0.15	0.44	0.43												
Protest. bkgrd. of childhood	5	0.05	0.03	0.04	−0.02											0.07
Protest. education	6	0.20	−0.06	−0.09	−0.04	0.23										0.30
Relig. behaviour	7	−0.07	0.07	0.15	0.10	0.33	0.17									0.39
Pietism	8	0.08	−0.02	0.01	−0.04	0.39	0.16	0.63								0.67
Ethnic communal	9	0.11	0.07	0.10	0.02	0.22	0.10	0.22	0.22							0.35
Trad. beliefs	10	−0.05	−0.25	−0.16	−0.10	0.34	0.11	0.41	0.46	0.15						0.60
Protest. org. activ.	11	0.03	0.10	0.10	0.10	0.11	0.36	0.47	0.34	0.20	0.19					0.58
Protest. educ. for children	12	−0.14	0.03	0.13	0.10	0.23	0.08	0.34	0.28	0.16	0.19	0.21				0.42
General com. org. activity	13	−0.01	0.35	0.22	0.30	0.05	0.02	0.16	0.10	0.17	−0.05	0.21	0.14			0.45
Anomie	14	0.08	−0.34	−0.34	−0.28	−0.02	0.12	−0.18	−0.11	−0.07	0.13	−0.18	0.02	−0.13		0.49
Liberalness	15	−0.23	−.16	0.19	0.15	0.11	0.03	0.12	0.07	0.04	−0.04	0.10	0.05	0.01	−0.34	0.44

ational membership was added to the identity block. The presence of the new control variables of sex and generations in the United States did not alter the recursive system relations that have just been reported.[16] In the Protestant system, generations urban did not prove to be a meaningful variable.[17]

While present denominational membership also does not alter the relationships among the other variables, such membership does add somewhat to the explanatory power of the recursive systems.[18]

The four-category grouping of Protestant denominational preferences produces a rank pattern quite like that for the four Jewish denominational groupings. Jews and Protestants with no denominational preferences have the lowest mean scores on the identity variables. The Orthodox Jewish denomination and the fundamentalist group both usually have the highest scores on their respective identity dimensions. The Orthodox Jews, unlike the fundamentalists, also lead on religious education, religious behaviour, and ethnic organisation activities. Those who prefer the Reform Jewish denomination and the liberal Protestant denominations rank first on activity in general community organisations. Also, Reform Jews match the lead of liberal denomination Protestants on activities in ethnic organisations by tying the Jewish organisation mean score of the Orthodox denomination. Again, Reform Jews and liberal Protestants, conservative Jews and Protestants, Orthodox Jews and fundamentalist Protestants are paired in rank, going from the lowest to highest mean scores on anomie. The exception here is for the no-preference people. Jews with no denominational preferences score equally high with Orthodox Jews on anomie while no-preference Protestants have a mean anomie score (2.6) falling between those for Reform Jews (2.4) and liberal Protestants (2.9).

Jews and Protestants differ somewhat on mean liberalness scores. The most liberal are Reform Jews who have a mean score of 5.3. Next come a grouping of no-preference Jews (mean score 4.9); conservative Jews (4.8) and no-preference Protestants (4.8). Fundamentalist Protestants follow with a mean score of 4.5. Bringing up the rear are conservative denomination Protestants (mean score of 4.2), liberal denomination Protestants (4.1) and Orthodox Jews (4.0).[19]

Two New Models

Much of Lenski's thinking about religious and ethnic factors and effects is supported by the Protestant recursive system. There does appear to be evidence of a secondary identification branch moving through ethnic communal involvement, as Lenski maintains, which is weakly related to the religious variables. But contrary to Lenski's findings, pietism and traditional beliefs are strongly related.

These data indicate a weak, perhaps zero, relationship between religious behaviour and liberalness. There are only weak relations between ethnic communal involvement and the three consequence variables, contrary to Lenski's finding that this dimension linked with less liberalness.

Furthermore, Lenski maintains that pietism should be related to a more liberal attitude while traditional beliefs should display weak relationships with liberalness. Here, we find that both have weak relationships with liberalness. Finally, we support Lenski by finding a positive association between religious behaviour and Protestant organisation activities.

The Jewish data provide still less support for Lenski. Jewish identity is a more tightly related complex of variables and does not provide any sign of a secondary, secular, identity path through ethnic communal involvement nor through Jewish organisations as Sklare has stated. As with Protestant data, we find a strong association between pietism and traditional beliefs.

Among Chicago Jewry there are three factors making for a positive stance on welfare and civil rights issues. The strongest factor is social status. The second derives from growing up in an ethnic community with traditionally liberal norms. Apart from negative effects from ethnicity and traditional beliefs, their other Jewish identity components have little effect on liberalness among upper- and middle-status Jews. That smaller group of the Chicago Jewish community which does not taste the milk and honey of success is distinctly less liberal and has more anomie than their more successful brethren. But, when members of this less successful group become involved in the communal and organisational activities of Chicago Jewry, the 'non-religious' Jewish identity components have increased positive effects. For them, the non-religious organisations and communication network of the Jewish community becomes the weakest third factor making for a more liberal stance. Liebman (1973) discusses the variety of factors that have produced liberal attitudes among Jews and is in agreement with these findings.

These rather limited supports for the models proposed in Chart 1 demand a new set of hypothesised relations which appear in Chart 2.

The new Jewish model in Chart 2, Part A now registers the dominance of childhood background and religious behaviour along with additional links involving pietism, Jewish organisation activities, and Jewish education for one's children. In this chart, a double arrow indicates a strong impact, a

Religious Identification and its Ethnic Correlates   107

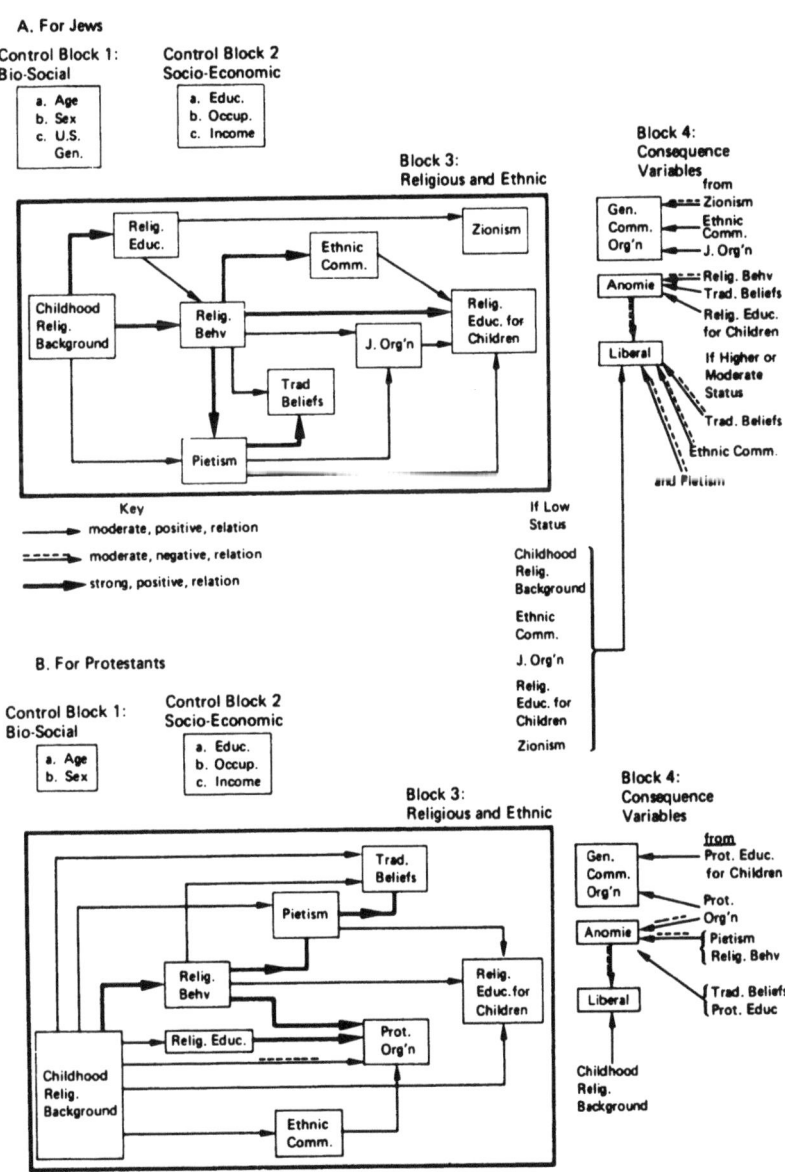

single arrow a moderate impact, and no arrow a weak or zero impact. A minus sign by an arrow indicates an expected negative effect.

Chart 2, Part B, presents the new model for Protestants. Here we have the dominance of childhood home background and religious behaviour as in the new Jewish model. However, childhood background is considerably more influential among Protestants than among Jews. Then, Jewish organisations are related to Jewish education for one's children, while Protestant organisations are not. A major difference between the two models is in the hypothesised independence of the ethnic communal variable from the religious mainstream among Protestants in contrast to its closer ties among Jews.

What this expected differential relationship of ethnic communal involvement and religious behaviour means is gasoline for our theoretical engines. Two contrasting possibilities exist:

1. That a majority group, like United States Protestants, will develop a separation of their ethnic community from their religious life as maintained by Lenski. By way of contrast, minority groups will be more tightly organised and will bind together their community and religious lives. This conceptualisation predicts that equivalent measurement of Jewish identity in Israel, or Catholic identity in Italy, would produce a separation of the ethnic and religious behaviour dimensions. It also expects US Catholics to reveal a model akin to the Jewish one.
2. That the Jewish model with its close ties between ethnic communal involvement and religious behaviour pictures a minority group whose religious behaviour pictures a minority group whose religious institution has been considerably secularised. The Protestant model represents the situation of a strong, independent, religious structure and a strong, independent, ethnic community. In essence, this means that there are two somewhat separated Protestant subcommunities—one expressing itself through religion and one expressing itself through a communal, non-religious, structure. Again this adopts Lenski's position for both Protestants and Catholics. This American Jewish model would represent the special case of a group whose communal structure now dominates its religious life. Future research will have to decide which of these two possibilities are nearer reality.

Looking at the consequence variables for both new models, one quickly notes that activity in ethnic organisations enhances activity in general community organisations. Also that traditional beliefs consistently have positive associations and religious behaviour negative associations with anomie. Again, there is just a weak, or no, causal link between activity in general community organisations and the other two consequence variables.[20]

Still another gain from these models is their ability to show researchers a way to a better allocation of research efforts. Future research can best profit by searching for what there is in childhood home backgrounds that results in strong, moderate, or weak religious and ethnic identities. Is a well-organised household permeated with religious concern, the crucial variable set? Does it help or hinder to have parents who are quite active in religious and ethnic affairs?

As measured here, pietism seems to be an extension of religious behaviour. But, rather than combining the two, the measurement of pietism ought to be considerably improved by careful probing into the characteristics of religious experiences. The ideological dimension, here limited to the traditional—atraditional range, needs to be expanded beyond a Zionism dimension and has to be introduced into the Protestant model. At this stage of model development, it is too early to recommend the dropping of dimensions from those regression equations in which they have little direct effects. Instead, such simplications ought to be tried in future model applications which employ more developed dimension measurements.[21]

As mentioned in the discussion of the extended model, denominational preference is an influential variable and ought to be included in future model testing.

Better dimension measurements, larger, more varied, probability samples, and a broader universe than just the Chicago area, especially for Protestants, should be research design priorities for another round of model construction.

One can try to clarify the persistent debate over the consequences of religious and ethnic identification by pointing out:

1. The relations among the recursive block components of identification and the various consequence variables are frequently weak ones. Such weak (or even moderate) relationships can be considerably influenced by study design, measurement bias, sampling bias, and sampling errors. Hence, results from limited studies, such as those cited above, have a fair chance of yielding differing conclusions.
2. The determination of relations among identity components and consequence variables requires the introduction of controls for biosocial and socioeconomic variables (which usually have substantial impact on such relations).
3. In addition, it seems necessary to introduce intervening variables, such

as anomie, that can serve to link identity components with potential consequences such as positions on political issues.

4. The possible interactions among the several identity model factors must be located, and handled, before specific identity effects can be evaluated.

An examination of the research literature on the consequences of religious and ethnic involvement shows that seldom are these four complications taken into account. Clearly, the consequences of involvement are the result of a complicated chain of variables, and need to be teased out by quite careful research procedures. Failure to do this will continue to yield inconclusive results as to the effects of religious and ethnic involvement on the total national community.

Reprinted from Social Forces (52(2), December, 1973)
Copyright © University of North Carolina Press.

Notes

* This research was made possible by National Science foundation grants GS 637 and GS 1766 and by the Florence G. Heller—Jewish Welfare Board Research Center. The author wishes to thank Professors James Grimm, Edward Malecki, Morris Axelrod, Jack Fowler, and Edward C. Lehman, Jr, for their help with various project phases; Mildred Karler for her field work supervision; Richard Curran and Arthur Norton for their many months of able research assistance; Dina Bedi and Warren Glimpse for their programming assistance.

[1] These citations cover only recent major works. A very large number of other materials are, in turn, cited in the publications referred to in this article.

[2] For example, these varieties of measurements have been used in Sklare and Greenblum (1967), Rothman (1965), Lazerwitz (1953; 1969), and Herman (1971). These Jewish studies prefer to use the term identification rather than involvement. Such a usage will be continued in this article.

[3] For recursive model presentations see Blalock and Blalock (1968) or Land in Borgatta (1969).

[4] Since the Protestant data to be discussed do not include the dimension on concern about coreligionists in the rest of the world, it is not included in recursive block 3 of Chart 1B. Were it so included, it would come after religious educations for one's children, as does Zionism. The numbers by arrows in Chart 1 are path coefficients, which will be discussed later on.

[5] A full discussion of the survey design, multistage probability sample selection, field tribulations, and response rates are available in Lazerwitz (1969).

[6] Half of the Jewish non-response was concentrated in large apartment structures in Chicago. Protestant non-response was more widely scattered.

[7] Space limitations do not permit a more detailed statement about the

allotment of questions to each Protestant and Jewish dimension, their scoring, and combination into identity scores, and the formation of scores for the other items. This detailed material is available upon request.

[8] Of course, the standard item analysis technique of checking the association of each question's score with its total dimension score was performed.

[9] Another advantage of using both AID and MCA is that they are members of the same computer program package. A discussion of a joint AID-NCA analysis approach to inductive model building can be found in Sonquist (1970).

[10] To use MCA, respondents were grouped into those under 40 years; those 40 to 59; and those 60 years old or older. The three social status variables and the nine Jewish and eight Protestant identity variables were broken into high, moderate, and low levels. The details of such break points are available upon request.

[11] To simplify an already complex Chart 1, unexpected path coefficients are not put into it. In other words, if analysis turns up a moderate or strong relationship between two variables that has not been hypothesised, the path coefficient is presented in the text but not in the Chart. This Chart deals solely with those relationships initially hypothesised.

[12] The various variable branches through which the total indirect effects are expressed will not be gone into in this article. First of all, the large number of variables available for indirect paths considerably lessens the meaning of any specific path. Also, the strength of any specific indirect path is a product of the total correlation between two independent variables and the size of the direct effect upon the dependent variable of that independent variable through which the other independent variable indirectly expresses itself. Hence, study of total correlations between independent variables and their associated direct effects quickly gives a statistical picture of the various specific indirect paths.

[13] This strong impact of religious behaviour upon Jewish identification has also been found by Simon Herman (1971) in his study of Israeli Jews. Indeed, in his work Herman found it to be the single most influential variable and to display considerable impact upon what is here called beliefs about and concern for co-religionists in the rest of the world.

[14] Controls were obtained through use of the high, moderate, low status occupation index mentioned in introducing the MCA procedure. Such a control also gave, for all practical purposes, controls on education and income.

[15] This impact of Jewish communal life upon liberal attitudes of Jews is discussed by Liebman (1973).

[16] Sex and generations in the United States have previously been treated in single factor analyses in Lazerwitz (1970).

[17] Among Protestants, number of generations urban did not reveal any consistent patterns when the first, second, and third generations were compared with one another because their mean scores oscillated back and forth.

[18] Protestant respondent denominational preferences are grouped into those expressing no denominational preferences (5 per cent); those

preferring the so-called liberal denominations such as the United Church of Christ, Episcopal, Methodist or Presbyterian (48 per cent); and those respondents preferring the more fundamentalist denominations such as the Pentecostal, Baptist, Nazarene, Jehovah Witnesses, Latter-Day Saints, and Missouri Synod Lutheran Church (19 per cent). The Jewish denominations are Reform (31 per cent of the Jewish sample), Conservative (44 per cent), Orthodox (16 per cent), and no denominational preference (9 per cent of the Jewish sample). Denomination was placed between religious education and religious behaviour in the two causal systems.

[19] Using the AID technique, each new MCA equation was checked for interactions arising from the three variables of sex, generation, and denomination. No meaningful interactions could be detected.

[20] Detailed comments about the relationships among the variables of the biosocial and socioeconomic control blocks and the identification dimensions can be found in Lazerwitz (1970).

[21] This dropping of low beta variables has been done for Jews and Protestants. The resultant regression equations do not undergo meaningful changes on multiple correlation values nor on the relative importance of the retained variables.

3 Regression Analysis for the Comparison of School and Home Effects

Editor's Introduction and Commentary

In this paper, the author first criticises the interpretations given to certain variance measures in regression analysis used in the influential American IEA research studies, and then goes on to suggest new measures which better suit the required interpretation.

The essence of the problem is that $R_{4(12)}^2 - R_{41}^2$, say, is the variance accounted for by X_2 when all the effects of X_1 on X_4 are subtracted out (we assume here linear unconstrained regression). This will include the effect that X_1 has on X_4 through X_2, so that 'indirect effects' though X_2 are missing. This means that we cannot validly compare the effects of X_1 and X_2 by comparing R_{41}^2 and $R_{4(12)}^2 - R_{41}^2$, for in the former case effects of X_1 on X_4 through X_2 are included. Careful analysis is needed to understand what is being compared here, and Coleman provides that analysis. (Note that Coleman uses R_1^2 and R_{12}^2 for R_{41}^2 and $R_{4(12)}^2$, and later he uses $R_{4.1}^2$ and $R_{4.12}^2$.)

The data is evaluated in terms of a causal model between four blocks of variables. It would be possible to use block recursive methods in this case, the relationship between variables in any block being irrelevant (see the introduction to the previous chapter). However, in this case such methods would not serve the purpose, for what is required is a measure of the composite effect of one block on another; block recursive methods give the single effects of each variable in one block upon each variable in another. The task, then, is to formulate some composite measure of blocks 1, 2 and 3 in order to measure their effect on the single variable in block 4.

Coleman achieves the formulation conceptually by using the hypothetical experiment idea, already intrdouced in Part I of this book. Considering block 1, for instance (home background variables), we can compound these by forming their linear regression equation on X_4. This linear regression equation will take a particular value for each child measured. If we put these values in numerical order (from smallest to largest) we get a frequency table. From this frequency table we can obtain a cumulative frequency for any value t, say, being the number of children with a value of t or less. If we plotted a graph of values against cumulative frequency we would obtain a cumulative frequency graph. If we now divide the cumulative frequency scale into 100 parts, then the value for the 84th part, say, will be that value which 84 per cent of the sample of children do not exceed. This value at the 84th part is called the 84th percentile.

The hypothetical experiment now is to ask for the expected performance (i.e. value on X_4) of a child at the 84th percentile of home background. The reason we use percentiles is that there is no natural interval level meaning to the composite of scores in terms of home background — any given score can be made up of many different combinations of the individual variables making up home background. There is an ordinal level interpretation, however, and thus the use of percentiles, which rest only upon our acknowledging that one person's composite score is more or less than another's.

Coleman chooses the 84th percentile because in a distribution that is approximately normal (i.e. the frequency distribution is approximately bell-shaped), the value equal to one standard deviation above the mean is approximately the 84th percentile. This is the value $\bar{x}_1 + \sigma_{x_1}$. (Coleman uses σ_{x_1} but he is referring to the sample estimate of this which we have labelled s_{x_1}.)

The value of x_4 is given by the regression equation of x_4 on the composite variable x_1, where b_{41} allows for the rescaling of x_1 i.e.

$$x_4^* = a_{4.1} + b_{41} x_1$$

where x_4^* is the predicted value of x_4. Now, since $\bar{x}_4 = a_{4.1} + b_{41}\bar{x}_1$ and since $b_{41}\sigma_{x_1} = \beta_{41}\sigma_{x_4}$ (where β_{41} is the standardised regression coefficient $(\sigma_{x_1}/\sigma_{x_4})b_{41}$, obtained when the variables are standardised) then, at the value $\bar{x}_1 + \sigma_{x_1}$, the 84th percentile, $x_4^* = \bar{x}_4 + \beta_{41}\sigma_{x_4}$. This is generally less than the 84th percentile of performance, which is $\bar{x}_4 + \sigma_{x_4}$, since β_{41} is usually less than one. What this amounts to is that β_{41} is the ratio of the expected distance of X_4 above its mean for the 84th percentile of X_1 to the distance above the mean for the 84th percentile of X_4. Clearly, this is a valid measure then of the total effect of home background on performance, for this is true at all percentiles, not just the 84th.

Coleman then goes on to assess the direct effect of X_2 on X_4 in a similar way, except that X_2 is formed by taking the regression coefficients for variables in X_2 found in the regression equation of X_4 on X_1 and X_2. Coleman describes this as finding that linear combination of the variables comprising X_2 which have the maximum pmcc with X_4 when the variables comprising X_1 are constant. In Appendix 2(II), it is shown that these statements are equivalent given some conditions (labelled B and C in that Appendix) and clearly Coleman implicitly assumes these conditions. Indeed, the conditions are satisfied if the variables comprising X_1 and X_2 together with X_4 are multivariate normal, and it is this which Coleman probably assumes.

Coleman then goes on to analyse the various effects which can be estimated through his analysis, and an appendix discusses various algorithms for calculating the coefficients.

The article gives a very clear insight into the meaning and use of correlation and regression, an understanding of which is not as commonplace as it ought to be, and a careful reading of it will greatly benefit the reader.

ARTICLE 3

Regression Analysis for the Comparison of School and Home Effects[1]

JAMES S. COLEMAN *University of Chicago*

In this paper, I want to ask what are appropriate measures for comparing home and school effects in regression analysis. I will do so by examining the methodology used in three IEA studies, on science education (Comber and Keeves, 1973), reading comprehension (Thorndike, 1973), and literature (Purves, 1973). These studies continue the distinguished series that began with the comparative study of mathematics achievement a few years ago (Husen, 1967).

In all three of these studies, a particular strategy was employed in evaluating the relative importance of different classes of variables. In both the between-school analyses and overall analyses, variables were divided into four 'blocks,' labelled Blocks 1, 2, 3, and 4. The blocks are roughly defined as follows (the operational definitions differ somewhat from study to study, from between-school to overall analysis, and from Population I to II to IV, but the intent is the same in all cases):

Block 1 – Home background, including age and sex of child.

Block 2 – Type of school and type of programme, for all countries and grade levels in which there was differentiation of programme or of school or both.

Block 3 – School and instructional variables.

Block 4 – 'Kindred' variables, that were not seen as either necessarily prior to achievement nor necessarily consequent upon it, but as possibly either. These were variables such as motivation.

Interest is centered primarily on variables in Block 3, because they are the variables which can be affected by educational policy and practice. However, interest is also great in Block 2 variables, for somewhat different reasons. Since the type of school a student is in and the type of programme he is in (when there are differing school types and differing programmes, as there were in most of the countries) are ordinarily determined on the basis of his performance up to that point, the measure for type of school and type of programme shows primarily the degree of selection of high- and low-performing students into different schools.

The reason for separating these variables into blocks of this sort is to bring some kind of order into the regression analyses. The problems confronting the analysts were very great, and the number and variety of variables potentially affecting achievement were enormous. Complex analyses prior to the regression analyses themselves were necessary merely to create a reasonably small set of variables without throwing out variables that were important in their effects on achievement. I will not dwell on that elaborate process of data reduction except to commend the analysts.

However, some serious questions remain concerning the methodology used in the regression analyses of the three studies. For unless it is fully clear what is done through use of this methodology, it will not be possible to draw substantive conclusions about the effect of schools on learning. It will be my contention that the authors were not fully clear about what they were doing, and that this lack of clarity has led them to carry out analyses that prevent one from answering certain important questions about the effect of schools on learning.

The problem that I want to examine goes to the heart of the procedures used in the regression analyses in all three studies, in both the between-school and between-student analyses. This is the way in which blocks of variables were entered into the analysis. The blocks were used not merely to group variables into sets that were similar in type and interpretation, but also to allow a sequential order in the regression analysis. Block 1 variables, home background and age and sex of child, were entered first, and measures were reported for a regression equation including only them. The measure was explained variance or its square root, the multiple correlation coefficient, and in some analyses, more detailed measures of variables within this block. Block 2 variables, type of programme and type of school, were entered second, and measures were reported for them using equations containing Block 1 *and* Block 2 variables. The measure was the increment to explained variance, a measure obtained by subtracting the explained variance with Block 1 variables alone (R_1^2) from the explained variance with Block 1 and Block 2 variables (R_{12}^2), that is, $R_{12}^2 - R_1^2$. Next were entered Block 3 variables, school variables of numerous sorts, in an equation including Block 1 *and* Block 2 *and* Block 3 variables. The measure reported was analogous to that of type of school and programme, that is, the increment in variance explained, $R_{123}^2 - R_{12}^2$. One might immediately ask, apart from the order of blocks used in the analysis: Why did the studies not use raw or standardised regression coefficients instead of the measures used? But these alternatives are not so simple, for the blocks are not single variables, but sets of variables that together define the variable of 'home background', 'school type', or 'school resources'. Each variable within a block will have a regression coefficient, but these cannot be added within blocks to provide any meaningful measure.

Given the procedure actually used, the major question is an obvious one: What kind of inferences were drawn from the measures reported $(R_1^2, R_{12}^2 - R_1^2,$ and $R_{123}^2 - R_{12}^2)$, and what kind can be properly drawn? First, note that the measures are asymmetric for the three blocks. Despite this, inferences were made in each of the studies about the relative effects of home background and school variables, i.e. Blocks 1 and 3. In all three studies, the inferences were that home background (Block 1) is more important than school variables (Block 3) and that school variables showed little effect. The terms used to describe school effects varied from study to study, but the characterisation of school effects on the basis of these analyses had a certain consistency: 'disappointing' (Comber and Keeves, 1973; p. 298), 'largely negative results' (Thorndike, 1973; p. 100), 'there is little the school seems to be able to do to enhance or inhibit' (Purves, 1973; p. 184).

The quantitative results appear to bear these statements out, and as in earlier studies, the home background variables appear much stronger than the school variables. Furthermore, I am sure that, just as other studies have showed, the home background variables would still have showed great power and the school variables still been 'disappointing' if the analysis had been more symmetric. All regression analyses I have seen on these questions, analysed in whatever way imaginable, would have shown this. But the fact remains that these comparisons are made on the basis of an analysis that is very asymmetric. The measure for the Block 1 variables is R_1^2, while the measure for the Block 3 variables is $R_{123}^2 - R_{12}^2$. It is not the case that R_1^2 *is compared with* R_3^2, or $R_{123}^2 - R_{23}^2$ with $R_{123}^2 - R_{12}^2$. The fixed order is maintained throughout.

I want to take issue with the use of this asymmetric approach for comparing the relative effects of home background and school variables, and to suggest just what kind of inference can properly be drawn from the analysis as carried out.

In an attempt to discover effects of school factors on achievement, perhaps the principal villain is the fact that student populations in different schools differ at the outset, and because of this difference, it is not possible merely to judge the quality of a school by the achievements of the students leaving it. It is necessary to control in some way for the variations in student input with which the teachers and staff of the school are confronted. In some way, it is the *increment* in achievement that the school provides, which should be the measure of the school's quality. If we had good measures of that increment, as well as good measures of the level of various school resources in the same school, it would be possible to establish a relation between the size of the increment and the level of certain resources, and thus to determine which school resources were most important to learning.

The problem lies in establishing the appropriate baseline so that some estimate of the achievement increment can be made, and most cross-sectional studies have, like the IEA studies, attempted to use factors in the student's own background or possible in the community which can provide an estimate of the student input to the school and thus allow an estimate of the increment of achievement.

To see the logic by which school effects can be assessed in a cross-sectional analysis while controlling for student characteristics, it is helpful to use a causal diagram similar to that presented for Japan (in Comber and Keeves, 1973; pp. 280–284). Assume a home background variable (Block 1), a school type variable (Block 2), and two school variables (Block 3), arbitrarily labelling school achievement Block 4 for convenience. The diagram indicates the causal reasoning behind the use of the sequence of blocks in IEA, and I have no quarrel whatsoever with this set of *a priori* causal assumptions. All analyses of school effects that I know suggest this kind of scheme, in which home background precedes, in a causal sequence, both the type of school and particular variables of the school, and in which the type of school (in a differentiated system) precedes the particular school variables.

The question arises, then, of just what the analyses carried out in IEA correspond to in this diagram.

(1) First, an equation with Block 1 as independent and school achievement as dependent (R_1^2) shows the total effect of the Block 1 variable, through these paths: direct: 14; 2-step: 124 and 134; and 3-step: 1234. The variance explained by Block 1 is explained through these four paths.

(2) Second, the equation with Block 1 and Block 2 as independent variables (R_{12}^2) shows the effect of two paths from equation 1 (14 and 134) plus those from school type, both direct and 2-step: direct: 23; 2-step: 234. When the variance accounted for in Equation 1 is subtracted out, what is left ($R_{12}^2 - R_1^2$) is all due to school type, that is, 24 and 234; that due to 14 and to 134 is subtracted out. But also subtracted out is a portion of the variance that operated through school type: 124 and 1234. These paths are much less strong than 24 and 234 whenever 12 is itself small; and it usually is not very large. Nevertheless, some portion of the effect of 24 and 234 is subtracted out, the portion depending on the size of 12.

(3) The third equation includes Block 1, 2, and 3 variables (R_{123}^2), and includes variance from two paths in Equation 2 (14 and 24) plus that from Block 3 variables: 34. When the variance accounted for in Equation 2 is subtracted out ($R_{123}^2 - R_{12}^2$), what is left is all due to Block 3, that is 34: that due to 14 and 24 is subtracted out. But also subtracted out is a portion of the variance due to 34. Variance due to both the 134 and 234 paths is subtracted out. Thus what is left after Equation 2 variance is subtracted out is [var(34) − var(134) − var(234)]. [I am using var( ) to mean the variance accounted for by a given causal relation denoted by the bracketed symbols.]

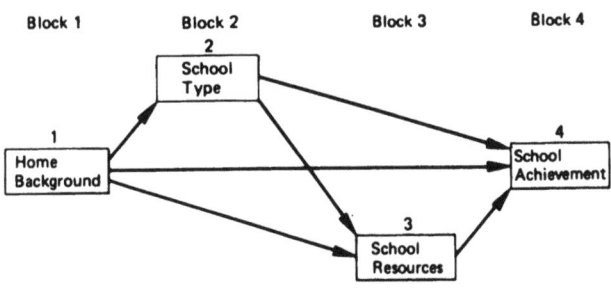

Now, let us summarise what variance is contained in the numbers reported for Blocks 1, 2, and 3 in these studies. This table shows the asymmetry introduced by the procedure used in these studies. Note that asymmetry exists in two ways: the variance for Block 1 includes all the variance due both to the direct path and all indirect paths; the variance for Block 3 not only is limited to that from direct paths, but excludes that due to indirect paths from earlier steps.

There is nothing wrong with such asymmetry, as the IEA analyses show, but it is important to be aware of its implications. One implication is this: it is not possible to make a comparison of the amount of variance accounted for in different blocks, and, say, for example, that Block 1, home background, accounts for much more variance than Block 3. Thus the statements in these studies about the small effects of school variables compared to the effects of home background, which 'account for much of the variance' (Purves, 1973; p. 152), are of 'decided importance' (Thorndike, 1973; p. 100), or are 'quite considerable' (Comber and Keeves, 1973; p. 235), are not appropriate statements on the basis of the analyses reported. The statements are very likely true, as inspection of the zero-order correlations, the path analysis for science in Japan, or any of numerous other indicators suggest, but in order to make an explicit comparison, a symmetric analysis would be necessary — for example, a commonality analysis of the variance R_{123}^2, showing both the unique variance and total variance accounted for by each block in that equation. As it stands, the variance estimates at Block 1 are of *total* variance due to Block 1 variables, while those at Block 3 are of the *unique* variance due to Block 3 variables, with those at Block 2 being somewhere in between.

But it is perhaps not even appropriate to want to make symmetric comparisons between 'effect of home' and 'effect of school' if one has in mind the kind of causal diagram as shown in Figure 1, because the home and school occupy quite different places in it: home variables partly

Table 1

Block 1	Block 2	Block 3
R_1^2	$R_{12}^2 - R_1^2$	$R_{123}^2 - R_{12}^2$
var(14)		
var(124)	var(24) − var(124)	
var(134)		var(34) − var(134) − var(234)
var(1234)	var(234) − var(1234)	

determine school variables, but not the other way around. What one might want to specify for Block 1 and 3 are these effects:

(a) The *total effect* of variations in Block 1 (home background) variables on achievement both through its impact on school variables and independent of those variables (effects 14, 124, 134, and 1234 in Figure 1).

(b) The *direct effect* of variations in Block 3 (school) variables on achievement (effect 34), whether this effect is merely implementing the force of home background (effects 134, 1234) or independent of it. This may be thought of as the potential direct effect of school variables if they were distributed independently of home background.

(c) The direct effect of variations in Block 3 (school) variables as distributed *independent of* or *over and above* the force of home background and school type (effect 34 minus effects 134 and 1234).

(d) The *direct effect* of variations in Block 1 (home background) variables on achievement apart from the force of home background in shaping or selecting schools (effect 14).

Perhaps other effects are desired as well, but these appear to me the most important. One might then want (i) to compare effects (b) and (d): the direct effect of school and the direct effect of home apart from its effects through school. But if one did so he should realise that this does not express the total effect of home, because the home acts to determine the school resources themselves. Consequently, one might want (ii) to compare (a) and (b), the *total* effect of variations in home background with the direct effect of variations in school resources. One might also want (iii) to compare effects (a) and (d), to determine the proportion of the home's effect that takes place through shaping or selecting the school the child goes to, and the proportion that takes place directly through its impact on the child himself.[2] And one might want (iv) to compare effects (b) and (c), to compare the total direct effect of school resources to the effect of school resources that is distributed independently of differences in family background. In addition, one might want (v) to compare effects (a) and (c), recognising that these are total effects of home background variations, but only partial effects of school variations. The idea here might be to compare the total effects of family variations on achievement with the effect on the child's achievement of other variations in society that act through the schools but independent of the home. Finally, one of the most important comparisons one might want to make lies within a block: for example, one might want to compare the relative sizes of the total direct effects of different Block 3 variables [comparisons within (b) above], or comparison of the relative sizes of the effects of different Block 3 variables that, as distributed, are independent of the force of home background [comparisons within (c) above].

That is, given a set of *a priori* assumptions about causal flows, the kind of comparisons one wants to make may very well not be symmetric, and it is not reasonable to think only of comparing 'home background effects' and 'school effects' without further specification. Furthermore, it is not possible to capture in a single measure or parameter or coefficient all of the effects specified in (a) through (d) above.

Given the kind of analyses that have in fact been carried out in these studies, which of the comparisons I have described is possible? What has been measured through the sequential introduction of blocks, and the reporting of R_1^2, $R_{12}^2 - R_1^2$, and $R_{123}^2 - R_{12}^2$ are effects (a) and (c) listed above. Consequently, it is possible among countries to show two things, if we consider blocks as wholes and neglect Block 2 for the present, or combine it with 1: the *total effect* of home background, independently of whether it operates through shaping the school or shaping the child, and the effect of school variables *over and above* the transmitted force of home background. Of the various comparisons, (i) through (iv) above, this is only one, (v). The only other possible comparison in two of the studies is (vi), comparison of relative size of effects of specific variables within blocks.

Now this is not disastrous in any way. If the analyses had been carried out so that all comparisons (i) through (vi) could be made, then there would have been far more to do than possible within the confines of these volumes. But it is important to recognise what kind of comparisons the data do allow, so that the inferences drawn are not incorrect.

The relation of the measures presented to the comparisons desired can be illustrated by comparing the IEA studies to another study of similar character, Equality of Educational Opportunity (Coleman, *et al.*, 1966), in which I participated. In that study we too introduced blocks of variables sequentially, always entering home background before any school variables, although among the school variables themselves, varying the sequence extensively. This gave 'variance added' measures comparable to those of the IEA studies, and measured effects (a) and (c) in the tabulation above, as did IEA. The difference, however, was that in that study the principal comparisons desired were of type (vi), that is, the relative sizes of the effects of different school variables, not the relative size of home and school variables. Part of the subsequent methodological debate surrounding that study (see, for example, Cain and Watts, 1970; Hanushek and Kain, 1972; Bowles and Levin, 1968; and Coleman, 1968, 1970, 1972) arose from a confusion over this point. If the aim of the research had been to compare effects of school and home (as some critics implicitly assumed), then certainly effects (b) and (d) should have been measured, and not only effects (a) and (c), which were measured. As a general rule, it appears that in such studies, all effects of types (a)–(d) should be reported so that comparisons other than those for which the study was designed may be subsequently made.

The Hypothetical Experiments

As stated above, these studies used measures of variance added, that is, R_1^2 and $R_{123}^2 - R_{12}^2$, to measure effects (a) and (c). But now the question arises, even for measuring effects are these the best measures? I believe the answer is no. The use of the 'variance added' measure, $R_{12}^2 - R_1^2$ and $R_{123}^2 - R_{12}^2$, is dictated, in part, by the fact that it is one of the few easily obtained measures of the effect of a set of variables, as distinct from the effect of a single variable (for which regression coefficients and standardised regression coefficients are available). For a set of independent variables, e.g. 'home background' or 'school resources' in a regression equation, no single overall measures of their combined effect, other than variance added, is ordinarily available.

Consider, however, the following alternative, using as an example the results of a set of three regression equations such as the ones below for England (Purves, 1973; p. 163). The variance explained by a given set of variables, s, is denoted by R_s^2, and the variance explained by that set excluding Block i variables is denoted by R_{s-i}^2, (Table 2). Now suppose, looking first at the first row, we consider an attempt to explain cognitive achievement in literature by a single composite variable, 'home background'. That composite variable is a linear combination of the variables that go into it which minimises the sum of squared deviations of the predicted dependent variable from the actual one. That is, it is a composite variable which is a weighted sum of the various home background variables, the weights being the regression coefficients themselves. Now since we conceive of such a variable, 'home background', we can conceive of a hypothetical experiment to determine the expected performance of a child at a given percentile of home background — say the 84th percentile.[3] What is meant by the '84th percentile of home background' is a family background high in those resources that contribute to a child's performance in literature. The particular combination of resources might differ: one child with a family background at the 84th percentile might have low father's education and high mother's education, while another might have high father's

Table 2

	R_s^2 (variance explained)	$R_s^2 - R_{s-i}^2$ (variance added)
1. Block 1 (home background)	0.252	0.252
2. Blocks 1 and 2 (+ type of school and programme)	0.371	0.119
3. Blocks 1, 2, 3 (+ instructional variables)	0.410	0.039

education and low mother's education. The two backgrounds are equivalent only in that on the average, homes with these two combinations of resources both produce children at the 84th percentile of the distribution of predicted performance.

Now, the answer to the question of what would be the predicted performance of a child at the 84th percentile of family background is not, as one might at first expect, the 84th percentile of actual performance. Predicted performance has a smaller standard deviation than the distribution of actual performance. We can see just what the predicted performance of some one at the 84th percentile would be by an equation based on the regression analysis. If $\bar{x}_1$ is the average value of the home background composite, σ_{x_1} is the standard deviation, then the predicted performance, x_4, when home background is one standard deviation above its mean (the 84th percentile), can be obtained from the regression equation:

$$x_4^* = a_{4.1} + b_{41}(\bar{x}_1 + \sigma_{x_1})$$
$$= a_{4.1} + b_{41}\bar{x}_1 + b_{41}\sigma_{x_1}$$

But $a_{4.1} + b_{41}\bar{x}_1$ is simply the mean performance, $\bar{x}_4$, and $b_{41}\sigma_{x_1}$ is equal to the standardized regression coefficient, β_{41}, times the standard deviation of performance, $\sigma_{x_4}: x_4^* = \bar{x}_4 + \beta_{41}\sigma_{x_4}$. Thus the predicted performance at the 84th percentile of home background is not the 84th percentile of performance, which is $\bar{x}_4 + \sigma_{x_4}$, but a lesser distance above, depending on the size of the standardised regression coefficient, β_{41}. The fraction of the distance that the 84th percentile of *actual* performance is above the mean is $\bar{x}_4 + \sigma_{x_4} - \bar{x}_4$, or σ_{x_4}. The distance above for *predicted* performance is $\bar{x}_4 + \beta_{41}\sigma_{x_4} - \bar{x}_4$, or $\beta_{41}\sigma_{x_4}$. Thus the fraction is $(\bar{x}_4 + \beta_{41}\sigma_{x_4} - \bar{x}_4)/(\bar{x}_4 + \sigma_{x_4} - \bar{x}_4) = \beta_{41}$. Thus the fraction of the distance above the mean in this hypothetical experiment is simply the standardised regression coefficient, β_{41}, of the composite or block of variables, Block 1. For an equation that contains only a single composite, such as the equation with

Block 1 alone, the value of β_{41} is identical to the multiple correlation coefficient between performance and this composite variable, R_{41}. However, since what I have called a 'composite variable' is actually a set of variables describing the home background, it is necessary to ask what is meant by the 'standardised regression coefficient' for this set of variables. This coefficient, β_{41}, is the standardised regression coefficient for a newly defined variable, x_1 (defined up to a scale constant), which is the linear combination of home background variables created by the regression analysis. Above, this linear combination is denoted by x_1.

Returning to Figure 1 and the types of effects outlined on page 121, the standardised regression coefficient β_{41} is an appropriate measure for the first effect described there, the *total effect* of home background, whether direct or through school variables.

For example, if the average performance is 50, and the standard deviation is 10, then assuming a normal distribution, a child at the 84th percentile will score 60 while a child at the 16th percentile will score 40, that is 10 points below and above the average, respectively. If the multiple correlation between achievement and the home background variables in England is $0.502 = (0.252)^{\frac{1}{2}}$, then a child in England at the 84th percentile of home background will score at 50 plus (10)(0.502), or 55.02, while a child at the 16th percentile of home background will score 50 minus (10)(0.502), or 44.98. That is, if we know that the score for a given percentile is a certain distance below or above the mean, then the score for that same percentile on this composite variable will be R_{41} (or β_{41}) times that distance — in this case, 50.2 per cent of that distance. Thus we can reasonably say that this composite variable, home background, accounts for 50.2 per cent of the variation (not variance) in achievement. What is true at the 84th percentile is true at all percentiles — the child at a given percentile on home background is R_{41} times the distance from the mean in achievement that the child at the same percentile of actual achievement is. Or to look at it differently, if we know the difference in achievement score between any two percentiles (a difference of 20 points for the 16th and 84th in the example above), then the difference in achievement score of the average child with a home background at those same two percentiles will be R_{41} times that difference, or (20)(0.502) = 10.04 in this case.

By extension, the same argument given above now holds if we create a composite variable from home background *and* type of programme and school, that is, from the Block 1 and Block 2 variables combined. We can conceive of a new hypothetical experiment, asking about two children at the 84th and 16th percentile of a new compound variable, made up of home background and type of programme and school: what proportion of the total distance above the mean to the 84th percentile is the child who is at the 84th percentile in this combination of home background and school type? That proportion is $R_{4(12)}$ where $R_{4(12)}$ is the multiple correlation of achievement with home background and type of program and school.[4] $R_{4(12)}$ again is a standardised regression coefficient $\beta_{4(12)}$, for composite variable made up of Blocks 1 and 2, when no other variables are controlled. Of course it may not make much sense to define a new variable as 'home background and school type'. If not, then the usefulness of $R_{4(12)}$ or $\beta_{4(12)}$ is not very great. But in any case, our interest is not so much in the explanatory power of the best combination of home background and school types as in the explanatory power of school type itself, apart from home resources.

Direct Effect of School Type (Block 2) or School Resources (Block 3)

How can one assess the direct effect of Block 2 variables, that is, the effect of type (b)? What would such an effect be? We can think of an hypothetical experiment something as follows: suppose for two children, the Block 1 variables, home background, were at their average position for the population. Then if for one of the children the Block 2 variables were held at the population average, his predicted score would be exactly at the population average. But for the other child, the Block 2 variables are put at their 84th percentile level. What we mean by 'their 84th percentile level' is this: in this equation, including the Block 1 variables, we find the linear combination of Block 2 variables that in the presence of Block 1 variables has the highest partial correlation with achievement. This becomes for us a new variable which we labelled 'type of programme and school', or 'Block 2'. Then we find the 84th percentile position on this new variable (which we can assume is normally distributed, for purposes of the hypothetical experiment and the measure that this experiment is leading toward). And the second child is at the 84th percentile level on this variable, along with his 50th percentile family background level. Our question then becomes, what is the predicted achievement of this child at the 50th percentile of family background (Block 1) and the 84th percentile of Block 2? Further, thinking of the difference between the average achievement (50th percentile of Block 1 and 50th percentile of Block 2) and the 84th percentile achievement (which is one standard deviation above the mean of achievement), what proportion of that distance is covered by the score of the second child? Whatever measure will give us the answer to that question is the measure of the direct effect of the type of programme and school compound variable.

Regression Analysis of School and Home Effects 127

We can easily see how, if we truly went to the trouble of making up the compound variables as described above, such a measure would be directly forthcoming from the regression equation. We can see how by directly calculating the three scores in question:

(1) 84th percentile score: $x_4 + \sigma_{x_4}$;
(2) 50th percentile or average score (with average Block 1 and Block 2 variables): $\bar{x}_4$;
(3) predicted score of a child with average Block 1 variables (x_1) and 84th percentile on Block 2 variables (x_2): x_4^* as calculated below.

If the regression equation is $x_4 = a_{4.12} + b_{41.2}x_1 + b_{42.1}x_2$, then predicted achievement score, x_4^*, is given by:

$$x_4^* = a_{4.12} + b_{41.2}\bar{x}_1 + b_{42.1}(\bar{x}_2 + \sigma_{x_2})$$

$$= a_{4.12} + b_{41.2}\bar{x}_1 + b_{42.1}\bar{x}_2 + b_{42.1}\sigma_{x_2}$$

$$= \bar{x}_4 + b_{42.1}\sigma_{x_2}$$

But if $b_{42.1}$ is the raw regression coefficient of Block 2 variables, controlling on Block 1, and $\beta_{42.1}$ the standardised one, then $b_{42.1}\sigma_{x_2} = \beta_{42.1}\sigma_{x_4}$. Thus $x_4^* = \bar{x}_4 + \beta_{42.1}\sigma_{x_4}$. Therefore, the proportion of the distance between scores (1) and (2) covered by (3) is $(\bar{x}_4 + \beta_{42.1}\sigma_{x_4} - \bar{x}_4)/(\bar{x}_4 + \sigma_{x_4} - \bar{x}_4)$. Thus the desired measure, showing the proportion of variation in achievement that the Block 2 variables will explain when Block 1 variables are held fixed is merely the standardised regression coefficient for Block 2 in the equation containing Block 1 and Block 2.

The approach taken here toward carrying out hypothetical experiments with blocks of variables can be carried further. Some examples will show the generality of this approach toward measures of effects in regression analysis, and will make evident that it should not be practised merely through blind calculation of standardised regression coefficients without regard for precisely what is the desired measure. One hypothetical experiment would be to ask the achievement difference between a child who is at the 16th percentile in home background (Block 1), and at the 84th percentile in school type and programme (Block 2). Is this score above or below the mean, and what proportion of the distance from the mean to the 84th or 16th percentile is it? The score is:

$$x_4^* = a_{4.12} + b_{41.2}(\bar{x}_1 - \sigma_{x_1}) + b_{42.1}(\bar{x}_2 + \sigma_{x_2})$$

$$= a_{4.12} + b_{41.2}\bar{x}_1 + b_{42.1}\bar{x}_2 - b_{41.2}\sigma_{x_1} + b_{42.1}\sigma_{x_2}$$

$$= \bar{x}_4 - b_{41.2}\sigma_{x_1} + b_{42.1}\sigma_{x_2}$$

But $b_{41.2}\sigma_{x_1} = \beta_{41.2}\sigma_{x_4}$, and $b_{42.1}\sigma_{x_2} = \beta_{42.1}\sigma_{x_4}$, so that

$$x_4^* = \bar{x}_4 + \sigma_{x_4}(\beta_{42.1} - \beta_{41.2})$$

If the quantity in parentheses is positive, the score is above the mean. The score at the 84th percentile is $x_4 + \sigma_{x_4}$, so that the proportion of distance from $\bar{x}$ to the 84th percentile is $[\bar{x}_4 + \sigma_{x_4}(\beta_{42.1} - \beta_{41.2}) - \bar{x}_4]/[\bar{x}_4 + \sigma_{x_4} - \bar{x}_4] = \beta_{42.1} - \beta_{41.2}$. If the quantity is below the mean, the proportion of the distance to the 16th percentile would be calculated in the same way, but would be $\beta_{41.2} - \beta_{42.1}$.

A second hypothetical experiment would be this: suppose a child is one standard deviation below the mean in home background (Block 1) resources, and at the mean in school type (Block 2). Then how many standard deviations above the mean should his school resources (Block 3) be to make his predicted score be at the mean? This is answered by setting up the appropriate equation with the desired number of standard deviations represented by an unknown, c.

$$\bar{x}_4 = a_{4.123} + b_{41.23}(\bar{x}_1 - \sigma_{x_1}) + b_{42.13}\bar{x}_2 + b_{43.12}(\bar{x}_3 + c\sigma_{x_2})$$

$$= a_{4.123} + b_{41.23}\bar{x}_1 + b_{42.13}\bar{x}_2 + b_{43.12}\bar{x}_3 - b_{41.23}\sigma_{x_1} + cb_{43.12}\sigma_{x_2}$$

$$\therefore \bar{x}_4 = \bar{x}_4 - b_{41.23}\sigma_{x_1} + cb_{43.12}\sigma_{x_2}$$

$$\therefore 0 = -\beta_{41.23}\sigma_{x_4} + c\beta_{43.12}\sigma_{x_4}$$

$$\therefore c = \beta_{41.23}/\beta_{43.12}$$

These hypothetical experiments show the generality of manipulations among standardised regression coefficients as a way of measuring the effects of changing various independent variables by some standard distance related to their distribution in society, such as one standard deviation.

It is important to recognise that even if we had the standardised regression coefficients, they would be no panacea. It tells us only the effect of type (b) on page 121. Suppose it is empirically the case that children in the high-performance school and programme types (Block 2) are nearly always from good home backgrounds (Block 1). Then it is quite artificial, in one sense, to perform the first hypothetical experiment discussed above, for seldom does a child from an average home background attend an 84th percentile school. To know the potential for higher performance of a child in a high-resource secondary school with average home background is of purely academic interest if it infrequently happens. What is of greater interest is the amount of variation that the schools in fact account for independently of the family. But if there is not such a high correspondence between Block 1 and Block 2, the potential effect is, in fact, realised for some children, and it is of more than academic interest.

Independent effect of school resource variables. To obtain measures of the independent effect of school variables [effect (c) in the list on page 121] is complicated by the fact that the total effect of school variables, $\beta_{43.12}$, cannot be merely divided into two additive components, the effects that reinforce Block 1 and 2 variables and the effects that are independent of these variables. But the independent effect can be found through the operational meaning of the hypothetical experiments themselves, and another hypothetical experiment is useful in doing so. Consider one student with average values of Block 1, Block 2, and Block 3 variables. His predicted achievement will be exactly average, $\bar{x}_4$. Now consider another student with average values of Block 1 variables and average values of Block 2 variables. His values for the Block 3 compound, on the other hand, are above average. We do not put it one standard deviation, σ_{x_3}, above the average of the compound, because we want it to be only that distance above represented by the part of Block 3 that is independent of Blocks 1 and 2. If $R_{3(12)}$ is the multiple correlation of Blocks 1 and 2 with 3, then variance in Block 3 not associated with 1 and 2 is $1 - R^2_{3(12)}$, and the fraction of Block 3 that is independent of blocks 1 and 2 is $(1 - R^2_{3(12)})^{\frac{1}{2}}$. Thus we want the value of the Block 3 compound to be $(1 - R^2_{3(12)})^{\frac{1}{2}}$ times σ_{x_3} above average. Thus the equation for the predicted achievement is:

$$x_4^* = a_{4.123} + b_{41.23}\bar{x}_1 + b_{42.13}\bar{x}_2 + b_{43.12}(\bar{x}_3 + \sigma_{x_3}(1 - R^2_{3(12)}))^{\frac{1}{2}}$$

$$= \bar{x}_4 + b_{43.12}\sigma_{x_3}(1 - R^2_{3(12)})^{\frac{1}{2}}$$

$$= \bar{x}_4 + \beta_{43.12}\sigma_{x_4}(1 - R^2_{3(12)})^{\frac{1}{2}}$$

Then to see the fraction of the distance above the mean from $\bar{x}_4$ to $\bar{x}_4 + \sigma_{x_4}$ that this student's predicted achievement lies, we subtract $\bar{x}_4$ and divide by the total distance $\bar{x}_4 + \sigma_{x_4} - x_4$. This is $[\bar{x}_4 + \beta_{43.12}\sigma_{x_4}(1 - R^2_{3(12)})^{\frac{1}{2}} - \bar{x}_4]/[\bar{x}_4 + \sigma_{x_4} - \bar{x}_4] = \beta_{43.12}(1 - R^2_{3(12)})^{\frac{1}{2}}$. Thus the measure for the independent effect of school resources on achievement is simply the total direct effect discounted by the variation in school resources that is unexplained by Blocks 1 and 2.

But $\beta_{43.12}$ can be expressed as $(R^2_{4(123)} - R^2_{4(12)})^{\frac{1}{2}}/(1 - R^2_{3(12)})^{\frac{1}{2}}$ so that $\beta_{43.12}(1 - R^2_{3(12)})^{\frac{1}{2}} = (R^2_{4(123)} - R^2_{4(12)})^{\frac{1}{2}}$. That is, the independent effect (on the left) equals the square root of the added explained variance (on the right). Thus the effect of Block 3 variables on achievement independent of Blocks 1 and 2 is simply the square root of the 'added variance explained' reported in Husen (1967), Comber and Keeves (1973) and Thorndike (1973), that is, $(R^2_{4(123)} - R^2_{4(12)})^{\frac{1}{2}}$.

Calculation of Standardized Regression Coefficients for a Compound of Variables

In the above discussion, it was assumed that Blocks 2 and 3 each consisted of a single variable. But if a block consists of a number of variables, how do we get the measures described above for the impact of the block of variables, considered conceptually as a compound variable (e.g. 'school variables', 'instructional variables', or 'learning conditions', as the authors termed Block 3 variables), but in practice left as a set of variables? One of the appealing aspects of 'added explained variance' ($R_s^2 - R_{s-i}^2$) is that it serves as a global measure for the whole set of variables that are entered in a given block. Since the blocks have a coherent meaning or interpretation it is useful to have a measure, comparable to the standardised regression coefficient, for the block considered as a compound variable, even though it is a number of separate variables. This measure would tell us the proportion of variation that Block 2 or 3 variables, considered as the best-predicting compound, will explain when all Block 1 or Block 1 and Block 2 variables are held fixed. But it turns out this is not quite so simple to obtain as the added explained variance, $R_{123}^2 - R_{12}^2$. Conceptually, there is no problem. To calculate the standardised regression coefficient $\beta_{43.12}$ for Block 3, it would be possible to first carry out the full regression of achievement on Block 1, 2, and 3 variables, then to create a new compound variable from the Block 3 variables, by using the regression coefficients as weights, recalculate the correlation matrices including the newly-defined variable, and then carry out another regression analysis, in which the new compound Block 3 variable replaces the set of variables from which it was compounded. The new regression equation is identical to the preceding one, in total variance explained and in regression coefficients for the unaffected Block 1 and 2 variables. For the Block 3 compound, the raw regression coefficient and the standardised coefficient are identical (since the compound uses the regression coefficients of the individual variables as weights), and are the desired measure: the proportion of variation in achievement that will be accounted for by Block 3 variables when Block 1 and 2 variables are held fixed.

This kind of recalculation is, however, technically cumbersome. It involves recalculation of the covariance matrix every time a new compound is created. Instead of that, it is possible to proceed in any of several ways that make it possible to calculate these standardised regression coefficients without recalculating the correlation matrices. Two such ways are discussed in the Appendix.

Now it becomes possible to indicate what would be the appropriate measures for the four kinds of effects discussed for Blocks 1 and 3 earlier in the paper. The notations used will be subscript i for Block i, with subscript 4 denoting the dependent variable, achievement; $R_{4(ijk)}$ as the multiple correlation of Blocks i, j, k with achievements; $\beta_{4i.jk}$ as the standardised multiple regression coefficient of achievement on the Block i variables, considered as a compound, when Blocks j and k are controlled.

(a) *Total effect* of variations in Block 1 variables, both through school and outside it: $R_{41}(=\beta_{41})$;

(b) *Direct effect* of Block 3 variables, whether this implements the force of home and school type through its distribution, or not: $\beta_{43.12}$;

(c) *Independent direct effect* of Block 3 variables as distributed, in implementing societal variations beyond the home: $\beta_{43.12}(1 - R^2_{3(12)})^{1/2}$;

(d) *Direct effect* of Block 1 variables, apart from their effects through shaping or selecting schools: $\beta_{41.23}$.

With these effects now laid out as above, it is possible to see just what the 'added explained variance' or 'unique variance' measures used in these studies involves. Although they are not estimates, as are the measures I have proposed here, of the amount of variation explained by particular variables or blocks of variables, they are close to it. That is best seen by writing again the equation for $\beta_{43.12}$: $\beta_{43.12} = (R_{4(123)}^2 - R_{4(12)}^2)^{1/2} / (1 - R_{3(12)}^2)^{1/2}$. Now the added, or unique variance is simply $\beta_{43.12}^2 (1 - R_{3(12)}^2)$, that is, the square of the standardised regression coefficient, times the variance in Block 3 which is not accounted for by the other independent variables, Blocks 1 and 2. The added variance is simply the square of effect (c) in the list above. This discounting gives a measure which is not the direct effect of Block 3 (effect b), but the independent direct effect of Block 3 (effect c). Thus it is hardly appropriate to compare with effect (a), the total effect of Block 1. Yet by comparing R_{41}^2 with $R^2_{4(123)}$, as was done in the three studies, this is the comparison made (in squared form). That is, the comparison of 'home background effects' in the studies (R_{41}^2) with 'school effects' ($R^2_{4(123)} - R^2_{4(12)}$) is a comparison of the effects of types (a) and (c). What would be more appropriate is a comparison of effects of types (a) and (b), or possible even (b) and (d).

The regression coefficient $\beta_{43.12}$ (effect b) says to take (the square root of) the added explained variance, but to take into account that a portion of the variance of Block 3, $R_{3(12)}^2$, had no chance to be effective, because that variance coincided with the variance of Blocks 1 and 2 which already accounted for variance $R_{4(12)}^2$. Thus it multiplies (the square root of) the added explained variance by a ratio $1/(1 - R_{3(12)}^2)^{1/2}$, which inflates $(R_{4(123)}^2 - R_{4(12)}^2)^{1/2}$ back up to what its estimated value would be if variables 1 and 2 were not correlated with it.

The added explained variance, $R_{4(123)}^2 - R_{4(12)}^2$, if put in non-squared form, is a valuable statement about the *relative* effects of different school variables which have different correlations with home background variables, and for which the extrapolation due to $R_{3(12)}^2$ might be very different, and possibly a bad extrapolation to use. It is used in this way in these studies (particularly Purves, 1973) for the examination of individual variables. However, its depressed value due to $R_{3(12)}^2$, and due to the use of the squared rather than the square root form, leads to an unwarranted pessimism about the size of the effects.

It is preferable to use the square root, because that has an explicit meaning in terms of variation of the dependent variable as described earlier [effect of type (c)]. The meaning is this: $(R_{4(123)}^2 - R_{4(12)}^2)^{1/2}$, or equivalently $\beta_{43.12} (1 - R_{3(12)}^2)^{1/2}$, is the proportion of the distance between the score of the student average on achievement and the score of the student at percentile A which would be covered by changing the Block 3 composite variable for a student from its average value to the value it takes when the forces on Block 3 independent of Blocks 1 and 2 are at percentile A. (If there is a strong correlation between Block 3 and Blocks 1 and 2, these independent forces are small, and Block 3 will be near the average. If not, $R_{3(12)}^2$ will be close to zero, then the forces independent of Blocks 1 and 2 will be great, and the Block 3 composite will be close to percentile A.)

Thus, the use of added explained variance, but in its square root form, consititues a useful statement about the effect of Block 3 variables as distributed.

From the three studies under consideration, it is possible, with the published data, to obtain one measure of the effect of school resources (c above) and an approximation for the other (b above). The measure $R_{4(123)}^2 - R_{4(12)}^2$ shows the direct effect of school variations on achievement that is *distributed independently* of home background and type of school, and the approximation to $\beta_{43.12}$, which is a function of $R_{4(123)}^2$ and $R_{4(12)}^2$, shows the direct effect of school variations on achievement, including both those that are an indirect consequence of the school working through the home, and those that are independent of it. The first may be called 'independent direct effect' and the second 'direct effect'. The direct effect will always be larger than the independent direct effect, because it includes the latter.

It is useful to see what happens to a country when the measures I have proposed are used for measuring the effect of school variables, in place of the measure used by the authors. In England, for example, for Population II in Purves (1973, p. 163) the measure for home effects (R_{41}^2) is 0.252 while the measure for effects of school resources $(R_{4(123)}^2 - R_{4(12)}^2)$ is only 0.039. However, using the measures proposed here, a more appropriate comparison is between the effects (a) (β_{41}) and (b) $(3_{43.12})$ discussed earlier. Using the approximation to $\beta_{43.12}$ given earlier, the comparison would show 0.502 for the total effect of home background (effect a) and 0.223 for the direct effect of school resources (effect b). The comparison of these two numbers gives quite different conclusions than the comparison of 0.252 with 0.039. Although home background total effects are greater than the direct effects of school resources, they are only 2.2 times as great, rather than 6.5 times as great, as the comparison of 0.252 with 0.039 indicates.

Conclusion

In this paper, I have examined the various possible comparisons of effects of school and home variables that one might want to carry out, using three IEA studies as a starting point. There has been some confusion in the literature, including these IEA studies, about just what comparisons are desired, and how particular measures relate to the desired comparisons. The desired comparisons may be conceived in terms of hypothetical experiments, and through these hypothetical experiments, measures for the comparisons may be developed. The appropriate hypothetical experiments and the resulting measures are presented in the paper.

The confusion in the literature about appropriate measures is increased by the fact that measures of effects are ordinarily desired for sets of variables that taken together measure 'home background' or 'school resources', rather than for single variables. This precludes use of raw or standardised regression coefficients that are normally calculated for each variable of the set when regression analyses are carried out. Methods for calculating from the correlation matrix and variances of each variable standardised regression coefficients for the combined set of variables for which a measure is desired (e.g. 'school resources') are presented in the appendix.

Appendix

Calculation of Standardized Regression Coefficient for a Compound of Variables, Controlling on Another Set of Variables

Let the variables be labelled as follows:

1. a linear combination of Block 1 variables, created as the best-fitting combination for predicting achievement;
2. a combination of Block 2 variables, the best-fitting combination for predicting achievement;
3. achievement.

Then $\beta_{42.1}$ is the standardised regression coefficient for Block 2 variables in explaining achievement, with Block 1 variables fixed.

$R_{4(12)}$ is the multiple correlation of Blocks 1 and 2 together with achievement.

R_{41} is the multiple correlation of Block 1 variables with achievement.
R_{42} is the multiple correlation of Block 2 variables with achievement.
R_{12} is the correlation of the compound of Block 1 variables with the compound of Block 2 variables. Then

$$\beta_{42.1} = \frac{(R_{4(12)}^2 - R_{41}^2)^{1/2}}{(1 - R_{12}^2)^{1/2}}. \qquad (1)$$

$R_{4(12)}$, R_{41}, and R_{42} may be obtained directly as the multiple correlations of regressions of achievement on Blocks 1 and 2, Block 1, and Block 2, respectively. R_{12} may be obtained from these three quantities by use of the following equation:

$$R_{12} = \frac{1}{R_{4(12)}^2} [R_{42}R_{41} - (R_{42}^2 R_{41}^2 + R_{4(12)}^4 \\ - R_{4(12)}^2 (R_{41}^2 + R_{42}^2))^{1/2}] \qquad (2)$$

Having $R_{4(12)}$, R_{41}, and R_{42}, one may calculate R_{12} and then $\beta_{42.1}$ [or alternatively $\beta_{41.2}$ by use of the R_{42}^2 in place of R_{41}^2 in Equation (1)].[5]

Another method by which $\beta_{42.1}$ may be calculated is to use the regression weights from the regression equation including Blocks 1 and 2 to calculate zero-order correlations of the new compound (Block 2) with all other variables not in the compound. The equation for doing so is given below, where:

r_{ij} = zero-order correlation between variables i and j;
r_{cj} = zero-order correlation between variable j and the new compound variable, c;
σ_i = standard deviation of variable i;
$b_{4i.s}$ = multiple regression coefficient of variable i with the dependent variable in the presence of a set of variables $1, \ldots, n$, the set of variables to be labeled s.

Variables $1, 2, \ldots, n$ are not to be compounded, and variables $n+1, n+2, \ldots, m$ are to be compounded into compound variable c. Then,

$$r_{cj} = \frac{\sum_{i=n+1}^{m} b_{4i.s}\, r_{ij}\, \sigma_i\, \sigma_j}{\sigma_j \left[\sum_{i=n+1}^{m} b_{4i.s}^2\, \sigma_i^2 + 2 \sum_{k=n+1}^{m} \sum_{g=k+1}^{m} b_{4g.s}\, b_{4k.s}\, r_{gk}\, \sigma_g\, \sigma_k \right]^{\frac{1}{2}}}.$$

These two methods of calculating standardised regression coefficients for new compounds may, of course, be incorporated into a computer program so that calculations for the compound are automatically done by specifying in advance the compounds for which standardised coefficients are desired. With neither method is it necessary to calculate new sums of squares for the compound variable.

When only $R_{4(12)}$ and R_{41} have been presented, as in the studies under consideration, then some reasonable bounds for $\beta_{42.1}$ may be calculated as follows:

The minimum of R_{12}^2 is 0, so that the maximum of the denominator of Equation (1) is 1.0, and thus the minimum of $\beta_{42.1}$ is $(R_{4(12)}^2 - R_{41}^2)^{\frac{1}{2}}$. As an estimate of the maximum of $\beta_{42.1}$, we note that R_{41} is ordinarily greater than R_{12}, since the variables 1 and 2 have been selected to correlate with 4, and not with each other. Thus ordinarily, $(1 - R_{12}^2)^{\frac{1}{2}}$ will be smaller than $(1 - R_{41}^2)^{\frac{1}{2}}$. Consequently, an estimate of a maximum value for $\beta_{42.1}$ will be $(R_{4(12)}^2 - R_{41}^2)^{\frac{1}{2}}/(1 - R_{41}^2)^{\frac{1}{2}}$. Thus the following inequalities can be used to obtain an estimate for $\beta_{42.1}$:

$$\frac{(R_{4(12)}^2 - R_{41}^2)^{\frac{1}{2}}}{(1 - R_{41}^2)^{\frac{1}{2}}} > \beta_{42.1} > (R_{4(12)}^2 - R_{41}^2)^{\frac{1}{2}}.$$

One might then estimate $\beta_{42.1}$ by averaging these two estimates. For the case of England in Purves (1973) given earlier, the estimates are:

$$0.399 > \beta_{42.1} > 0.345$$

$$\beta_{42.1} \approx 0.372$$

These bounds are not extremely wide, and thus provide some useful information.

FOOTNOTES

[1] An expansion and elaboration of this paper, which also examines substantive results, has appeared in *Review of Educational Research*. Coleman, 1975. The reader is referred to that paper for an examination of some aspects of the substance of the three studies, the methodology of which I examine here.

[2] When Block 2 is included in the consideration, for differential school systems, further possibilities exist, some of which may be quite important for example, the effect of home (through whatever means, including direct effects on the child's earlier performance) in determining the type of school attended vs the home's effect apart from this; the effect of the type of school in itself on achievement (for example, through the selected student body), apart from the specific resources that exist in that type of school, vs the effect of type of school through the school resources it provides.

[3] Note that for an independent variable that was not a composite but had explicit operational meaning, such as a number of siblings, one could ask the expected performance of a child with a given number of siblings, rather than 'at the x percentile on sibling distribution', because the variable does have explicit meaning. In such a case, a (raw) regression coefficient will provide the answer. But in the present case, like most analyses of school achievement, the independent variable is a composite one, without a natural metric other than a distributional one, i.e. percentile.

[4] In preceding pages, '4' and parentheses have been left implicit in multiple correlations 'R_{12}' and 'R_{123}'. Here and in succeeding pages, they will be explicit, to prevent confusion. Thus, what was before labeled R_{12} is labeled $R_{4(12)}$; R_{123} becomes $R_{4(123)}$; and R_1 becomes R_{41}.

[5] It should be noted that this method for calculating $\beta_{42.1}$ involves an approximation; it treats 'variable 1' and 'variable 2' in $R_{4(12)}$ as the same as those in R_{41} and R_{42}. The second method involves no approximations.

Appendices

Appendix 1: Some Further Reading

In Part I, all the specified causal relationships between variables were been one-way: thus if X_i is a causal factor of X_j then we assume that X_j cannot be a causal factor of X_i. This assumption can be relaxed, but only at the expense of making other assumptions. This gives rise to what are called simultaneous equation techniques. The statistical ideas involved in this are not easy, but the reader can do no better than begin by referring to Part III of Blalock (1971), where Blalock's introduction plus a series of revealing articles should help to introduce the major ideas to the reader. Appendix 3, on matrix algebra, should be a help here, together with the fundamental ideas examined in the other sections of this book. The reader should not, however, regard recursive methods (the ones used in this book) as necessarily inferior to simultaneous equation methods. Block recursivity (discussed on p. 37 and also in the introduction to Chapter 2, Part II) can often be used when certain variables are suspected to be causally related; and if the bicausal relationship can be assumed to be heavily weighted in one direction, recursive techniques provide quite satisfactory approximations without the further assumptions necessary with simultaneous equation methods having to be invoked.

We have had nothing to say in this book about the effects of various errors in causal models. Possible errors include: that the residual variables are not conditionally normal; that the variables are measured inexactly, to some degree of error; that some of the assumptions about causal priority are incorrect (this is called specification error); and that one or more of the residuals are correlated with one or more of the explicit variables. All these errors are discussed in an excellent introductory article by Bohrnstedt and Carter (1971). Measurement error is a particularly important issue, and Part IV of Blalock (1971) contains some excellent discussions.

Related to measurement error is the issue of unmeasured or unobserved variables. These often occur when a variable is defined at a theoretical level, and attempts to measure it are made by proposing that sets of other variables are causes of or are caused by the variable. As well as Part IV of Blalock (1971), Hauser and Goldberger (1971) and Werts et al. (1974) provide some interesting, if difficult, discussions.

Much has been written on the possibilities of using non-interval variables in causal analysis, but there is little here that I can really recommend. Exceptions, however, are Blalock (1974, 1975) and Goodman (1975). A useful introduction to Goodman's work is provided by Davis (1974).

Readers interested in finding out more about significance tests in causal analysis should refer to the instructive article by Bielby and Kluegal (1977). In connection with simultaneous equation techniques, the articles by Jöreskog (1973) and Goldberger (1973 a, b) should be studied carefully, though they are rather heavy going.

All the recursive models discussed in the book have assumed that the causal parameters are fixed for the entire theoretical domain under consideration. This might be regarded as a rather unrealistic assumption in some circumstances, and we would then want to assume that variables have different effects for different units of analysis; the causal parameters themselves become random variables. Among other things, this assumption overcomes the problem of discrete cardinal endogenous variables discussed on p. 43. Readers interested in this generalisation of recursive systems can refer to Birnbaum (1977) and Birnbaum (1979), the latter article also containing discussion on the philosophy of statistical inference in causal analysis.

There is a great deal more to multivariate analysis than causal analysis, of course. By far the best book on the subject is by Kendall (1975), and also worth reading is the book of Gnanadesikan (1977). Knowledge of matrices is required for both these books — and indeed for all the references cited in this Appendix — and the reader can refer to Appendix 3 for most of the matrix results he is likely to need.

Appendix 2(I): Review of Some of the Basic Statistical Results Used in Part I

As far as we are concerned, a random variable or variate is a set of values with which are associated a set of probabilities. In the continuous case this has to be modified slightly, but this need not concern us here. In what follows, the results given are valid for continuous as well as discrete variables but the discussion is restricted to discrete variables to avoid the use of calculus. We shall generally use a capital letter, like X, for a random variable, and a small letter, like x, for one of its values. It should be noted, however, that since x can be any one of its values, the distinction between X and x is rather academic and, while in the text we have attempted to be consistent, generally X and x can be used interchangeably without confusion.

We understand by a function $h(X)$ of a random variable, a new random variable, the values of which are $h(x)$ and the associated probabilities those of X. The expectation of $h(X)$, $E(h(X))$, is defined as the sum of the products of $h(x)$ and its probability over all values of x. In the discrete case this is

$$E(h(X)) = \sum_{i=1}^{n} p_i h(x_i),$$

where X takes n values $x_1, \ldots, x_n$ with associated probabilities $p_1, \ldots, p_n$, and $\sum_{i=1}^{n}$ denotes the sum for i varying from 1 to n. Thus in full,

$$E(h(X)) = p_1 h(x_1) + p_2 h(x_2) + \cdots + p_n h(x_n)$$

Two important expectations are the mean μ and variance σ^2, where $h(X)$ is X and $(X - \mu)^2$ respectively. The variance of X is sometimes written $\text{Var}(X)$.

Some results worth noting are

$$E(c) = c$$
$$E(cX) = cE(X)$$
$$\text{Var}(X + c) = \text{Var}(X)$$
$$\text{Var}(cX) = c^2 \text{Var}(X)$$

where c is a constant.

Given two random variables, we can consider their joint distribution. If X_1 and X_2 are two random variables then we shall write the values of X_1 as x_{11}, x_{21}, etc. and of X_2 as x_{12}, x_{22} etc.; also we let p_{ij} be the probability that $X_1 = x_{i1}$ and $X_2 = x_{j2}$. We can extend this to any number of random variables, whence $p_{ijk} \ldots$ is the probability that $X_1 = x_{i1}$, $X_2 = x_{j2}, \ldots$. We define the covariance of two variables X_1 and X_2, written σ_{12} or $\text{Cov}(X_1, X_2)$ as $E(X_1 - \mu_1)(X_2 - \mu_2)$. To the extent that X_1 and X_2 vary in the same way, so is σ_{12} correspondingly positive, and to the extent that they vary in opposite ways, so is σ_{12} correspondingly negative.

If we restrict the possible joint values of X_1 and X_2 to those where $X_2 = x_2$, say, then we can ask for the probability distribution conditional on X_2 equalling x_2. It is natural to calculate the conditional probabilities on the basis that they be proportional to the unconditional probabilities, and this gives rise to the definition of the conditional probability of X_1 given $X_2 = x_2$ as

$$p(X_1 = x_{i1} \mid X_2 = x_2) = \frac{p_{i2}}{p_2}, \text{ where } p_2 = p(X_2 = x_2).$$

This is easily extended to any number of variables.

If $p_{i2}/p_2 = p_i$ for all values of x_i and of x_2 then we say that X_1 and X_2 are statistically independent. We note that if X_1 and X_2 are statistically independent then

$$E(X_1 X_2) = E(X_1)E(X_2)$$

$$\text{Cov}(X_1, X_2) = 0$$

$$\text{Var}(X_1 + X_2) = \text{Var } X_1 + \text{Var } X_2$$

These results do not hold if X_1 and X_2 are not statistically independent, but the relationship $E(X_1 + X_2) = E(X_1) + E(X_2)$ always holds.

We can now introduce the notion of conditional expectation, of great importance in the text. We have, for two variables,

$$E(h(X_1) \mid X_2 = x_2) = \sum_{i=1}^{n} \frac{p_{i2}}{p_2} h(x_i).$$

This can be extended easily to the conditional expectation given two or more variables. Thus

$$E(h(X_1) \mid X_2 = x_2, X_3 = x_3, \ldots, X_k = x_k) = \sum_{i=1}^{n} \frac{p_{i23\ldots k}}{p_{23\ldots k}} h(x_i)$$

where $p_{23\ldots k}$ is $p(X_2 = x_2, X_3 = x_3, \ldots, X_k = x_k)$.

When $h(X_1) = X_1$, we get the conditional mean of X_1, written $\mu_{1.23\ldots k}$. We can now show that the unconditional expectation of $\mu_{1.23\ldots k}$ is μ_1. For,

$$E(\mu_{1.23\ldots k}) = \sum_{X_2, X_3, \ldots, X_k} p_{23\ldots k} \mu_{1.23\ldots k}$$

$$= \sum_{X_2, X_3, \ldots, X_k} p_{23\ldots k} \left[\sum_{i=1}^{n} \frac{p_{i23\ldots k}}{p_{23\ldots k}} x_i \right]$$

$$= \sum_{i=1}^{n} \sum_{X_2, X_3, \ldots, X_k} p_{i23\ldots k} x_i = \sum_{i=1}^{n} p_i x_i = \mu_1$$

Similarly,

$$E(\mu_{1.23\ldots k} \mid X_2 = x_2, X_3 = x_3, \ldots, X_j = x_j) = \mu_{1.23\ldots j}.$$

Another important result is that

$$E(X_1 X_2) = E[X_1 E(X_2 \mid X_1)]$$

This is so since

$$E[X_1 E(X_2 \mid X_1)] = \sum_i p_i x_i \left[\sum_j \frac{p_{ij}}{p_i} x_j \right] = \sum_{ij} p_{ij} x_i x_j$$

Similarly,

$$E(X_1 X_2 \ldots X_k) = E[X_1 E(X_2 \mid X_1) E(X_3 \mid X_1 X_2) \ldots$$
$$E(X_k \mid X_1 \ldots X_{k-1})]$$

Finally, we define the conditional variance of X_1 given $X_2, \ldots, X_k$ as $E[(X_1 - \mu_{1.2\ldots k})^2 \mid X_2, \ldots, X_k]$ and the conditional covariance of X_1 and X_2 given $X_3, \ldots, X_k$ as $E[(X_1 - \mu_{1.3\ldots k})(X_2 - \mu_{2.3\ldots k}) \mid X_3, \ldots, X_k]$. We write these as $\sigma_{1.2\ldots k}^2$ and $\sigma_{12.3\ldots k}$, respectively. Thus, the conditional correlation between X_1 and X_2 given $X_3, \ldots, X_k$, $\rho(X_1, X_2 \mid X_3, \ldots, X_k)$, is $\sigma_{12.3\ldots k} / \sigma_{1.3\ldots k} \sigma_{2.3\ldots k}$.

Appendix 2(II): Proofs of Asterisked Results in Part I

1. *Proof that $\rho^2 \leq 1$ (see p. 11)*

Let

$$M = E\left[\frac{(s - \mu_s)}{\sigma_s} + \theta \frac{(t - \mu_t)}{\sigma_t} \right]^2,$$

so that M is a function of θ.

Then $M = 1 + 2\theta\rho + \theta^2$.

When $\theta = -\rho$, $M = 1 - \rho^2$.

Since M must be greater than or equal to zero,

$$1 - \rho^2 \geq 0 \text{ or } \rho^2 \leq 1.$$

Moreover, when $\rho = \pm 1$ and $\theta = \rho$, then M equals zero. Hence $\text{Var}(s' \mp t') = 0$, where dashes indicate standardised variables. It follows that $s' \mp t'$ is a constant, so that s is a linear function of t (or vice versa). In consequence, if $\rho = \pm 1$ then s is a linear function of t, and clearly the converse also holds.

2. *Proof that $f(x_1) = E(X_2 \mid x_1)$ minimises $E[(X_2 - f(x_1))^2 \mid x_1]$ and that it maximises $\rho(f(X_1), X_2)$ (see p. 12)*

(a) $E[(X_2 - f(x_1))^2 \mid x_1] = E(X_2^2 \mid x_1) - 2f(x_1) E(X_2 \mid x_1) + f^2(x_1)$

$= [f(x_1) - E(X_2 \mid x_1)]^2 + E(X_2^2 \mid x_1) - \{E(X_2 \mid x_1)\}^2$

Only the first term depends on f, and its minimum value is zero; whence $f = E(X_2 \mid x_1)$ provides the minimum value, which is $\text{Var}(X_2 \mid x_1)$.

(b) Let $M = E(X_2 \mid x_1)$.

Then $E(M) = \mu_2$.

Also, $E(X_2 M) = E[ME(X_2 \mid x_1)] = E(M^2)$.

Since $\text{Cov}(X_2, M) = E[(X_2 - \mu_2)M]$, we have that, $\text{Cov}(X_2, M) = E(M^2) - [E(M)]^2 = \sigma_M^2$.

Hence

$$\rho(X_2, M) = \frac{\sigma_M}{\sigma_2}.$$

Now $E(fM) = E\{fE(X_2 \mid x_1)\} = E(fX_2)$.

Hence $\text{Cov}(f, M) = E[f(M - \mu_2)] = E(fX_2) - \mu_f \mu_2 = \text{Cov}(f, X_2)$.

So $\quad \rho(f, M) = \dfrac{\text{Cov}(f, X_2)}{\sigma_f \sigma_M}$.

Hence $\rho(X_2, M)\rho(f, M) = \dfrac{\sigma_M}{\sigma_2} \times \dfrac{\text{Cov}(f, X_2)}{\sigma_f \sigma_M}$

$\qquad\qquad = \rho(f, X_2)$.

Since $\rho(f, M) \leqslant 1$, $\rho(f, X_2) \leqslant \rho(M, X_2)$.

Thus $\rho(f, X_2)$ is a maximum when $f = M$, the value of ρ^2 being then σ_M^2 / σ_2^2. This value of f is unique to within linear functions of M, since $\rho(f, M) = 1$ only if f is a linear function of M (see (1) above).

Finally,

$$\eta_{21}^2 = \rho^2(M, X_2) = \frac{\sigma_M^2}{\sigma_2^2}.$$

Now $\tau_2 = X_2 - M$, so $\text{Var}(\tau_2) = \text{Var}(X_2) + \text{Var}(M) - 2\,\text{Cov}(X_2, M) = \text{Var}(X_2) - \text{Var}(M)$, since $\text{Cov}(X_2, M) = \text{Var}(M)$.

Hence $\eta_{21}^2 = 1 - \dfrac{\text{Var}(\tau_2)}{\text{Var}(X_2)}$.

3. To show that $E(X_2 - \mu_2)^2 = E(X_2 - M)^2 + E[(M - E(M)]^2$ *(see p. 13)*

$E(X_2 - \mu_2)^2 = E(X_2 - M + M - \mu_2)^2$

$\qquad\qquad = E(X_2 - M)^2 + E(M - \mu_2)^2 + 2E(X_2 - M)(M - \mu_2)$

Now $E(X_2 - M)(M - \mu_2) = E(MX_2) - E(M^2) - \mu_2 E(X_2) + \mu_2 E(M) = 0$, since $E(MX_2) = E(M^2)$ and $E(M) = \mu_2$.

So $\quad E(X_2 - \mu_2)^2 = E(X_2 - M)^2 + E(M - E(M))^2$.

4. *Proof that for linear regression, $b_{21} = (\sigma_{12}/\sigma_1^2)$ and $a_2 = \mu_2 - b_{21}\mu_1$* *(see p. 15)*

We wish to minimise $E(X_2 - b_{21}X_1 - a_2)^2$. This equals

$$E(X_2 - b_{21}X_1)^2 - 2a_2 E(X_2 - b_{21}X_1) + a_2^2$$
$$= [a_2 - E(X_2 - b_{21}X_1)]^2 + E(X_2 - b_{21}X_1)^2$$
$$- [E(X_2 - b_{21}X_1)]^2$$

Only the first term depends on a_2, and its minimum value is zero whence $a_2 = E(X_2 - b_{21}X_1)$ or $a_2 = \mu_2 - b_{21}\mu_1$.
The second and third terms equal $\mathrm{Var}(X_2 - b_{21}X_1)$, which depends only on b_{21}. This equals

$$\mathrm{Var}(X_2) - 2b_{21}\mathrm{Cov}(X_1, X_2) + b_{21}^2 \mathrm{Var}(X_1)$$

$$= \sigma_1^2 \left\{ b_{21} - \frac{\sigma_{12}}{\sigma_1^2} \right\}^2 + \sigma_2^2 - \frac{\sigma_{12}^2}{\sigma_1^2}$$

Only the first term depends on b_{21} and its minimum value is zero whence $b_{21} = \sigma_{12}/\sigma_1^2$. (Note these results can also be obtained by calculus.)
Note that the minimum value of $E(X_2 - b_{21}X_1 - a_2)^2$ is $\sigma_2^2 \times (1 - \sigma_{12}^2/\sigma_1^2\sigma_2^2) = \sigma_2^2(1 - \rho^2)$, i.e. $\rho^2 = 1 - \mathrm{var}(\xi_2)/\sigma_2^2$.

5. *To show that $\rho(G, X_2) = \rho(X_1, X_2)$ if G is a linear function of X_1* *(see p. 17)*

Let $\quad G = aX_1 + b$, where a and b are constants.
Then $\quad E(X_2 G) = aE(X_1 X_2) + bE(X_2)$
$\therefore \quad \mathrm{Cov}(X_2, G) = aE(X_1 X_2) + b\mu_2 - \mu_2(a\mu_1 + b)$

$\quad\quad\quad = a\sigma_{12}$

Also $\quad \mathrm{Var}(G) \quad = \mathrm{Var}(aX_1 + b) = a^2 \mathrm{Var}(X_1)$, so

$$\rho^2(G, X_2) = \frac{a^2 \sigma_{12}^2}{a^2 \mathrm{Var}(X_1) \mathrm{Var}(X_2)} = \rho(X_1, X_2).$$

6. *Proof that* $f(x_1, x_2, x_3) = E(X_4 \mid x_1, x_2, x_3)$ *minimises*
$E[(X_4 - f)^2 \mid x_1, x_2, x_3]$ *and that it maximises* $\rho(f, X_4)$ (see p. 18)

(a) The proof here is exactly parallel to that in (2a) above, with $f(x_1, x_2, x_3)$ replacing $f(x_1)$ and $E(X_4 \mid x_1, x_2, x_3)$ replacing $E(X_2 \mid x_1)$. The minimum value is $\text{Var}(X_4 \mid x_1, x_2, x_3)$.

(b) The proof here is similar to that in (2b) above, but it is sketched here for convenience.

Let $M = E(X_4 \mid x_1, x_2, x_3)$. Then $E(M) = \mu_4$ and $E(X_4 M) = E[ME(X_4 \mid x_1, x_2, x_3)] = E(M^2)$.
So $\text{Cov}(X_4, M) = \sigma_M^2$ and so $\rho(X_4, M) = \sigma_M/\sigma_4$.

Now $E(fM) = E[fE(X_4 \mid x_1, x_2, x_3)] = E(fX_4)$.

So $\text{Cov}(f, M) = \text{Cov}(f, X_4)$, hence $\rho(f, M) = \text{Cov}(f, X_4)/\sigma_f \sigma_M$

Hence $\rho(M, X_4)\rho(f, M) = \rho(f, X_4)$.

Since $\rho(f, M) \leq 1, \rho(f, X_4) \leq f(M, X_4)$.

Hence $\rho(f, X_4)$ is maximum when $f = M$, and it equals σ_M^2/σ_4^2.

Hence $\eta_{4(123)}^2 = \sigma_M^2/\sigma_4^2$.

Finally $\tau_4 = X_4 - M$.

So $\text{Var}(\tilde\tau_4) = \sigma_4^2 + \sigma_M^2 - 2\,\text{Cov}(X_4, M)$
$= \sigma_4^2 - \sigma_M^2$, since $\text{Cov}(X_4, M) = \sigma_M^2$

Hence $\eta_{4(123)}^2 = 1 - \text{Var}(\tau_4)/\text{Var}(X_4)$.

This proof is easily extended to any number of variables.

7. *Proof that F.3 gives the values of the coefficients to minimise* $E(\xi_4^2)$ *(see p. 20)*

$$E\left(X_4 - \sum_{i=1}^{3} b_{4i}X_i - a_4\right)^2$$

$$= E\left(X_4 - \sum_{i=1}^{3} b_{4i}X_i\right)^2 - 2a_4 E\left(X_4 - \sum_{i=1}^{3} b_{4i}X_i\right) + a_4^2$$

$$= \left[a_4 - E\left(X_4 - \sum_{i=1}^{3} b_{4i}X_i\right)\right]^2 + E\left(X_4 - \sum_{i=1}^{3} b_{4i}X_i\right)^2$$

$$- \left[E\left(X_4 - \sum_{i=1}^{3} b_{4i}X_i\right)\right]^2$$

Only the first term depends on a_4, and, its minimum value is zero, whence

$$a_4 = E\left(X_4 - \sum_{i=1}^{3} b_{4i}X_i\right) = \mu_4 - \sum_{i=1}^{3} b_{4i}\mu_i$$

which is the first equation of F.3.
The second and third terms equal

$$\text{Var}\left(X_4 - \sum_{i=1}^{3} b_{4i}X_i\right),$$

and this equals

$$\text{Var}(X_4 - b_{42}X_2 - b_{43}X_3) - 2b_{4i}\,\text{Cov}(X_1, [X_4 - b_{42}X_2 - b_{43}X_3]) + b_{41}{}^2\sigma_1{}^2$$

$$= \sigma_1{}^2\left[b_{41} - \frac{(\sigma_{14} - b_{42}\sigma_{12} - b_{43}\sigma_{13})}{\sigma_1{}^2}\right]^2$$

+ terms independent of b_{41}.

Only the first term depends on b_{41}, and its minimum value is zero, whence $b_{41} = (\sigma_{14} - b_{42}\sigma_{12} - b_{43}\sigma_{13})/\sigma_1{}^2$, which is equivalent to the second equation of F.3. (Note: these results can also be obtained by calculus.)
The other equations follow by symmetry, by permutating the relevant subscripts.
This process is easily generalised to any number of variables.

8. Conditions under which the partial correlation is a correlation for one or more variables constant (see p. 23)

Let us consider first $\rho_{42.1}$ and then generalise the result.
Let

$$X_4 = b_{41.2}X_1 + b_{42.1}X_2 + \epsilon_{4.12} \quad \text{(i)}$$

$$X_4 = b_{41}X_1 + \epsilon_{4.1} \quad \text{(ii)}$$

The necessary and sufficient conditions for $\rho(X_2, X_4 \mid X_1)$ to equal $\rho_{42.1}$ are: (a) $E(\epsilon_{4.12} \mid X_1, X_2) = 0$ and (b) $E(\epsilon_{4.12}{}^2 \mid X_1, X_2) = E(\epsilon_{4.12}{}^2)$ so that equation (i) is unconstrained linear and displays homoscedasticity; (c) $E(\epsilon_{4.1} \mid X_1) = 0$ and (d) $E(\epsilon_{4.1}{}^2 \mid X_1) = E(\epsilon_{4.1}{}^2)$, so that equation (ii) is unconstrained linear and displays homoscedasticity. (iii)

We shall here demonstrate them to be sufficient.

From (i),

$$X_4 - E(X_4 \mid x_1) = b_{42.1}[X_2 - E(X_2 \mid x_1)] + \epsilon_{4.12} \tag{iv}$$

since $E(\epsilon_{4.12} \mid x_1) = E[E(\epsilon_{4.12} \mid X_1 X_2) \mid x_1] = 0$, from (a).

Now $E[\epsilon_{4.12}(X_2 - E(X_2 \mid x_1)) \mid x_1)]$

$$= E(\epsilon_{4.12} X_2 \mid x_1) - E(X_2 \mid x_1) E(\epsilon_{4.12} \mid x_1).$$

The second term we have already shown to be zero. The first is also zero because $E(\epsilon_{4.12} X_2 \mid x_1) = E[X_2 E(\epsilon_{4.12} \mid x_1 x_2) \mid x_1] = 0$, from (a). So from (iv), multiplying by $X_2 - E(X_2 x_1)$ and taking expectations with X_1 constant,

$$\mathrm{Cov}(X_2, X_4 \mid x_1) = b_{42.1} \mathrm{Var}(X_2 \mid x_1) \tag{v}$$

Hence,

$$\rho^2(X_2, X_4 \mid x_1) = \frac{b_{42.1}{}^2 \mathrm{Var}(X_2 \mid x_1)}{\mathrm{Var}(X_4 \mid x_1)} \tag{vi}$$

So far, we have made use of only (a).

Now, squaring (iv) and taking expectations with X_1 constant,

$$\mathrm{Var}(X_4 \mid x_1) = b_{42.1}{}^2 \mathrm{Var}(X_2 \mid x_1) + \mathrm{Var}(\epsilon_{4.12}) \tag{vii}$$

using the result above and also (b).

From (ii), $X_4 - E(X_4 \mid x_1) = \epsilon_{4.1}$, using (c); and so, using (d),

$$\mathrm{Var}(X_4 \mid x_1) = \mathrm{Var}(\epsilon_{4.1}) \tag{viii}$$

So from (vii) and (viii)

$$b_{42.1}{}^2 \frac{\mathrm{Var}(X_2 \mid x_1)}{\mathrm{Var}(X_4 \mid x_1)} = 1 - \frac{\mathrm{Var}(\epsilon_{4.12})}{\mathrm{Var}(\epsilon_{4.1})} \tag{ix}$$

Now $\mathrm{Var}(\epsilon_{4.12}) = \sigma_4{}^2(1 - \rho_{4(12)}{}^2)$ and $\mathrm{Var}(\epsilon_{4.1}) = \sigma_4{}^2(1 - \rho_{41}{}^2)$ so from (vi) and (ix)

$$\rho^2(X_2, X_4 \mid x_1) = 1 - \frac{1 - \rho_{4(12)}{}^2}{1 - \rho_{41}{}^2} = \frac{\rho_{4(12)}{}^2 - \rho_{41}{}^2}{1 - \rho_{41}{}^2} = \rho_{42.1}{}^2$$

as required.

This result is generalised as follows.

If $X_n = L_1^{(1)} + L_2 + \epsilon_{n.12}$

and $X_n = L_1^{(2)} + \epsilon_{n.1}$

where $L_1^{(1)}$ and $L_1^{(2)}$ are linear combinations of variables $X_1, \ldots, X_m$

and L_2 of $X_{m+1}, \ldots, X_p (m < p < n)$ then given

(A) $E(\epsilon_{n.12} | X_1, \ldots, X_p) = 0$

then
$$\rho^2(L_2, X_n | X_1, \ldots, X_m) = \frac{\text{Var}(L_2 | X_1, \ldots, X_m)}{\text{Var}(X_n | X_1, \ldots, X_m)}$$

If, in addition,

(B) $E(\epsilon_{n.12}^2 | X_1, \ldots, X_p) = E(\epsilon_{n.12}^2)$ then the partial pmcc is
$$\rho^2(L_2, X_n | X_1, \ldots, X_m) = 1 - \frac{\text{Var}(\epsilon_{n.12})}{\text{Var}(X_n | X_1, \ldots, X_m)}$$

this being the minimum possible for each set of values $X_1, \ldots, X_m$ since $\text{Var}(\epsilon_{n.12})$ is the minimum possible.

If, in addition to (A) and (B),

(C) $E(\epsilon_{n.1} | X_1, \ldots, X_m) = 0$ and $E(\epsilon_{n.1}^2 | X_1, \ldots, X_m) = E(\epsilon_{n.1}^2)$

then
$$\rho^2(L_2, X_n | X_1, \ldots, X_m) = 1 - \frac{\text{Var}(\epsilon_{n.12})}{\text{Var}(\epsilon_{n.1})}$$
$$= \frac{\rho_{n(1 \ldots p)}^2 - \rho_{n(1 \ldots m)}^2}{1 - \rho_{n(1 \ldots m)}^2}$$
$$= \rho_{n(m+1 \ldots p) . 1 \ldots m}^2$$

this being what we might call the multiple partial correlation coefficient. Thus given (A), (B) and (C), the pmcc between X_n and a linear combination of $X_{m+1}, \ldots, X_p$, with $X_1, \ldots, X_m$ constant, is maximised when the coefficients of $X_{m+1}, \ldots, X_p$ are the regression coefficients in the equation of X_n on $X_1, \ldots, X_p$, this maximum value being the multiple partial correlation coefficient. These conditions are also necessary.

9. *Derivation of the Maximum Likelihood Estimates (Using Calculus)*
   (see p. 48)

We have
$$L(\theta_k) = \frac{\sum_{j=1}^{n} \left(x_{kj} - \sum_{i=1}^{k-1} b_{ki} x_{ij} - c_k\right)^2}{2 \text{Var}(U_k)} - \frac{n}{2} \log \text{Var}(U_k)$$

$$\frac{\partial L}{\partial c_k} = \frac{\sum_{j=1}^{n} \left(x_{kj} - \sum_{i=1}^{k-1} b_{ki} x_{ij} - c_k\right)}{\text{Var}(U_k)} = 0$$

148 An Introduction to Causal Analysis in Sociology

if $c_k = \hat{c}_k$ where

$$\sum_{j=1}^{n} \hat{c}_k = \sum_{j=1}^{n} x_{kj} - \sum_{i=1}^{k-1} b_{ki} \sum_{j=1}^{n} x_{ij}$$

$$\Rightarrow nc_k = n\bar{x}_k - \sum_{i=1}^{k-1} b_{ki} n \bar{x}_i$$

$$\Rightarrow \hat{c}_k = \bar{x}_k - \sum_{i=1}^{k-1} b_{ki} \bar{x}_i.$$

This is N.14. Substituting for c_k and using dashes for variables measured from their means,

$$\frac{\partial L}{\partial \operatorname{Var}(U_k)} = \frac{\sum_{j=1}^{n} \left(x_{kj}' - \sum_{i=1}^{k-1} b_{ki} x_{ij}' \right)^2}{2 \operatorname{Var}^2(U_k)} - \frac{n}{2 \operatorname{Var}(U_k)}$$

$$= 0 \quad \text{if } \operatorname{Var}(U_k) = \hat{\operatorname{Var}}(U_k)$$

where

$$\hat{\operatorname{Var}}(U_k) = \frac{1}{n} \sum_{j=1}^{n} \left(x_{kj}' - \sum_{i=1}^{k-1} b_{ki} x_{ij}' \right)^2. \quad \text{This is N.15.}$$

Finally,

$$\frac{\partial L}{\partial b_k} = \frac{\sum_{j=1}^{n} x_{lj}' \left(x_{kj}' - \sum_{i=1}^{k-1} b_{ki} x_{ij}' \right)}{\operatorname{Var}(U_k)} = 0$$

if $b_{ki} = \hat{b}_{ki}$ for all i, where

$$\sum_{j=1}^{n} x_{lj}' x_{kj}' = \sum_{i=1}^{k-1} \hat{b}_{ki} \sum_{j=1}^{n} x_{lj}' x_{ij}'$$

$$\Rightarrow s_{lk} = \sum_{i=1}^{k-1} \hat{b}_{ki} s_{il}.$$

This is N.16, for $l = 1, k - 1$.

All equations run from $k = s + 1$ to m, where $X_1, \ldots, X_s$ are exogenous.

10. *Proof that* $\dfrac{1}{n} \sum_{j=1}^{n} \left(x_{kj}' - \sum_{i=1}^{k-1} \hat{b}_{ki} x_{ij}' \right)^2$ *simplifies to*

$$s_k^2 - \sum_{i=1}^{k-1} \hat{b}_{ki} s_{ik} \quad \text{(se p. 49)}$$

$$\frac{1}{n}\sum_{j=1}^{n}\left(x_{kj}' - \sum_{i=1}^{k-1}\hat{b}_{ki}x_{ij}'\right)^2$$

$$= \frac{1}{n}\sum_{j=1}^{n}\left[x_{kj}'^2 - 2\sum_{i=1}^{k-1}\hat{b}_{ki}x_{ij}'x_{kj}' + \left(\sum_{i=1}^{k-1}\hat{b}_{ki}x_{ij}'\right)^2\right]$$

$$= s_k^2 - 2\sum_{i=1}^{k-1}\hat{b}_{ki}s_{ik} + \sum_{l=1}^{k-1}\sum_{i=1}^{k-1}\hat{b}_{ki}\hat{b}_{kl}s_{il}$$

$$= s_k^2 - 2\sum_{i=1}^{k-1}\hat{b}_{ki}s_{ik} + \sum_{l=1}^{k-1}\hat{b}_{kl}\left[\sum_{i=1}^{k-1}\hat{b}_{ki}s_{il}\right]$$

$$= s_k^2 - 2\sum_{i=1}^{k-1}\hat{b}_{ki}s_{ik} + \sum_{l=1}^{k-1}b_{kl}s_{kl} \quad \text{(from N.16)}$$

$$= s_k^2 - \sum_{i=1}^{k-1}\hat{b}_{ki}s_{ik}$$

11. *Combining Variances over Finite Populations*

Let one population have mean μ_1, variance σ_1^2 and size n_1, and the second μ_2, σ_2^2 and n_2 respectively.

The sum of squares for the first population is $n_1(\sigma_1^2 + \mu_1^2)$ and for the second $n_2(\sigma_2^2 + \mu_2^2)$. The mean of the combined population is

$$\frac{n_1\mu_1 + n_2\mu_2}{n_1 + n_2},$$

hence the variance for the combined population is

$$\frac{n_1(\sigma_1^2 + \mu_1^2) + n_2(\sigma_2^2 + \mu_2^2)}{n_1 + n_2} - \left(\frac{n_1\mu_1 + n_2\mu_2}{n_1 + n_2}\right)^2$$

$$= \frac{n_1\sigma_1^2 + n_2\sigma_2^2}{n_1 + n_2} + \frac{n_1 n_2(\mu_1^2 + \mu_2^2 - 2\mu_1\mu_2)}{(n_1 + n_2)^2}$$

$$= \frac{n_1\sigma_1^2 + n_2\sigma_2^2}{n_1 + n_2} + \frac{n_1 n_2}{(n_1 + n_2)^2}(\mu_1 - \mu_2)^2$$

If $n_1 \doteq n_2$, then this equals approximately

$$\frac{\sigma_1^2 + \sigma_2^2}{2} + \frac{(\mu_1 - \mu_2)^2}{4}.$$

150 *An Introduction to Causal Analysis in Sociology*

Appendix 3: Matrices

1. *Basic Definitions and Operations*

(a) A matrix (plural matrices) is simply a rectangular array of numbers. A matrix with r rows and c columns is said to have *order* $r \times c$. Thus, in general,

$$\begin{bmatrix} a_{11} & a_{12} & \ldots & a_{1c} \\ a_{21} & a_{22} & \ldots & a_{2c} \\ \cdot & \cdot & & \cdot \\ \cdot & \cdot & & \cdot \\ \cdot & \cdot & & \cdot \\ a_{r1} & a_{r2} & \ldots & a_{rc} \end{bmatrix}$$

is an $r \times c$ matrix, where a_{ij} is the number, or *element*, in the ith row and jth column. Matrices are often denoted by single bold face capital letters like $\mathbf{A}_{(r \times c)}$ (the order is often omitted unless ambiguity would result) or by a typical element, viz. $(a_{ij})_{r \times c}$.

(b) A matrix with order $r \times 1$ is called a *column vector*, dimension r, and a $1 \times c$ matrix is called a *row vector*, dimension c. As distinct from matrices and vectors, ordinary numbers are called *scalars*, ordinary variables, scalar variables, and ordinary functions, scalar functions. A matrix with the same number of rows as columns is called *square*. The set of elements on the diagonal, from top left to bottom right, of a square matrix is called the *leading diagonal*; the other elements being termed off-diagonal; thus for an $m \times m$ matrix, $a_{11}, a_{22}, a_{33}, \ldots, a_{mm}$ is the leading diagonal. A square matrix whose leading diagonal is $1, 1, 1, \ldots, 1$ and the rest of whose elements are zero is called *the identity matrix*, and is denoted by $\mathbf{I}_{(m \times m)}$. This is a special case of a diagonal *matrix* where all off-diagonal elements are zero, the leading diagonal consisting of any elements whatsoever.

Any matrix which consists entirely of zeros is called a *null matrix*, denoted by $\mathbf{0}_{(r \times c)}$. Any square matrix whose elements below its leading diagonal are zero is called *upper triangular* (*lower triangular* if those above are zero).

(c) Given any matrix $\mathbf{A}$, its *transpose*, denoted $\mathbf{A}'$ or $\mathbf{A}^T$, consists of the matrix formed from $\mathbf{A}$ by interchanging its rows and columns. Thus if $\mathbf{B} = \mathbf{A}'$, then $a_{ij} = b_{ji}$ for all elements. For example, if

$$A = \begin{bmatrix} -7 & 4 & -3 \\ 6 & 5 & 4 \end{bmatrix} \text{ then } A' = \begin{bmatrix} -7 & 6 \\ 4 & 5 \\ -3 & 4 \end{bmatrix}$$

For all matrices $\mathbf{A}$, it is clear that $\mathbf{A}$ and $(\mathbf{A}')'$ are the same matrix.

(d) Two matrices are equal if they have the same order and the same corresponding elements. Thus $\mathbf{A} = \mathbf{B}$ if and only if $a_{ij} = b_{ij}$ for all elements of both matrices.

A matrix which is equal to its transpose is called *symmetric*. Thus

$$\begin{bmatrix} 2 & 7 \\ 7 & 8 \end{bmatrix} \text{ is symmetric.}$$

Clearly, a symmetric matrix must be a square matrix A where $a_{ij} = a_{ji}$. Note that all diagonal matrices are symmetric.

If $\mathbf{A}$ is a matrix and $\mathbf{B}$ is its transpose, and if $b_{ij} = -a_{ij}$ for all off-diagonal elements, $\mathbf{A}$ is called *antisymmetric*. Thus if $\mathbf{A}$ is antisymmetric, $a_{ij} = -a_{ji}$ except for the leading diagonal.

(e) Given a matrix $\mathbf{A}$, $c\mathbf{A}$ where c is a scalar, means the matrix with elements $(ca_{ij})_{r \times c}$. Hence every element of $\mathbf{A}$ is multiplied by c — this is called *scalar multiplication*.

(f) To add (or subtract) two matrices, we add (or subtract) corresponding elements. Thus if $\mathbf{C} = \mathbf{A} + \mathbf{B}$, then $c_{ij} = a_{ij} + b_{ij}$ for all elements. Only matrices with the same order may be added or subtracted.

(g) Matrices may only be multiplied if the number of columns in the first equals the number of rows in the second. Then, if $\mathbf{A} = (a_{ij})_{m \times n}$ and $\mathbf{B} = (b_{ij})_{n \times p}$ then $\mathbf{C} = (c_{ij})_{m \times p}$ equals $\mathbf{A}$ times $\mathbf{B}$, written $\mathbf{C} = \mathbf{AB}$, if $c_{ik} = \sum_j a_{ij} b_{jk}$ for all $i = 1, \ldots, m$, $k = 1, \ldots, p$, where $\sum_j$ represents the sum over $j = 1, \ldots, n$.

For example, if

$$\mathbf{A} = \begin{bmatrix} 2 & 4 & 1 \\ 1 & 1 & 3 \end{bmatrix} \text{ and } \mathbf{B} = \begin{bmatrix} 1 & 3 \\ 2 & 2 \\ 4 & 0 \end{bmatrix},$$

then

$$\mathbf{AB} = \begin{bmatrix} (2 \times 1) + (4 \times 2) + (1 \times 4) & (2 \times 3) + (4 \times 2) + (1 \times 0) \\ (1 \times 1) + (1 \times 2) + (3 \times 4) & (1 \times 3) + (1 \times 2) + (3 \times 0) \end{bmatrix}$$

$$= \begin{bmatrix} 14 & 14 \\ 15 & 5 \end{bmatrix}.$$

Matrix multiplication is best remembered as rows times columns, the shape of the resulting matrix being given by the domino pattern —

$m \times \boxed{n \ n} \times p$.

In general, **AB** and **BA** will give different results

(BA above is $\begin{bmatrix} 5 & 7 & 10 \\ 6 & 10 & 8 \\ 8 & 16 & 4 \end{bmatrix}$)

and, indeed, unless $m = p$, only the first will be defined. Thus matrix multiplication is said to be non-commutative. It is however, associative, in that $A(BC) = (AB)C$, the multiplication in brackets being done first.

For any $m \times n$ matrix **A**, $I_{(m \times m)}A = A$ and $AI_{(n \times n)} = A$. Clearly $0_{(m \times m)}A = A0_{(n \times n)} = 0_{(m \times n)}$. Also, if $1_{(p \times m)}$ represents the $p \times m$ matrix consisting entirely of ones, $1_{(p \times m)}A$ gives a matrix each of whose p rows is identical, the rth member of each row being the sum of the elements in the rth column of **A**. Similarly, $A1_{(n \times p)}$ gives p identical columns, the rth element of each being the sum of the rth row of **A**.

If **D** is a diagonal matrix, $\text{diag}(d_1, d_2, \ldots, d_m)$, i.e.

$$\begin{bmatrix} d_1 & 0 & . & . & . & 0 \\ 0 & d_2 & . & . & . & 0 \\ . & . & . & . & . & . \\ . & . & . & . & . & . \\ . & . & . & . & . & . \\ 0 & 0 & . & . & . & d_m \end{bmatrix}$$

then **DA** gives a matrix where the first row of **A** is multiplied by d_1, the second row by d_2, etc. Similarly, $AD_{(n \times n)}$ multiplies the first column of **A** by d_1, the second by d_2, etc. If **D**, **E** and **F** are the diagonal matrices $\text{diag}(d_1, \ldots, d_m)$, $\text{diag}(e_1, \ldots, e_m)$, $\text{diag}(f_1, \ldots, f_m)$ respectively, then **DEF** is $\text{diag}(d_1 e_1 f_1, \ldots, d_m e_m f_m)$.

Note finally that $(AB)' = B'A'$.

(h) Given an $(m \times m)$ matrix **A**, if there exists a matrix **B** such that $AB = BA = I$, then **A** is said to be *non-singular* and **B** is called the *inverse* of **A**, usually written A^{-1}. Some matrices have no inverse and they are called *singular*. Calculations for the inverses of matrices of order (4×4) or higher are very tedious and are best left to the computer.

Note that $(AB)^{-1} = B^{-1}A^{-1}$. Also, if **D** is

$$\text{diag}[d_1, d_2, \ldots, d_m], \quad D^{-1} = \text{diag}\left[\frac{1}{d_1}, \frac{1}{d_2}, \ldots, \frac{1}{d_m}\right].$$

Finally, $(A^{-1})' = (A')^{-1}$, and if $A^{-1} = A'$, **A** is called *orthogonal*.

(i) If **A** is an $(m \times n)$ matrix and the first r rows and c columns of **A** are designated by the matrix A_{11}, the remaining $s = (m - r)$ rows and c

columns A_{21}, the r rows and the remaining $d = (n - c)$ columns A_{12} and the s rows and d columns remaining A_{22}, then A can be *partioned* into sub-matrices as follows:

$$A = \begin{bmatrix} A_{11} & A_{12} \\ A_{21} & A_{22} \end{bmatrix} \begin{matrix} r \\ s \end{matrix}$$
$$c \phantom{_{11}} d$$

If $B_{(m \times n)}$ is similarly partitioned, then A and B are said to be *conformably* partitioned for addition and we have

$$A + B = \begin{bmatrix} A_{11} + B_{11} & A_{12} + B_{12} \\ A_{21} + B_{21} & A_{22} + B_{22} \end{bmatrix}$$

If, instead, $B_{(n \times p)}$ is partitioned into c and d rows and t and u columns, then we say that A and B are conformably partitioned for premultiplication of B by A and we have

$$AB = \begin{matrix} r \\ s \end{matrix} \begin{bmatrix} A_{11} & A_{12} \\ A_{21} & A_{22} \end{bmatrix} \begin{bmatrix} B_{11} & B_{12} \\ B_{21} & B_{22} \end{bmatrix} \begin{matrix} c \\ d \end{matrix}$$
$$c d t u$$

$$= \begin{bmatrix} A_{11}B_{11} + A_{12}B_{21} & A_{11}B_{12} + A_{12}B_{22} \\ A_{21}B_{11} + A_{22}B_{21} & A_{21}B_{12} + A_{22}B_{22} \end{bmatrix} \begin{matrix} r \\ s \end{matrix}$$
$$t u$$

(j) The *rank* of a matrix is the order of the largest square sub-matrix which has an inverse. A square matrix is said to have full rank if it has an inverse. A rectangular matrix has full rank if its rank is equal to the smaller of its number of rows and columns.

(k) A point in two-dimensional space can be represented by a pair of numbers (x, y) – called the coordinates. Similarly, in three-dimensional space, (x, y, z). Although we cannot visualise higher dimensional spaces, we can clearly generalise our coordinates, and this gives rise to the algebraic representation of n-dimensional space.

Now, we can consider the coordinates as a vector, usually a column vector. Premultiplying this by a square matrix, order equal to the dimension of the space, will give a new set of coordinates. For instance, in two dimensions, the matrix might be

$$\begin{bmatrix} 0.867 & -0.5 \\ 0.5 & 0.867 \end{bmatrix}.$$

154   An Introduction to Causal Analysis in Sociology

Acting on the points (2, 1), written as vector $\binom{2}{1}$ this would give $\binom{1.234}{1.867}$. In fact, if the matrix were to act on a set of points which make up the boundary of some shape, then its effect would be to rotate the shape anticlockwise through 30°. The matrix is said to effect a *transformation* on the points.

The same idea can be extended to any number of dimensions, and any square matrix can be seen as producing a transformation of points. If the matrix is of full rank, and only if, then the dimension of the resulting points will be that of the original points. If the rank is k less than the order, the dimension will drop by k. For instance, if we begin in five dimensions and operate with a matrix rank two, all five-dimensional hypercubes will collapse into parallelograms.

In two dimensions, the ratio between the areas of the transformed shape and the original, which is constant for a given transformation, is called the *determinant* of the matrix of the transformation. In three dimensions, the determinant is the ratio of volumes. In four or more dimensions, we talk of ratios of n-dimensional hyper-volumes. If the rank of a matrix is not full, then the determinant will be zero, and vice-versa; the matrix will have no inverse, and neither will the transformation it represents. It is not possible to find a matrix to transform a parallelogram into a hypercube, for instance.

Most calculations of determinants are tedious and are best left to computers. The symbol used for the determinant of the square matrix $\mathbf{A}$ is $|\mathbf{A}|$, or sometimes det $\mathbf{A}$.

(l) A very important result is: for a square matrix $\mathbf{A}$, there exist matrices $\mathbf{U}$ and $\mathbf{D}$, such that $\mathbf{A} = \mathbf{U}\mathbf{D}\mathbf{U}^{-1}$, where $\mathbf{U}$ is non-singular (i.e. $|\mathbf{U}| \neq 0$) and $\mathbf{D}$ is diagonal. If, in addition, $\mathbf{A}$ is symmetric then $\mathbf{A} = \mathbf{T}\mathbf{D}\mathbf{T}'$, where $\mathbf{T}$ is orthogonal. This means if $\mathbf{A}$ is a symmetric matrix, then as a transformation it can be decomposed into a rotation, followed by a stretch, followed by another rotation.

(m) A function like $f(x_1, x_2) = ax_1^2 + bx_1x_2 + cx_2^2$ is called a degree two quadratic form. We can write

$$bx_1x_2 \text{ as } \frac{b}{2}x_1x_2 + \frac{b}{2}x_1x_2,$$

and then $f(x_1, x_2) = \mathbf{x}'\mathbf{A}\mathbf{x}$, where

$$\mathbf{A} = \begin{bmatrix} a & \frac{b}{2} \\ \frac{b}{2} & c \end{bmatrix} \text{ and } \mathbf{x} = \begin{pmatrix} x_1 \\ x_2 \end{pmatrix}$$

This can easily be generalised as follows. If A is order $(n \times n)$ and symmetric and x' is $(x_1, x_2, \ldots, x_n)$, then $x'Ax$ is an degree n quadratic form.

Quadratic forms are easily related to transformations. Let $y = Cx$, where x may be of greater dimension than y. Then the squared length of y is $y_1^2 + y_2^2 + \cdots + y_n^2$, which is $y'y$. But $y'y = (Cx)'Cx = x'C'Cx = x'Ax$, where $A = C'C$. It follows that $x'Ax$ gives the length of the vector Cx, where $A = C'C$. If, in addition, C is of full rank (it need not be square) then A is called *positive definite*, and $x'Ax$ is always positive for any x, an obvious requirement for lengths.

Now since A is symmetric, we have $A = TDT'$ (see (l)), so $x'Ax = x'TDT'x = (T'x)'D(T'x)$. So if $u = T'x$, we have $u'Du$. T' represents a rotation of the coordinate axes against which a point is designated by x to a new set of axes, leaving the point fixed. This is called the diagonal representation of the quadratic form, there being no cross-product terms, viz. $a_1 u_1^2 + a_2 u_2^2 + \cdots + a_n u_n^2$.

The rank of D is given by the number of non-zero elements, and this is also the rank of A. The number of non-zero coefficients in the diagonal representation is unique; if A is positive definite, they will all be positive. Matrices T and D are easily found using the computer, by finding eigenvectors (see (n) below).

(n) An *eigenvector* of a square matrix A is a (column) vector t such that $At = \lambda t$, where λ, a scalar, is called the associated *eigenvalue*. Eigenvalues are found by solving the equation $(A - \lambda I)t = 0$. This equation has solutions given by the determinant equation $|A - \lambda I| = 0$ (for if $(A - \lambda I)$ is non-singular, then $t = 0$) and this equation is called the *characteristic equation* of A. Eigenvectors can then be found from the eigenvalues.

Now, if T is the matrix whose columns are the eigenvectors, and if A is symmetric, then T is orthogonal (i.e. the eigenvectors are at right angles) and $A = TDT'$. Thus T is the matrix required in Section (m), and D is diag$(\lambda_1, \lambda_2, \ldots, \lambda_n)$, λ_i being the eigenvalue corresponding to the ith column of T. These results are easily proved, and you may wish to construct the proofs yourself (for the orthogonality of T, show that $t_2't_1 = 0$, where t_1 and t_2 are two different eigenvectors).

(p) *Some results on vector and matrix differentiation*

(A knowledge of calculus is required for this section.)

The following notation is used.

If A is matrix whose elements a_{ij} are functions of a scalar variable x, then $\partial A/\partial x$ is the matrix whose elements are $\partial a_{ij}/\partial x$.

If y is a scalar function of the vector x (i.e. y is a function of the elements of x) then $\partial y/\partial x$ is the vector whose components are $\partial y/\partial x_i$, where $x' = (x_i)$. By extension, if y is a scalar function of the matrix X, then $\partial y/\partial X$ is the matrix with elements $(\partial y/\partial x_{ij})$, where $X = (x_{ij})$.

156   An Introduction to Causal Analysis in Sociology

If z is an $m \times 1$ vector, each element of which is a scalar function of the $1 \times n$ vector x, where $x' = (x_1, x_2, \ldots, x_n)$ then $\partial z/\partial x$ is the matrix with elements $(\partial z_i/\partial x_j)$, $i = 1, 2, \ldots, m$ and $j = 1, 2, \ldots, n$.

Derivatives of matrices with respect to vectors or matrices are not defined.

The following results are useful. (x is $m \times 1$, y is $n \times 1$, unless stated otherwise. A is $m \times n$ and c is a constant $m \times 1$ vector):

(i) $\dfrac{\partial(c'x)}{\partial x} = c$

(ii) $\dfrac{\partial(x'Ay)}{\partial x} = Ay$ and $\dfrac{\partial(x'Ay)}{\partial y} = A'x$

(iii) $\dfrac{\partial(x'Ax)}{\partial x} = \begin{cases} (A + A')x, & \text{A square and non-symmetric} \\ 2Ax, & \text{A square and symmetric} \end{cases}$

(iv) $\dfrac{\partial(x'Ay)}{\partial A} = x'y$,   A square and y order $m \times 1$.

(v) $\dfrac{\partial}{\partial x}(x'x) = 2x$

(vi) $\dfrac{\partial}{\partial x}(x'A) = A$ and $\dfrac{\partial}{\partial y}(Ay) = A'$

2. *Some Basic Uses of Matrices in Statistics*

(a) *Fundamental results*

The matrix X, with a typical element x_{ij} representing the value taken by individual i on variable x_j is called the *fundamental data matrix*. Clearly, each column of the matrix represents the values taken by the entire sample on one variable, and each row the values taken by one unit on the entire set of variables.

The product $X'X$ will give on its diagonal the sum of squares of each variable, and off-diagonal the relevant sum of cross products. Thus, the (ij)th element of $X'X$ is $\Sigma x_i x_j$, the sum being taken over the entire sample, and the (ii)th element is Σx_i^2 (x_i and x_j are the values of variables X_i and X_j).

The mean values of the variables can be computed by finding $(1/n)X'\mathbf{1}$, where **1** is an $n \times 1$ vector consisting entirely of 1's, there being n individuals in the sample. Then the matrix S, consisting of the variances and covariances of the variates is given by

$$S = \left(\frac{1}{n}\right)X'X - \left(\frac{1}{n^2}\right)(X'1)(1'X)$$

or

$$S = \left(\frac{1}{n}\right)X'X - \left(\frac{1}{n^2}\right)X'1_{(n \times n)}X$$

where $1_{(n \times n)}$ consists of n rows of n ones. S is often called the variance–covariance matrix, and it is extremely important in any multivariate study.

Finally, the correlation matrix, R, is obtained from S by calculating $R = DSD$, where $D = \text{diag}(1/s_1, 1/s_2, \ldots, 1/s_k)$, s_i^2 being the variance of x_i and so the (ii)th element of S.

All these can be calculated very simply using a computer but note that problems of rounding error cause the programs to be somewhat complex.

(b) *Least squares in regression*

(Calculus is required in this section.)

Let z be an $n \times 1$ vector representing the values on the predicted variable taken by the n individuals constituting the sample. Let Y be the $n \times k$ data matrix, and **a** the $k \times 1$ vector of coefficients, there being k predictor variables. Then if c is a scalar, 1 is an $n \times 1$ vector of 1's and e is the $n \times 1$ vector of values taken on e by the sample members then we have

$$z = Y\mathbf{a} + c1 + e$$

as a concise way of writing the n regression equations for the n units sampled, e being such that $e'e$ is minimum.

We therefore need to minimise

$$(z - Y\mathbf{a} - c1)'(z - Y\mathbf{a} - c1)$$

with respect to **a** and c.

The terms in c are $c1'(-z + Y\mathbf{a} + c1) - c(z' - \mathbf{a}'Y')1$ giving, on differentiating by c and equating to zero,

$$2c1'1 = -1'z - z'1 + 1'Y\mathbf{a} + \mathbf{a}'Y'1$$

But $1'1 = n$, $1'z = z'1 = n\bar{z}$ and $1'Y\mathbf{a} = \mathbf{a}'Y'1 = n\Sigma a_j\bar{x}_j$. Hence $c = \Sigma a_j\bar{x}_j - \bar{z}$.

Thus we may write

$$y = X\mathbf{a} + e$$

where y and X are z and Y measured from their means.

We must now minimise $(y - X\mathbf{a})'(y - X\mathbf{a})$, and the terms in **a** are $-\mathbf{a}'X'y - y'X\mathbf{a} + \mathbf{a}'(X'X)\mathbf{a}$. Differentiating by **a** and equating to zero we obtain

$$2(X'X)a = X'y + X'y = 2X'y$$

$$\therefore \quad a = (X'X)^{-1}X'y$$

Now the variance of Xa is $(1/n)a'X'Xa = (1/n)y'X(X'X)^{-1}X'y$ which is a quadratic form in y with the symmetric matrix $X(X'X)^{-1}X'$. The covariance of y and Xa is

$$\left(\frac{1}{n}\right)y'Xa = \left(\frac{1}{n}\right)y'X(X'X)^{-1}X'y.$$

Hence, the correlation between y and Xa — the multiple correlation coefficient — is

$$R^2 = \frac{y'X(X'X)^{-1}X'y}{y'y}$$

Finally, matrices make it easy for us to see the connection between the observed residuals e and the theoretical ones ϵ.

We have $y = Xb + \epsilon$, say, where b is the vector of 'true' values. Now,

$$a = (X'X)^{-1}X'y = (X'X)^{-1}X'(Xb + \epsilon) = b + (X'X)^{-1}X'\epsilon$$

which shows immediately that if $E(\epsilon \mid X) = 0$ then a is unbiased, and also that if ϵ is conditionally normal, then so is a. We have $\epsilon - e = X(a - b) = X(X'X)^{-1}X'\epsilon$, so that

$$e = [I - X(X'X)^{-1}X']\epsilon$$

Hence conditional on X, e is distributed like ϵ.

(c) *Causal Analysis*

The rth equation of a recursive system with k variables can be written

$$-a_{r1}x_1 - a_{r2}x_2 - \cdots - a_{r\,r-1}x_{r-1} + 1x_r + 0x_{r+1} + \cdots + 0x_k = 0$$

This equation holds for the n units of analysis sampled, and these n equations can be written in matrix form as

$$X(-a_{r1}, -a_{r2}, \ldots, -a_{r\,r-1}, 1, 0, \ldots, 0)' = U_r$$

where X is the k-variable data matrix (so that a row of X gives the set of values taken on the k variables by one unit of analysis), and U_r is the $n \times 1$ vector of values taken on U_r.

Now, we have k such equations (the first being $x_1 = U_1$, where U_1 is a 'dummy' implicit term). If we define the matrix **A** as

$$\begin{bmatrix} 1 & 0 & 0 & \ldots & 0 \\ -a_{21} & 1 & 0 & \ldots & 0 \\ -a_{31} & -a_{32} & 1 & \ldots & 0 \\ \cdot & \cdot & \cdot & \cdot & \cdot \\ \cdot & \cdot & \cdot & & \cdot \\ \cdot & \cdot & \cdot & & \cdot \\ -a_{k1} & -a_{k2} & -a_{k3} & \ldots & 1 \end{bmatrix}$$

so that the rth row of **A** is the row vector in the equation for x_r above, then we can write the entire system for the n units sampled as

$$\mathbf{XA'} = \mathbf{U}$$

where **U** is an $n \times k$ matrix, the rth column of which is $\mathbf{U}_r$.

(This formulation can easily be used to express the theoretical system rather than the sample; we replace matrices **X** and **U** by vectors **x** and **u**, **x** being $(X_1, \ldots, X_k)'$ and **u** being $(u_1, \ldots, u_k)'$.)

If there is more than one exogenous variable, then on some lines all the a-coefficients will be zero. If assumptions are made as to zero causation then some of the a-coefficients on some other lines will be zero.

It is possible to generalise this to give what is called a simultaneous equation system (see Appendix 1) in the following way.

We split our k variables up into those k_1 which are exogenous and those k_2 which are not, giving associated data matrices **Z** and **X** respectively, and then we write

$$\mathbf{XA_1'} + \mathbf{ZA_2'} = \mathbf{U}$$

U being $n \times k_2$, $\mathbf{A_1}$ being $k_2 \times k_2$, and $\mathbf{A_2}$ being $k_2 \times k_1$. Saying the variables in **Z** are exogenous means that they are causally independent of all elements of **U**.

Moreover, if we write $\mathbf{w}_i$ for the $k \times 1$ vector consisting of the scores taken on $U_1, U_2, \ldots, U_k$ for the ith unit of analysis, then we assume $E(\mathbf{w}_i \mathbf{w}_i') = \Sigma$ for all i. Σ is the theoretical variance–covariance matrix for the set of implicit variables U_k, U_{k-1}, etc. We can now say that the recursive system is a special case of this where (i) $\mathbf{A}_1$ is triangular and (ii) Σ is diagonal. (In this formulation we need no dummy **U**'s for exogenous variables since the latter are incorporated in **Z**.)

References

Allen, R. and B. Spilka (1967) 'Committed and Consensual Religion: A Specification of Religion-Prejudice Relationships', *Journal for the Scientific Study of Religion*, Vol. 6. (Fall), 191–206.

Allinsmith, W. and B. Allinsmith (1948) 'Religious Affiliation and Politico–Economic Attitudes', *Public Opinion Quarterly*, Vol. 12 (Fall), 378–89.

Andrews, F., J. Morgan and J. Sonquist (1969) *Multiple Classification Analysis* (Ann Arbor: Survey Research Center, University of Michigan).

Axelrod, M., F. Fowler and A. Gurin (1967) *A Community Survey for Long Range Planning: A Study of the Jewish Population of Greater Boston* (Boston: Combined Jewish Philanthropies of Greater Boston).

Bartlett, M. S. (1947) 'The Use of Transformations', *Biometrics*, Vol. 3, 39–52.

Berelson, B., P. Lazarfeld and W. McPhee (1954) *Voting* (Chicago: University of Chicago Press).

Bielby, W. T. and J. R. Kluegal (1977) 'Statistical Inference and Statistical Power in Applications of the General Linear Model', in D. R. Heise (ed.), *Sociological Methodology, 1977* (San Francisco: Jossey–Bass).

Birnbaum, I. (1977) 'Greater Indeterminism in Causal Analysis', *Quality and Quantity*, Vol. 11, 119–34.

Birnbaum, I. (1979). 'Statistical Inference in Causal Analysis: Some Foundations', *Quality and Quantity* 13: 203–13.

Blalock, H. M., Jr (1964) *Causal Inferences in Nonexperimental Research* (Chapel Hill: The University of North Carolina Press).

Blalock, H. (1969) *Theory Construction* (Englewood Cliffs: Prentice-Hall).

Blalock, H. M. (1971) *Causal Models in the Social Sciences* (Chicago: Aldine).

Blalock, H. M. (1974) 'Beyond Ordinal Measurement: Weak Tests of Stronger Theories', in H. M. Blalock (ed.), *Measurement in the Social Sciences* (Chicago: Aldine).

Blalock, H. M. (1975) 'Can We Find a Genuine Ordinal Slope Analogue?', in D. R. Heise (ed.), *Sociological Methodology, 1976* (San Francisco: Jossey–Bass).

Blalock, H. and A. Blalock (eds) (1968) *Methodology in Social Research* (New York: McGraw-Hill).

Bohrnstedt, G. W. and T. M. Carter (1971) 'Robustness in Regression Analysis', in H. L. Costner (ed.) *Sociological Methodology, 1971* (San Francisco: Jossey–Bass).

Borgatta, E. (1969) *Sociological Methodology* (San Francisco: Jossey–Bass).

Bowles, S. and H. M. Levin (1968) 'The Determinants of Scholastic Achievement: An Appraisal of Some Recent Evidence', *Journal of Human Resources*, Vol. 3 (Winter), 3–24.

Cain, G. G. and Watts, H. W. (1970) 'Problems in Making Policy Inference from the Coleman Report', *American Sociological Review*, Vol. 35, 228–42.

Coleman, J. S. et al. (1966) *Equality of Educational Opportunity* (Washington, D.C.: Government Printing Office).

Coleman, J. S. (1968) 'Equality of Educational Opportunity: Reply to Bowles and Levin', *Journal of Human Resources*, Vol. 3, 237–46.

Coleman, J. S. (1970) 'Reply to Cain and Watts', *American Sociological Review*, Vol. 35, 242–9.

Coleman, J. S. (1972) 'The Evaluation of Equality of Educational Opportunity', in F. Mosteller and D. P. Moynihan (eds), *On Equality of Educational Opportunity* (New York: Random House).

Coleman, J. S. (1975) 'Methods and Results in the IEA Studies of Efforts of School in Learning', *Review of Educational Research*, Vol. 45, 335–86.

Comber, L. C. and J. P. Keeves (1973) *Science Education in Nineteen Countries. International Studies in Evaluation*, Vol. 1 (Stockholm: Almqvist & Wiksell).

Cooper, R. B. (1972) *Introduction to Queueing Theory* (New York: Macmillan).

Davis, J. A. (1974) 'Hierarchical Models for Significance Tests in Multivariate Contingency Tables: An Exegesis of Goodman's Recent Papers', in H. L. Costner (ed.) *Sociological Methodology, 1973–1974* (San Francisco: Jossey–Bass).

Demerath, N. J., III (1965) *Social Class in American Protestantism* (Chicago: Rand McNally).

Dohrenwend, B. P. and B. S. Dohrenwend (1969) *Social Status and Psychological Disorder: A Causal Inquiry* (New York: Wiley).

Duncan, O. D. (1966) 'Path Analysis: Sociological Examples', *American Journal of Sociology*, Vol. 72, 1–16.

Fichter, J. (1954) *Social Relations in the Urban Parish* (Chicago: University of Chicago Press).

Fuchs, L. (1956) *The Political Behaviour of American Jews* (Glencoe: Free Press).

Fukuyama, Y. (1961) 'The Major Dimensions of Church Membership', *Review of Religious Research*, Vol. 2 (Spring), 154–61.

Glock, C. and R. Stark (1965) *Religion and Society in Tension* (Chicago: Rand McNally).

Glock, C. and R. Stark (1966) *Christian Beliefs and Anti-Semitism* (New York: Harper & Row).

Glock, C., B. Ringer and E. Babbie (1967) *To Comfort and to Challenge* (Berkeley, Los Angeles: University of California Press).

Gnanadesikan, R. (1977) *Methods for Statistical Data Analysis of Multivariate Observations* (New York: Wiley).

Goldberger, A. S. (1973a) 'Structural Equation Models: An Overview', in A. S. Goldberger and O. D. Duncan (eds), *Structural Equation Models in the Social Sciences* (New York: Seminar Press).

Goldberger, A. S. (1973b) 'Efficient Estimation in Over-identified Models: An Interpretive Analysis', in A. S. Goldberger and O. D. Duncan (eds), *Structural Equation Models in the Social Sciences* (New York: Seminar Press).

Goldstein, S. and C. Goldscheider (1968) *Jewish Americans* (Englewood Cliffs: Prentice-Hall).

Goodman, L. A. (1953) 'Ecological Regression and the Behaviour of Individuals', *American Sociological Review*, Vol. 18, 663–6.

Goodman, L. A. (1975) 'The Relationships Between Modified and Usual Multiple-Regression Approaches to the Analysis of Dichotomous Variables', in D. R. Heise (ed.), *Sociological Methodology 1976* (San Francisco: Jossey–Bass).

Greeley, A. and P. Rossi (1966) *The Education of Catholic Americans* (Chicago: Aldine).

Hammond, J. L. (1973) 'Two Sources of Error in Ecological Correlations', *American Sociological Review*, Vol. 38 (December), 764–77.

Hannan, M. T. (1970) *Problems of Aggregation and Disaggregation in Sociological Research* (Chapel Hill: Institute for Research is Social Science, University of North Carolina).

Hanushek, E. A. and J. F. Kain (1972) 'On the Value of Equality of Educational Opportunity as a Guide to Public Policy', in F. Mosteller and D. P. Moynihan (eds), *On Equality of Educational Opportunity* (New York: Random House).

Hauser, R. M. and A. S. Goldberger (1971) 'The Treatment of Unobservable Variables in Path Analysis', in H. L. Costner (ed.), *Sociological Methodology, 1971* (San Francisco: Jossey–Bass).

Heise, D. (1969) 'Problems in Path Analysis and Causal Inference', in E. Borgatta (ed.), *Sociological Methodology: 1969* (San Francisco: Jossey–Bass).

Herman, S. (1971) *Israelis and Jews: The Continuity of an Identity* (Philadelphia: The Jewish Publication Society of America).

Husen, T. (ed.) (1967) *International Study of Achievement in Mathematics: A Comparison of Twelve Countries, Vols. 1 and 2* (Stockholm: Almqvist & Wiksell).

Jackson, D. D. (1960) 'Introduction', in D. D. Jackson (ed.), *The Etiology of Schizophrenia* (New York: Basic Books).

Jewell, W. S. (1967) 'A Simple Proof of $L = \lambda W$', *Operations Research*, Vol. 15, 1109–16.

Johnson, B. (1962) 'Ascetic Protestantism and Political Preference', *Public Opinion Quarterly*, Vol. 26 (Spring), 35–46.

Johnson, B. (1964) 'Ascetic Protestantism and Political Preference in the Deep South', *American Journal of Sociology*, Vol. 69 (January), 359–66.

Jöreskog, K. G. (1973) 'A General Method for Estimating a Linear Structural Equation System', in A. S. Goldberger and O. D. Duncan (eds), *Structural Equation Models in the Social Sciences* (New York: Seminar Press).

Kendall, M. (1975) *Multivariate Analysis* (London: Griffin).

King, M. (1967) 'Measuring the Religious Variable: Nine Proposed Dimensions', *Journal for the Scientific Study of Religion*, Vol. 6 (Fall), 173–90.

Kramer, J. (1957) 'A Discussion of the Concepts of Incidence and Prevalence as Related to Epidemiological Studies of Mental Disorders', *Americal Journal of Public Health*, Vol. 47, 826–40.

Lazerwitz, B. (1953) 'Some Factors in Jewish Identification' *Jewish Social Studies*, Vol. 15 (January), 3–24.

Lazerwitz, B. (1969) *An Investigation into the Associations Between Fertility and Religio–Ethnic Identification Among Protestants and Jews* (Columbia: Department of Sociology, University of Missouri).

Lazerwitz, B. (1970) 'Contrasting the Effects of Generation, Class, Sex and Age on Group Identification in the Jewish and Protestant Communities', *Social Forces*, Vol. 49 (September), 50–9.

Lenski, G. (1961) *The Religious Factor* (New York: Doubleday).

Lewin, K. (1948) *Resolving Social Conflicts* (New York: Harper).

Liebman, C. (1973) 'Jewish Liberalism', *Jewish Frontier*, Vol. 60 (January), 11–22.

Malzberg, B. (1958) *Cohort Studies in Mental Disease in New York State* (New York: National Association for Mental Health).

Malzberg, B. (1967) *Statistical Studies of Mental Disease in New York State, 1949–1951* (Albany: Research Foundation for Mental Hygiene).

Purves, A. C. (1973) *Literature Education in Ten Countries. International Studies in Evaluation. Vol. 2* (Stockholm: Almqvist & Wiksell).

Rothman, J. (1965) *Minority Group Identification and Intergroup Relations* (New York: Research Institute for Group Work in Jewish Agencies, National Jewish Welfare Board).

Sklare, M. and J. Greenblum (1967) *Jewish Identity on the Suburban Frontier* (New York: Basic Books).

Sonquist, J. (1970) *Multivariate Model Building* (Ann Arbor: Survey Research Center, University of Michigan).

Sonquist, J. and J. Morgan (1964) *The Detection of Interaction Effects* (Ann Arbor: Survey Research Center, University of Michigan).

Srole, L. (1956) 'Social Integration and Certain Corollaries: An Exploratory Study', *American Sociological Review*, Vol. 21 (December), 709–16.

Stark, R. and C. Glock (1968) *American Piety: The Nature of Religious Commitment* (Berkeley, Los Angeles: University of California Press).

Thorndike, R. L. (1973) *'Reading Comprehension Education in Fifteen Countries'*, International Studies in Evaluation, Vol. 3 (Stockholm: Almqvist & Wiksell).

Werts, C. E., R. L. Linn and K. G. Jöreskog (1974) 'Quantifying Unmeasured Variables', in H. M. Blalock (ed.), *Measurement in the Social Sciences* (Chicago: Aldine).

Winsborough, H. H. (1962) 'City Growth and City Structure', *Journal of Regional Science*, Vol. 4, 35–49.

Index

Allen, R., 94
Allinsmith, B., 93
Allinsmith, W., 93
Analysis of Variance, 26–7
Automatic Interaction Detection
  (AID), 87–8, 97, 101,
  111n9, 112n19
Axelrod, M., 88

Bartlett, M. S., 82n3
Berelson, B., 93
Bicausality, 35, 137
Bielby, W. T., 138
Birnbaum, I. B., 9, 10, 31, 138
Blalock, A., 110n3
Blalock, H. M., 82n4, 92, 110n3,
  137, 138
Bohrnstedt, G. W., 137
Borgatta, E., 110n3
Bowles, S., 122

Cain, C. G., 122
Carter, T. M., 137
Causal Analysis, 3, 12, 30ff, 138,
  158–9
Causal effect, 30–2, 39, 44
  non-constant, 44, 138
  and prevalence, 73–4
Causal model;
  decomposition of, 74–81
Causal priority, 30
Cause;
  explicit, 30
  implicit, 30
Cohort, 70, 75, 82–5
Coleman, J. S., 115–36
Comber, L. C., 115, 117, 118, 120,
  129

Consistency, 45
Cooper, R. B., 82n2
Correlation;
  correlation ratio, 13, 18
  linear correlation coefficient, 17, 49
  multiple correlation coefficient,
    21, 113, 117–35, 158
  partial correlation coefficient,
    23
  product moment correlation
    coefficient, 10,
    13, 17, 20–1, 23, 115
  conditional, 141
Covariance, definition of, 139
  conditional, 141
Cross-sectional data, 64–5, 70
Cumulative frequency, 114

Data-dredging, 24, 55
Davis, J. A., 138
Demerath, N. J., 90
Direct effect, 33, 39, 121, 125, 131
Dohrenwend, B. P., 76, 82n6
Dohrenwend, B. S., 76, 82n6
Ducan, O. D., 74, 75, 82n5

Eaton, W., 72–85
Efficiency, 45
Errors, 137
  measurement error, 137
  specification error, 137
Expectation, 138–9
  conditional expectation, 140–1

Fichter, J., 89
Fuchs, L., 93
Fukuyama, Y., 88

Glock, C., 88
Gnanadesikan, R., 138
Goldberger, A. S., 137, 138
Goldscheider, C., 88
Goldstein, S., 88
Goodman, L. A., 82n4, 138
Greeley, A., 89, 90, 91, 94
Greenblum, J., 88

Hammond, J. L., 82n4
Hannan, M. T., 82n4
Hanushek, E. A., 122
Hauser, R. M., 137
Herman, S., 91, 110n2, 111n13
Husen, T., 115, 129
Hypothesis testing, 44, 51–7, 60–1, 138
 piecemeal testing, 56
 as a test of theory, 53–5, 57
Hypothetical experiment, 32, 37, 63, 113–14, 123–9, 133

Independence;
 causal, 31–2, 34, 36
 statistical, 13, 31, 140
Indirect effect, 33–5, 113
Interaction, 26, 87–8, 97, 101, 112n19

Jackson, D. D., 72
Jewell, W. S., 82n2
Johnson, B., 93
Jöreskog, K. G., 138

Kain, J. F., 122
Keeves, J. P., 115, 117, 118, 120, 129
Kendall, M., 138
King, M., 88
Kluegal, J. R., 138
Kramer, J., 73

Land, K., 110n3
Lazerwitz, B., 88–112
Least squares, 27–9, 45, 157–8
Lenski, G., 88, 89, 90, 91, 92, 93, 100, 105–6, 108
Levin, H. M., 122
Lewin, K., 88

Liebman, C., 106, 111n15
Likelihood;
 likelihood ratio test, 52–7
 log-likelihood, 46ff
  constrained 52, 60
  unconstrained 52, 60
 maximum likelihood, 44–8
Linear causal model
 regression interpretation, 32–7
 variance interpretation, 37–40, 43
Longitudinal data, 70, 82

Malzberg, B., 75, 76, 82, 83, 84
Matrix, 137, 138, 150–9
 addition, 151
 antisymmetric, 151
 calculus, 155–6
 characteristic equation, 155
 conformable partition, 153
 converse, 152
 data matrix, 156
 determinant, 154
 diagonal, 150, 152
 eigenvalue, 155
 eigenvector, 155
 equality, 151
 identity, 150
 multiplication, 151
 non-singular, 152
 null, 150
 order, 150
 orthogonal, 152
 positive definite, 155
 quadratic form, 154
 rank, 153, 154
 scalar multiplication, 151
 singular, 152
 square, 150
 sub-matrix, 153
 symmetric, 151
 transformation, 154
 transpose, 150
 triangular, 150
 variance-covariance, 157
 vector, 150
Mean;
 conditional mean, 12–13, 24–5, 140

Mean *continued*
  definition of, 139
Measurement, 4–9, 40–1
  operational measurement, 90–1, 96–7
Morgan, J., 97
Multicollinearity, 33, 50
Multiple Classification Analysis (MCA), 87–8, 97–8, 103, 111nn, 112n19
Multivariate analysis, 138

Normal equations, 49

Parameters, 9, 15, 138
Path coefficients, 38, 43
  estimation of, 44–51
Path diagram, 34–6
Path regression coefficients, 34
  estimation of, 44–51
Percentile, 114, 123–8, 132, 136n3
Populations, 9
  combining variances over, 56–7
  comparing causal models over, 42–3, 51
Prediction, 11, 21, 24–5, 124
  and causality, 11–12, 30
Probability, 10, 45, 138–9
  conditional, 139
Purves, A. C., 115, 117, 120, 123, 132, 133, 135

Random variable, 139
Recursive systems, 137, 138, 159
  a-posteriori-trimmed, 36–7
  a-priori-trimmed, 35
    testing, 55–6
  block recursive, 37, 86–7, 92, 113, 137
  full, 35
  tested-a-priori-trimmed, 36
    testing, 52–5
Regression, 13, 18–19
  and cardinal variables, 24–5
  and dichotomous variables, 25
  estimating coefficients in, 27–9
  linear, 3
  constrained, 15–18, 19–21, 26, 27, 31
  unconstrained, 14–18, 19–21, 26, 27, 113ff
  and non-cardinal variables, 25
  step-wise, 23, 55
Replication, 24
Residual, 12, 15, 22, 158
Rossi, P., 89, 90, 91, 94
Rothman, J., 88, 93, 110n2

Sample, 9
  representative, 9
Sampling, 9, 11
Simultaneous equation techniques, 137, 138, 159
Sklare, M., 88, 90, 91, 92, 100, 106, 110n2
Sonquist, J., 97, 111n9
Spilka, B., 94
Srole, L., 96
Stability of causal model, 64–5
Standard error, 50
Standardisation, 37, 40–3
Standardised linear models, 40, 42–3
Stark, R., 88, 89, 94
Statistical inference, 9–10, 138
Structural coefficient, 33
Structural equation, 33

Thorndike, R. L., 115, 117, 120, 129
Time and causal analysis, 63–5

Unbiasedness, 28–9, 44, 45, 50
Units of analysis, 4, 32

Variables, 4
  cardinal, 6–9, 43, 87, 138
    interval, 7–8, 114
    ratio, 7–8
    and regression, 24–5
  composite, 113–14, 123–5, 130–2, 134–5
  continuous, 7
  dichotomous, 5–6
    and regression, 25–6
  discrete, 6–7, 43, 138
    and causal analysis, 43–4
  dummy, 26–7
  endogenous, 33

Variables *continued*
  exogenous, 33
  explicit, 32
  implicit, 32
  nominal, 5, 87–8
  non-cardinal
    and causal analysis, 43
    and regression, 25
  ordinal, 6, 114
  random, 139
  unobserved, 137

Variance;
  combining over populations, 42–3, 51
  conditional, 141
  definition of, 139
  minimum variance, 56–7

Watts, H. W., 122
Werts, C. E., 137
Winsborough, H. H., 81

GPSR Compliance

The European Union's (EU) General Product Safety Regulation (GPSR) is a set of rules that requires consumer products to be safe and our obligations to ensure this.

If you have any concerns about our products, you can contact us on

ProductSafety@springernature.com

In case Publisher is established outside the EU, the EU authorized representative is:

Springer Nature Customer Service Center GmbH
Europaplatz 3
69115 Heidelberg, Germany

www.ingramcontent.com/pod-product-compliance
Ingram Content Group UK Ltd.
Pitfield, Milton Keynes, MK11 3LW, UK
UKHW041417180426

11947UKWH00007B/188